D0178431

REWARD
Starter
Teacher's Book

WITHDRAWN

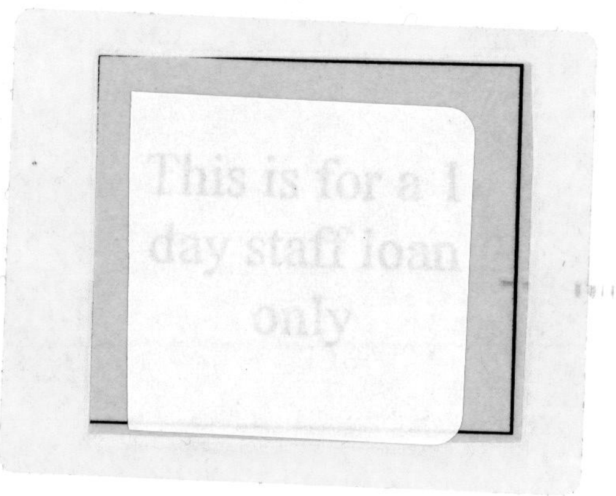

THE LEARNING CENTRE
HAMMERSMITH AND WEST
LONDON COLLEGE
GLIDDON ROAD
LONDON W14 9BL

0181 741 1688

Hammersmith and West London College
300261

Macmillan Heinemann English Language Teaching, Oxford

A division of Macmillan Publishers Limited

Companies and representatives throughout the world

ISBN 0 435 24223 7

HAMMERSMITH AND WEST
LONDON COLLEGE
LEARNING CENTRE

DAW B779330 £17.05
428.241
300261

Text © Simon Greenall, 1997
Design and illustration © Macmillan Publishers Limited 1998

Heinemann is a registered trademark of Reed Educational &
Professional Publishing Limited

First published 1997

All rights reserved; no part of this publication may be reproduced, stored in a retrieval system, transmitted in any form, or by any means, electronic, mechanical, photocopying, recording, or otherwise, without the prior written permission of the publishers.

Series design by Stafford & Stafford
Page Layout by eMC Design

Note to teachers
The four tests at the back of this book may be photocopied for use in class without the prior written permission of Macmillan Publishers Limited. However, please note that the copy-right law, which does not normally permit multiple copying of published material, applies to the rest of this book.

Author's Acknowledgements
I am very grateful to all the people who have contributed towards *Reward Starter*. Thank you so much to:
- All the teachers I have worked with on seminars around the world, and the various people who have influenced my work.
- Anne Rosenfeld for the efficient work she has done on producing the tapes, and the actors for their voices.
- Philip Kerr, for his comments on the material, which are especially helpful and well-considered.
- Chris Winter for his skilful design and management.
- Nicola Heaver for her efficient artwork commissioning.
- Douglas Williamson for his efficient design management.
- Emma Parker for tracking down some wonderful photos.
- Catherine Smith for her support and advice and her sensitive management of the project.
- Oonagh Wade for her hard work and commitment to the project.
- and last, but by no means least, Jill, Jack and Alex.

Printed and bound in Great Britain by Thomson Litho Ltd.

2003 2002 2001 2000 1999
11 10 9 8 7 6 5 4 3

300261

Introduction

Course organisation

Reward is a general English course which will take adult and young adult learners of English from beginner to upper intermediate level. British English is used as the model for grammar, vocabulary, spelling and pronunciation, but other varieties of English are included for listening and reading practice. The course components for each level are as follows:

For the student	For the teacher
Student's Book	Teacher's Book
Practice Book	Class cassettes
Practice Book cassette	Resource Pack
	Business Resource Pack

The Student's Book has forty teaching lessons and four Progress check lessons. After every ten teaching lessons there is a Progress check lesson to review the language covered in the preceding teaching lessons and to present new language work relevant to the grammar, functions and topics covered so far. Within the teaching lessons the main grammar or language functions and the most useful vocabulary are presented in boxes which allow easy access to the principle language of the lesson. This makes the focus of the lesson clearly accessible for purposes of presentation and revision. Each lesson will take between 45 to 60 minutes. *Reward* is designed to be very flexible in order to meet the requirements of learners.

The two **Class cassettes** contain the recorded material used in the Student's Book.

The Practice Book has forty practice lessons corresponding to the forty teaching lessons in the Student's Book. The activities are designed for self-access work and can be easily used to provide extra practice for the language presented in the Student's Book, either in the class or as self-study material. Each lesson will take between 40 and 60 minutes to do.

The **Practice Book cassettes** contain all the listening and sounds work in the Practice Book.

The Resource Pack provides extra teaching material to practise the main language points of the teaching lessons. Each pack contains a wide variety of communicative practice activities in the form of photocopiable worksheets with step-by-step Teacher's Notes on the back. There is at least one activity for each lesson in the Student's Book and the activities can be used to extend a core teaching lesson of 60 minutes from the Student's Book with an average of 30 minutes of extra material for use in the classroom. They can also be used to revise specific structures, language or vocabulary later in the course.

As well as a step-by-step Teacher's Notes for each activity, each Resource Pack includes an introduction which explains how to use the worksheets and offers tips on how to get the most out of the activities.

The **Teacher's Book** contains a presentation of the course design, methodological principles, and detailed teaching notes. There are four photocopiable tests. The teaching notes for each lesson include a step-by-step guide to teaching the lesson, a discussion of some of the difficulties the learners may encounter, and more detailed methodological issues arising from the material presented.

Course design

The course design is based on a broad and integrated multi-syllabus approach. It is broad in the sense that it covers grammar and language functions, vocabulary, reading, listening, speaking, writing, and sounds explicitly, and topics, learner training and socio-cultural competence implicitly. It is integrated in that each strand of the course design forms the overall theme of each lesson. The lessons always include activities focussing on grammar and language functions, and vocabulary. They will also include reading, listening, speaking, writing, and sounds. The inclusion of each strand of the syllabus is justified by its communicative purpose within the activity sequence. The methodological principles and approaches to each strand of course design are discussed below.

Methodological principles

Here is an outline of the methodological principles for each strand of the course design.

Grammar and language functions

Many teachers and learners feel safe with grammar and language functions. Some learners may claim that they want or need grammar, although at the same time suggest that they don't enjoy it. Some teachers feel that their learners' knowledge of grammar is demonstrable proof of language acquisition. But this is only partly true. Mistakes of grammar are more easily tolerated than mistakes of vocabulary, as far as comprehension is concerned, and may be more acceptable than mistakes of socio-cultural competence, as far as behaviour and effective communication is concerned. *Reward* attempts to establish grammar and language functions in their pivotal positions but without neglecting the other strands of the multi-syllabus design.

Vocabulary

There are two important criteria for the inclusion of words in the vocabulary boxes. Firstly, they are words which the beginner should acquire in order to communicate successfully in a number of social or transactional situations. Secondly, they may also be words which, although not in Threshold Level, are generated by the reading or listening material and are considered suitable for beginner level. However, an overriding principle operates: there is usually an activity which allows learners to focus on and, one hopes, acquire the words which are personally relevant to them. This involves a process of personal selection or grouping of words according to personal categories. It is hard to acquire words which one doesn't need, so this approach responds to the learner's individual requirements and personal motivation. *Reward* Starter presents approximately 450 words in the vocabulary boxes for the learner's active attention, but each learner must decide which words to focus on.

Reading

The reading passages are generally at a higher level than one might expect for learners at beginner level. Foreign language users who are not of near-native speaker competence are constantly confronted with difficult language, and to expose the learners to examples of real-life English in the reassuring context of the classroom is to help prepare them for the conditions of real life. There is always an activity or two which encourages the learner to respond to the passage either on a personal level or to focus on its main ideas. *Reward* attempts to avoid a purely pedagogical approach and encourages the learner to respond to the passages in an authentic way before using them for other purposes.

Listening

Listening is based on a similar approach to reading in *Reward*. Learners are often exposed to examples of natural, authentic English in order to prepare them for real-life situations in which they will have to listen to ungraded English. But the tasks are always graded for the learners' particular level. Learners at beginner level are often pleased by how much they understand. Furthermore, a number of different native and non-native accents are used in the listening passages, to reflect the fact that in real-life, very few speakers using English speak with British or American standard pronunciation.

Speaking

Many opportunities are given for speaking, particularly in pairs and groupwork. Learners are encouraged to work in pairs and groups, because the number of learners in most classes does not allow the teacher to give undivided attention to each learner's English. In these circumstances, it is important for the teacher to evaluate whether fluency or accuracy is the most important criterion. On most occasions in *Reward* Starter speaking practice in the *Grammar* sections is concerned with accuracy, and in the *Speaking* sections with fluency. In the latter case, it is better not to interrupt and correct the learners until after the activity is ended.

Writing

The writing activities in *Reward* are based on guided paragraph writing with work on making notes, turning notes into sentences, and joining sentences into paragraphs with various linking devices. The activities are quite tightly controlled; this is not to suggest that more creative work is not valid, but it is one of the responsibilities of a coursebook to provide a systematic grounding in the skill. More creative writing is covered in the Practice Book. Work is also done on punctuation, and most of the writing activities are based on real-life tasks, such as writing letters and cards.

Sounds

Pronunciation, stress and intonation work tends to interrupt the communicative flow of a lesson, and there is a temptation to leave it out in the interests of maintaining the momentum of an activity sequence. In *Reward* there is work on sounds in most lessons, usually just before the stage where the learners have to use the new structures orally in pair or group work. At this level, it seems suitable to introduce the straightforward system of English phonemes, many of which the learners will be able to reproduce accurately because the same phonemes exist in their own language. There are also activities which focus on stress in words and sentences. The model for pronunciation is standard British.

Topics

The main topics in *Reward* Starter include personal identification, house and home, daily life, leisure activities, travel, relations with other people, health, education, shopping, food and drink, geographical location and the environment. On many occasions the words presented in the vocabulary box all belong to a particular word fields or topic.

Learner-training

Implicit in the overall approach is the development of learner training to encourage learners to take responsibility for their own learning. Examples of this are regular opportunities to use mono- and bi-lingual dictionaries, ways of organising vocabulary according to personal categories and inductive grammar work.

Cross-cultural training

Much of the material and activities in *Reward* create the opportunity for cross-cultural training. Most learners will be using English as a medium of communication with other non-native speakers, and certainly with people of different cultures. Errors of socio-cultural competence are likely to be less easily tolerated than errors of grammar or lexical insufficiency. But it is impossible to give the learners enough specific information about a culture, because it is impossible to predict all the cultural circumstances in which they will use their newly acquired language competence. Information about *sample* cultures, such as Britain, America, as well as non-native English speaking ones, is given to allow the learners to compare their own culture with another. This creates opportunities for learners to reflect on their own culture in order to become more aware of the possibility of different attitudes, behaviour, customs, traditions and beliefs in other cultures. In this spirit, cross-cultural training is possible even with groups where the learners all come from the same cultural background. There are interesting and revealing differences between people from the same region or town, or even between friends and members of the same family. Exploring these will help the learners become not merely proficient at the language but competent in the overall aim of communication.

Level and progress

The core teaching lessons in the Student's Book may not provide the students with enough practice material to ensure that the given grammar, language functions and vocabulary have been firmly acquired. For these learners, extra practice may be needed and is provided in both the Practice Book (for self-study work) and by the Resource Packs (for classroom work).

Interest and motivation

Another important principle in the course design has been the intrinsic interest of the materials. Interesting material motivates the learners, and motivated learners acquire the language more effectively. The topics have been carefully selected so that they are interesting to adults and young adults, with a focus on areas which would engage their general leisure-time interests. This is designed to generate what might be described as authentic motivation, the kind of motivation we have when we read a newspaper or watch a television programme. But it is obvious that we cannot motivate all learners all of the time. They may arrive at a potentially motivating lesson with little desire to learn on this particular occasion, perhaps for reasons that have nothing to do with the teacher, the course or the material. It is therefore necessary to introduce tasks which attract what might be described as pedagogic or artificial motivation, tasks which would not usually be performed in real-life, but which engage the learner in an artificial but no less effective way.

Variety of material and language

Despite the enormous amount of research done on language acquisition, no one has come up with a definitive description of how we acquire either our native language or a foreign language which takes account of every language learner or the teaching style of every teacher. Every learner has different interests and different requirements, and every teacher has a different style and approach to what they teach. *Reward* attempts to adopt an approach which appeals to differing styles of learning and teaching. The pivotal role of grammar and vocabulary is reflected in the material but not at the expense of the development of the skills or pronunciation. An integrated multi-syllabus course design, designed to respond to the broad variety of learners' requirements and teachers' objectives, is at the heart of *Reward's* approach.

RESEARCH

Heinemann ELT is committed to continuing research into coursebook development. Many teachers contributed to the evolution of *Reward* through piloting and reports, and we now want to continue this process of feedback by inviting users of *Reward* – both teachers and students – to tell us about their experience of working with the course. If you or your colleagues have any comments, queries or suggestions, please address them to the Publishing Director, Adult Group, Heinemann ELT, Halley Court, Jordan Hill, Oxford OX2 8EJ or contact your local Heinemann representative.

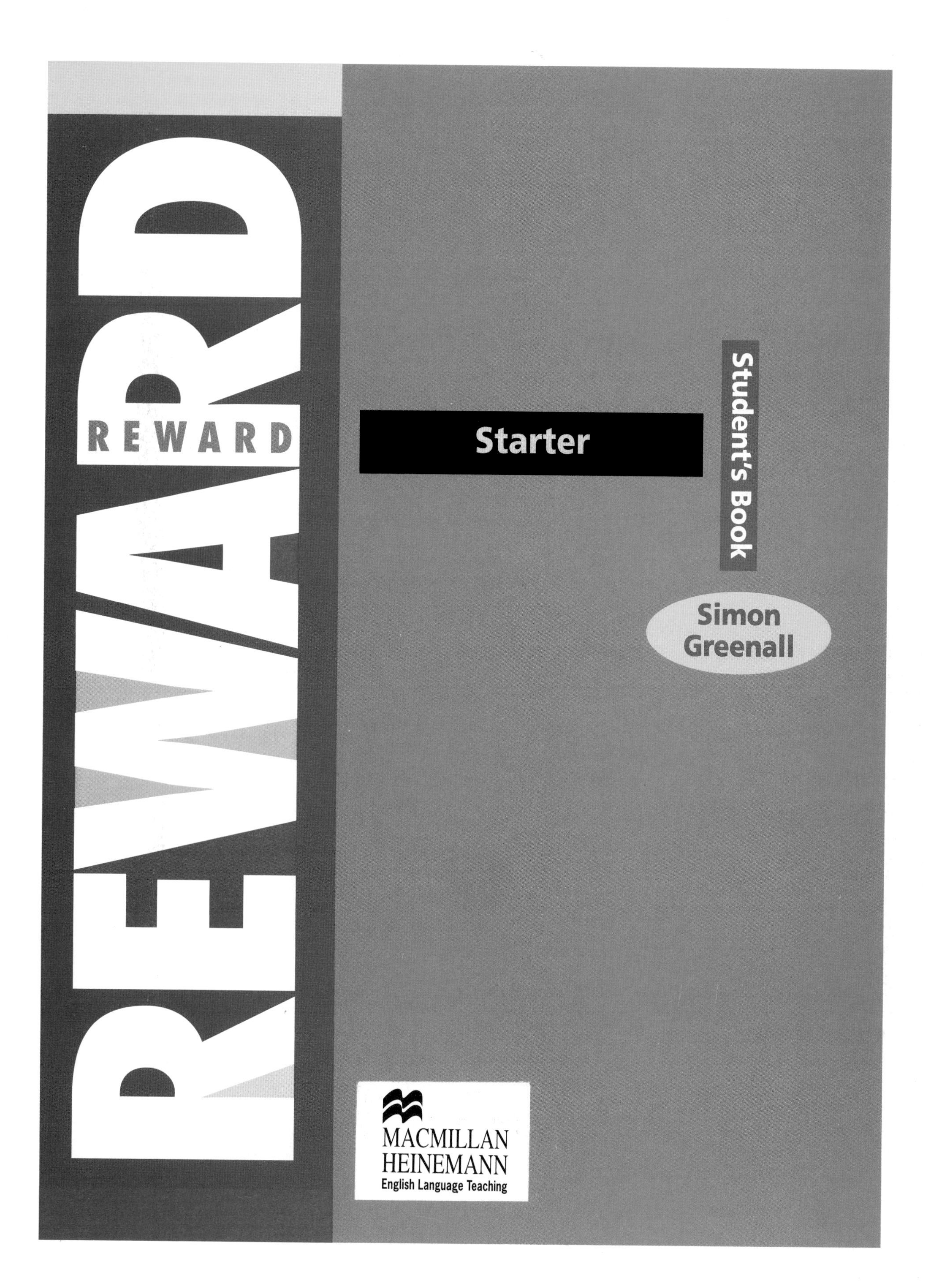
REWARD
REWARD
Starter
Student's Book
Simon Greenall
MACMILLAN HEINEMANN
English Language Teaching

Map of the book

Lesson	Grammar and functions	Vocabulary	Skills and sounds
1 *Hello, I'm Frank* Greeting people you don't know	Asking and saying names	*Hello, goodbye*	**Listening:** listening and matching; word recognition **Sounds:** pronouncing phrases **Reading:** inserting sentences **Speaking:** acting out a conversation
2 *I'm a student* Jobs	The indefinite article *a/an* Talking about jobs	Jobs	**Sounds:** stressing syllables in words **Listening:** listening and reading; ordering sentences **Reading:** reading and matching **Speaking:** acting out conversations
3 *How are you?* Greeting people you know	Greeting people Asking for and saying telephone numbers	Numbers 1-10	**Sounds:** pronouncing and recognising numbers **Listening:** listening and reading; ordering sentences **Reading:** reading telephone numbers **Speaking:** asking and saying telephone numbers
4 *Are you James Bond?* Asking and saying names	Asking and saying names Spelling	The alphabet	**Sounds:** pronouncing the alphabet; spelling names **Listening:** listening and repeating a conversation **Speaking:** acting out a conversation; finding out other people's professions
5 *She's Russian* Talking about where people are from	Saying where people are from Saying what nationality people are	Countries Nationalities	**Sounds:** pronouncing countries and nationalities **Listening:** listening and reading; listening and correcting wrong information **Reading:** reading and matching; completing charts **Writing:** writing sentences about people and their nationalities
6 *Is she married?* Asking and giving personal information	*Yes/no* questions and short answers	Numbers 11-20 Personal information	**Sounds:** pronouncing and recognising numbers **Listening:** listening and following a conversation; putting sentences in the right order **Writing:** copying and completing a membership form
7 *How old is he?* Talking about ages	Asking and saying how old people are Present simple (review)	Numbers 21-100	**Sounds:** pronouncing and recognising numbers **Listening:** listening and matching; listening and noting down personal information **Writing:** writing a poster of someone famous
8 *His favourite car is a Porsche* Talking about favourite people and things	*Who* and *what* Possessive adjectives: *my, your, his, her*	Favourite people and things	**Sounds:** pronouncing words; pronouncing questions **Listening:** listening and reading **Reading:** reading and answering a questionnaire **Listening:** listening and answering questions **Writing:** writing questions **Speaking:** talking about favourite people and things
9 *We're twins* Common interests	Present simple: *we're, you're, they're* Plurals	Words for people and their relationship to each other, eg *friend, twin, brother*	**Reading:** inserting sentences; reading and correcting wrong information **Listening:** listening and following a conversation
10 *What are these?* Finding out what the word for something is	Asking and saying what things are *This, that, these,* and *those*	Personal possessions Loan words	**Sounds:** pronouncing words; /æ/, /ɒ/, /ɪ/ **Listening:** listening and reading **Speaking:** asking and saying what things are in the classroom; playing *Word Bingo*
Progress check lessons 1-10	Revision	Word categories quiz	**Sounds:** /æ/, /e/, /əɪ/; stressing syllables in words; stressing words in sentences **Listening:** listening to a song - *Rock around the clock*

Lesson	Grammar and functions	Vocabulary	Skills and sounds
11 *How much are they?* The price of clothes and other items	Talking about prices Position of adjectives The definite article *the*	Clothes Money	**Sounds:** stressing words in sentences **Listening:** listening and correcting a conversation; listening for specific information to complete a chart **Speaking:** comparing prices
12 *Where are Jane's keys?* Personal possessions	Prepositions of place: *in, on, under* Possessive *'s*	Personal possessions Furniture *table, chair*	**Sounds:** pronouncing words **Listening:** listening and matching **Speaking:** asking and saying where things are **Writing:** writing sentences saying where things are in a picture
13 *We've got three children* Talking about families	*Have got* Possessive adjectives: *our, your, their*	Members of the family	**Reading:** reading and matching; completing a chart **Listening:** inserting sentences **Sounds:** /ə/ **Speaking:** talking about families; completing a chart
14 *She's got fair hair and blue eyes* Appearance and character	Talking about appearance and character *Has got*	Adjectives to describe appearance and character Colours Modifiers *quite, very*	**Speaking:** describing people **Listening:** listening and following a conversation **Reading:** completing charts; reading and matching **Writing:** writing about your family
15 *Stand up!* Instructions in the classroom	Imperatives	Features of a room Personal possessions	**Listening:** listening and following instructions **Sounds:** /əʊ/; stressing words in sentences; pronouncing instructions **Reading:** reading and checking comprehension **Writing:** writing instructions for a Students' Charter
16 *We live in a flat in Florence* Where people live and work	Present simple: regular verbs *I, we, you, they* Prepositions of place: *in, to*	Places where people live and work	**Sounds:** pronouncing words; /æ/, /əʊ/, /ɒ/, /uː/, /ɪ/, /ɜː/ **Reading:** reading and matching **Listening:** listening and checking **Reading:** reading and answering a game *What's my name?* **Writing:** writing your own *What's my name?*; writing about where you live
17 *What's the time?* Meal times in different countries	Telling the time (1) Present simple: *have* Prepositions of time: *at, in*	Meals Times of the day: hours	**Listening:** listening and reading **Reading:** reading and completing a chart **Speaking:** talking about when people around the world have meals
18 *I don't like Monday mornings* Weekly routines	Present simple: negatives Preposition of time: *on*	Days of the week Routine activities	**Sounds:** pronouncing days of the week; pronouncing expressions of time **Reading:** reading and matching **Listening:** listening and reading **Writing:** writing about weekly routines **Speaking:** talking about weekly routines
19 *Do you like running?* Likes and dislikes	*Yes/no* questions and short answers	Sports	**Sounds:** pronouncing words **Listening:**: completing a chart; putting sentences in the right order **Writing:** completing a conversation **Speaking:** finding people who like and don't like sports
20 *She likes her job* Daily routines	Telling the time (2) Present simple: *he, she, it*	Times of the day: *quarter past/to, half past* Routine activities	**Speaking:** talking about routine activities; deducing information about someone **Reading:** reading and matching; reading and completing sentences **Listening:** listening and checking; listening for specific information **Writing:** writing a paragraph about two people's daily routines
Progress check lessons 11-20	Revision	Word categories quiz	**Sounds:** /ɑː/, /ʌ/, /ɜː/, /eə/; stressing syllables in words; stressing words in sentences **Listening:** listening to a song - *Three Little Birds*

Lesson	Grammar and functions	Vocabulary	Skills and sounds
21 *Does she go to work by boat?* Transport in cities	*He, she, it* *Yes/no* questions and short answers *By*	Means of transport	**Sounds:** pronouncing words and sentences; /eɪ/, /əʊ/, /ɑː/, /ɑɪ/, /ʌ/, /ɔː/, /æ/ **Reading:** reading and completing a chart **Listening:** listening and completing a chart **Speaking:** acting out conversations; completing a questionnaire on how people get to work
22 *What do they eat in Morocco?* Food and drink in different countries	Present simple: *Wh*-questions	Food and drink Food from different countries	**Reading:** reading and matching; completing a chart **Listening:** listening and checking **Writing:** writing a paragraph about food and drink **Speaking:** talking about food and drink
23 *I don't like lying on the beach* Holiday activities	*Like + ing* Present simple: negatives	Holiday activities	**Reading:** reading and checking comprehension **Listening:** listening and completing a chart **Speaking:** asking and answering questions about holidays **Writing:** writing about your partner's holiday
24 *There's a telephone in the hall* Homes	*There is/are* *Any*	Rooms of the house Furniture	**Sounds:** pronouncing words **Reading:** reading and checking comprehension **Listening:** listening to a commentary; listening and deducing **Speaking:** describing a room in your house **Writing:** writing a description of a room in your house
25 *I usually have a party* Birthday celebrations	Present simple: adverbs of frequency	Months of the year Ordinal numbers	**Sounds:** pronouncing words **Reading:** reading and answering questions **Listening:** listening and completing a chart **Speaking:** asking and answering questions about birthdays
26 *I can cook* Abilities for jobs	*Can* for ability	Abilities eg *cook, draw, drive, sing*	**Sounds:** pronouncing the strong and weak form of *can* **Reading:** reading and making notes **Listening:** listening for specific information **Speaking:** acting out a job interview
27 *Can I have a sandwich, please?* Restaurant menus	Talking about food and drink	Food and drink	**Sounds:** pronouncing expressions such as *a cup of tea, a glass of wine* **Listening:** listening and inserting sentences; listening for specific information **Speaking:** acting out conversations in a restaurant
28 *Where's the station?* Finding your way around town	Asking for and giving directions	Shops Directions, eg *go straight ahead, turn left*	**Sounds:** pronouncing words; stressing syllables in words **Listening:** listening and matching; following a route on a map **Reading:** reading and following a route on a map **Writing:** writing a guided tour of your city
29 *He's buying lunch* Times and actions around the world	Present continuous (1)	Words for actions such as *buy, drive, sit, run*	**Reading:** reading and matching **Sounds:** pronouncing the present continuous **Speaking:** describing what people are doing in a picture and around the world
30 *He isn't having a bath* Talking about what's happening at the moment	Present continuous (2): negatives; questions	Nouns which go with certain verbs, *have, make*	**Reading:** reading and matching **Listening:** listening for specific information **Speaking:** saying the differences between two pictures **Writing:** writing the differences between two pictures
Progress check lessons 21-30	Revision	Identifying parts of speech Verbs and nouns which go together Word categories quiz	**Sounds:** /əɪ/, /ɪ/, /uː/, /iː/, /ʊ/; stressing syllables in words; stressing words in sentences: contrastive stress **Listening:** listening to a song - *Daniel*

Lesson	Grammar and functions	Vocabulary	Skills and sounds
31 *We're going to Australia* A visit to Australia	Present continuous (3): future plans	Words for travel	**Reading:** reading and answering questions **Listening:** listening and checking; listening for specific information **Speaking:** planning a trip to somewhere special
32 *Let's go to the cinema* Entertainment	Making suggestions Accepting and refusing Talking about the cinema and theatre	Places and forms of entertainment	**Listening:** listening and checking **Sounds:** using suitable intonation; stressing words in sentences **Speaking:** making, accepting and refusing suggestions to do things in your town
33 *Yesterday, I was in Paris* Weekends	Past simple (1) *be*: *was/were* affirmative Expressions of time	Adjectives to describe moods and feelings, such as *happy, cold*	**Listening:** listening and reading **Sounds:** pronouncing the strong and weak forms of *was* and *were*; pronouncing sentences **Reading:** reading and answering questions **Writing:** completing a passage
34 *Was she in the kitchen?* A murder mystery	Past simple (2): *yes/no* questions and short answers	New words from the murder mystery	**Reading:** predicting, reading and matching **Listening:** listening and checking; completing a chart **Speaking:** talking about the murder mystery
35 *They didn't have any computers* Technology and household goods in the past	Past simple (3): *had*	Household equipment	**Sounds:** stressing syllables in words **Reading:** reading and completing a chart **Listening:** listening for specific information **Speaking:** talking about an anachronistic picture; talking about inventions and discoveries
36 *We listened to the radio* Childhood	Past simple (4): regular verbs	Expressions of past time	**Reading:** reading and matching; correcting sentences **Sounds:** pronouncing the endings of regular verbs **Listening:** listening for specific information **Writing:** writing sentences about yourself ten years ago
37 *Picasso didn't live in Spain* The life of Pablo Picasso	Past simple (5): negatives	Verbs to describe the life of Picasso	**Reading:** predicting; reading and checking **Sounds:** stressing words in sentences: contrastive stress **Speaking:** talking about the life of a famous person **Writing:** writing about the life of a famous person
38 *Did you take a photograph?* Animal mysteries	Past simple (6): *yes/no* questions and short answers	Animals	**Reading:** inserting sentences **Listening:** listening and checking **Sounds:** using suitable intonation for questions **Reading:** reading and answering questions; predicting a story
39 *We went to New York* A visit to New York	Past simple (7): questions; irregular verbs	Paper documents, such as *bills, ticket, receipts*	**Sounds:** pronouncing words **Listening:** listening and reading **Reading:** reading and answering questions **Writing:** completing a letter; writing about a visit **Speaking:** checking information
40 *The end of the world?* A short story	Tense review: present simple, present continuous, past simple	New words from *The end of the world?*	**Reading:** reading and answering questions **Listening:** listening and checking **Speaking:** predicting the end of the story
Progress check lessons 31-40	Revision	Different ways of recording vocabulary Survival vocabulary Word categories quiz	**Sounds:** /ɪ/, /iː/, /ɑ/, /ʊ/and /ɔː/ **Listening:** listening to a song – *Yesterday*

Classroom language

Listen

Say

Look

Write

Read

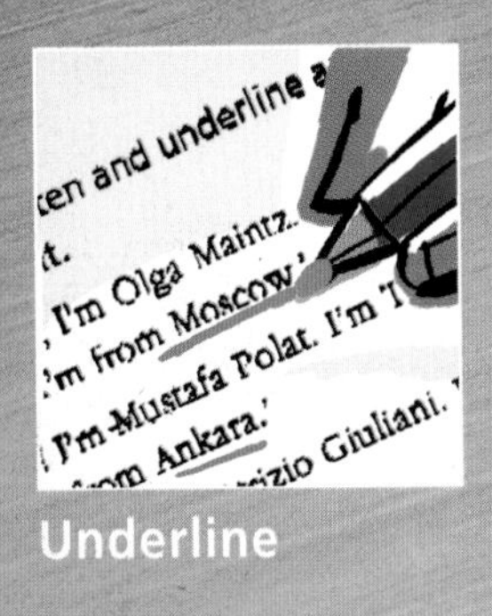

Underline

Tick

Check

Punctuate

Spell

Answer

Work in pairs

Complete

Ask

Copy

Repeat

Correct

Point

Act

Count

Match

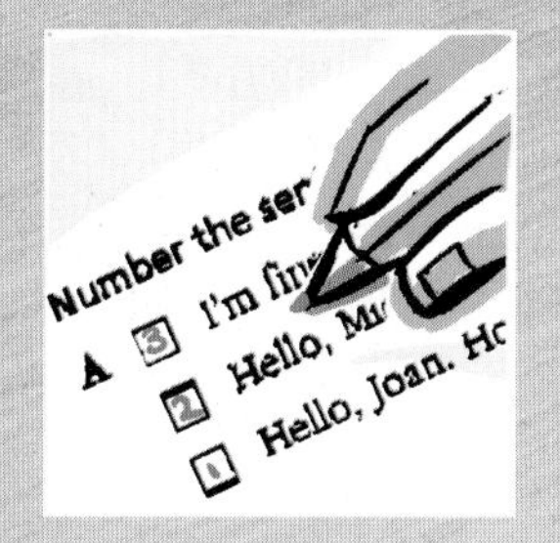

Number

Put in order

Turn to page 3

Translate

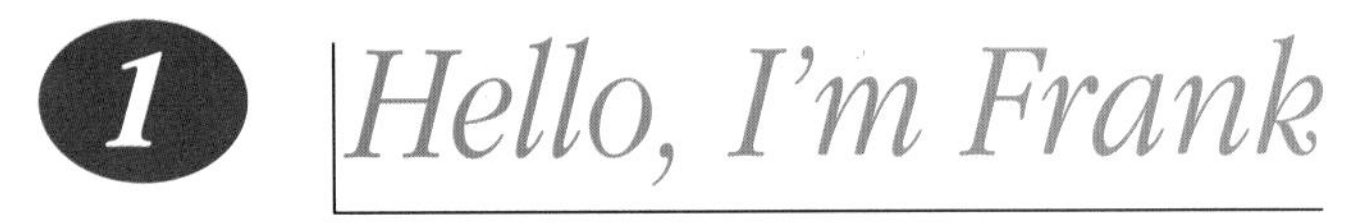

1 Hello, I'm Frank

Asking and saying names

LISTENING AND READING

1

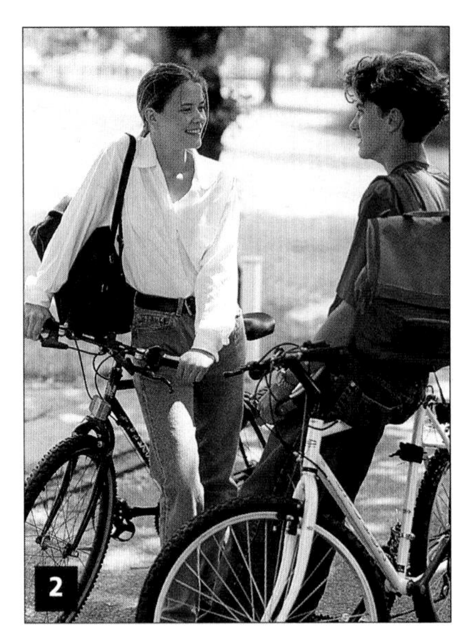

2

1 Match the conversations with the photos.

A FRANK Hello, I'm Frank. What's your name?
SARAH Hello, Frank. I'm Sarah.

B KATE Goodbye Pete!
MIKE Goodbye!

Now listen and read.

2 Listen and match.

Anna	David
Tony	Steve
Judy	Jane

3 Read and match.

Hello, I'm Anna. What's your name?	Hello, Tony. I'm Jane.
Hello, I'm Tony. What's your name?	Hello, Judy. I'm Steve.
Hello, I'm Judy. What's your name?	Hello, Anna. I'm David.

Now listen again and check.

VOCABULARY AND SOUNDS

1 Listen and repeat.

hello goodbye

2 Listen and repeat.

name your name What's your name?
Hello, what's your name?
Frank I'm Frank.
Hello, what's your name?
Judy I'm Judy. Hello, I'm Judy.
Goodbye, Judy!

1

GENERAL COMMENTS

Level

Reward Starter is designed for students who have never had any formal instruction in English. Each lesson includes the presentation of a simple structure or two, (in Lesson 1, the language is the first and third person of the verb *be*) and a few words. The subsequent lessons build on the structures presented in the preceding lessons, with the effect that all the language covered in each lesson is productive and undergoing constant recycling.

You may like to show the learners that they have already acquired a little more vocabulary than that presented in the lesson by writing on the board some common English words which are often seen in your country. Point out that even names of people (President Clinton, Boris Yeltsin) and trade names (Coca Cola, MacDonalds) constitute items of vocabulary.

Design and layout

Draw the students' attention to the fact that the target language for each lesson is presented in boxes, the vocabulary box and the grammar or functions box. There is a further grammatical explanation in the *Grammar Review* at the back of the book. Also at the back of the book are the *Tapescripts*, a list of *Irregular verbs* and the *Pronunciation guide*. Discourage the students from reading the tapescripts while they listen to the listening passages, as this will lead them to an over dependence on the printed word and the assumption that they have to understand every word in order to understand the main ideas.

LISTENING AND READING

1 Aim: to present the target structures; to practise reading for main ideas.

● Ask the students to read the conversations silently, and to match them with the photos.

● Ask the students to check their answers in pairs, and then with the whole class.

Answer
Photo 1: conversation B
Photo 2: conversation A

● Play the tape and ask them to follow the conversation.

● It may be wiser at this stage not to ask the students to act out these conversations, or even to repeat them. This stage is the receptive presentation of the target structures. There will be plenty of opportunities to produce language at a later stage.

2 Aim: to practise listening for main ideas.

● Explain that it isn't necessary to understand every word when you listen and read English, although for the moment, all the language presented in passages and conversation is carefully graded.

● Write the six names on the board. Play the tape and ask one student to draw lines matching the people who are speaking to each other.

Answers
Anna - David Tony - Jane Judy - Steve

3 Aim: to practise reading for specific information.

● This activity repeats the information checked in activity 2, and focuses on word recognition, in this case, the recognition of people's names.

● Ask the students to read and match the two sides of each conversation.

Answers
Hello, I'm Anna. What's your name?
- Hello, Anna. I'm David.
Hello, I'm Tony. What's your name?
- Hello, Tony, I'm Jane.
Hello, I'm Judy. What's your name?
- Hello, Judy. I'm Steve.

● Ask the students to write out the conversations in full. This may be a suitable moment to focus on some key points of punctuation. Point out that:

- the first letter of the first word in each sentence has a capital letter
- all names begin with a capital letter
- the first person singular *I* is always written with a capital letter
- all sentences end with a full stop (period) except questions which end with a question mark, and exclamations which end with an exclamation mark
- commas are used to represent a slight pause in spoken language.

VOCABULARY AND SOUNDS

1 Aim: to present the pronunciation of the target structures.

● Play the tape and ask the students to repeat the two words.

● Ask students to translate the words into their own language.

2 Aim: to practise the pronunciation of the target structures.

● This technique is known as *back chaining*. You can do it using chorus repetition, which students find reassuring at this level, as pairwork or as individual practice. A mixture of all three is often best, providing variety.

● Play the tape and ask students to repeat.

FUNCTIONS

1 Aim: to present the target structures.

● Ask the students to look at the information in the functions box and then to do the exercises. You may like to ask the students to do them in writing or orally with the whole class.

● Ask the students to complete the sentences. Check their answers with the whole class.

Answers
1 Hello, what's your name?
2 I'm John.
3 What's your name?
4 Hello, I'm Petra.

● You may need to explain that the contracted form is extremely common in spoken and informal written English. It's not regarded as sloppy or incorrect.

2 Aim: to focus on punctuation.

● Remind the students of the information about punctuation which you gave them in *Listening and reading* activity 3.

● Ask the students to punctuate the sentences. You may like to ask individual students to write their answers on the board.

Answers
1 What's your name?
2 I'm Sarah.
3 Hello, I'm Gerry. What's your name?
4 Hello, Gerry, I'm Henry.

3 Aim: to practise using the target structures.

Answers
1 – c
2 – a, b

4 Aim: to practise using the target structures.

● This should be the first time the students use the target structures productively and in a communicative context. If the circumstances of the classroom allow it, ask the students to get up and move around the class, meeting and greeting people. This type of activity is known as a *mill drill*, in which people *mill* around.

READING AND SPEAKING

1 Aim: to practise reading for understanding text organisation.

● This activity type is known as *inserting sentences* and involves an appreciation of the logical order of a reading passage.

● Ask the students to do this on their own and then correct their versions with the whole class.

Answers
1 – c 2 – b 3 – a

2 Aim: to practise using the target structures.

● Ask the students to act out the conversations in pairs. Ask two or three pairs to perform their conversations in front of the class.

3 Aim: to practise using the target structures.

● Ask the students to change partners and to continue to act out the conversation, but using their own names.

4 Aim: to practise word recognition.

● Explain that words from this lesson can be found in the word search. You may like to point out one or two words.

Answers

c	b	n	k	n	h	m	n	h	k	p	o
h	j	k	l	g	e	b	k	j	l	a	s
g	q	f	r	s	l	d	z	x	v	k	l
m	k	l	t	h	l	d	f	g	v	i	f
h	a	t	s	y	o	u	r	n	a	m	e
q	b	o	y	f	d	s	h	j	a	k	c
i	o	p	b	f	g	h	k	d	f	a	u
s	d	g	h	c	v	n	b	g	j	t	l
x	c	v	g	b	g	o	o	d	b	y	e

5 Aim: to practise using the target structures.

● Only do this activity if it coincides with the end of the lesson.

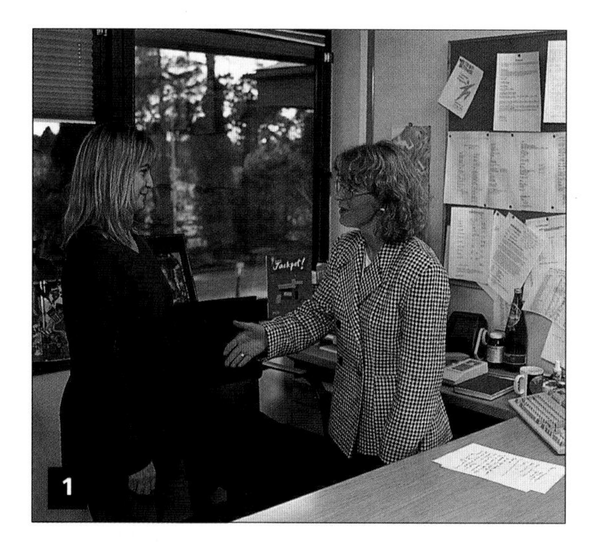

1

2

FUNCTIONS

> **Asking and saying names**
> *What's your name?*
> *(= What is your name?)*
> *I'm Kate. (= I am Kate.)*

1 Complete.

1 Hello. What's ____ name?
2 ____ John.
3 ____ your name?
4 Hello. I ____ Petra.
1 Hello. What's your name?

2 Write and punctuate.

1 whats your name
2 im sarah
3 hello im gerry whats your name
4 hello gerry im henry

3 Match the sentences with the speakers in the photos above.

a Hello,Val, I'm Katy.
b Hello, Katy.
c Hello, I'm Val. What's your name?

4 Ask and say your names.

Hello, I'm ____. What's your name?
Hello, ____. I'm ____.

READING AND SPEAKING

1 Read and complete.

STEVE Hello. What's your name?
SEMA (1) ____
STEVE Hello, Sema.
SEMA (2) ____
STEVE I'm Steve.
SEMA (3) ____

a Hello, Steve.
b What's your name?
c I'm Sema.

2 Work in pairs. Act out the conversation in 1.

3 Find three more words and phrases from this lesson.

X	C	B	N	K	N	H	M	N	H	K	P	O
G	H	J	K	L	G	E	B	K	J	L	A	S
G	G	Q	F	R	S	L	D	Z	X	V	K	L
N	M	K	L	T	H	L	D	F	G	V	I	F
W	H	A	T	S	Y	O	U	R	N	A	M	E
D	Q	B	O	Y	F	D	S	H	J	A	K	C
Y	I	O	P	B	F	G	H	K	D	F	A	U
Q	S	D	G	H	C	V	N	B	G	J	T	L
A	X	C	V	G	B	G	O	O	D	B	Y	E

4 Say goodbye to people at the end of the lesson.

Goodbye, Yildiz. *Goodbye, Frank.*

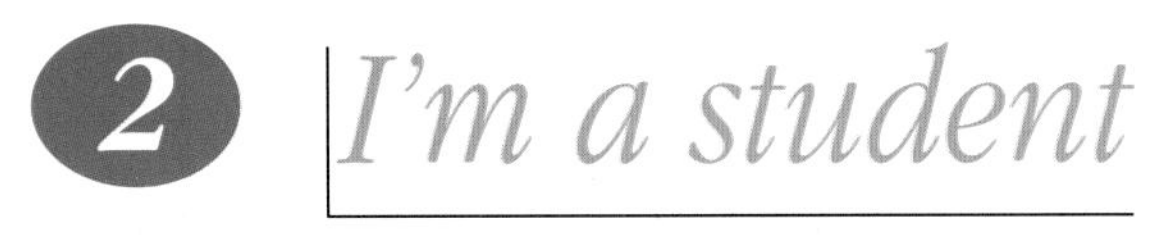

2 I'm a student

The indefinite article *a/an*; talking about jobs

VOCABULARY AND SOUNDS

1 Listen and repeat.

doctor teacher secretary actor
journalist singer student waiter
actress engineer job

2 Listen and match.

Pete	a teacher
José	b doctor
Hillary	c journalist
Maria	d student
Yıldız	e waiter
Hashimi	f singer
	g secretary
	h actor
	i engineer
	j actress

Pete – c

Now write the four extra jobs.

3 Listen and repeat.

job what's What's your job?
doctor a doctor I'm a doctor.
engineer an engineer
I'm an engineer.

2

GENERAL COMMENTS

Correction

You may want to explain your policy on correction to your students as early as possible. Decide if you'll correct them every time they make a mistake or only on the occasions when you are testing the manipulation of the target structure. It's possible at this stage that you'll want the students to be as accurate as possible at the expense of fluency. In any case, they do not yet have much language to use for fluency practice.

VOCABULARY AND SOUNDS

1 Aim: to present the pronunciation of the words in the vocabulary box.

- Explain to the students that the words in the box are all jobs. Ask them if they recognise any of them.
- Play the tape. Ask the studentsto listen and repeat the words. Are they similar to words in their own language?

2 Aim: to present the meaning of the words in the vocabulary box.

- In activity 1, the students were presented with the pronunciation of the words. In this activity, the students are presented with their meaning.
- Before you do the listening with the students, ask them to look at the drawings and match them to the list of jobs.

Answers
1 - b 2 - a 3 - g 4 - h 5 - c 6 - f 7 - d
8 - e 9 - j 10 - i

- Play the tape and ask the students to match the names and the jobs. There are four extra jobs.

Answers
Pete - c
José - b
Hillary - g
Maria - a
Yildiz - d
Hashimi - I
Extra jobs: e, f, h, j

3 Aim: to practise the pronunciation of the target structures.

- Play the tape and ask the students to repeat the phrases. Do this with the whole class and with individual students.

LISTENING

1 Aim: to practise listening for main ideas; to present a model conversation for activity 2.

- The students have simply to listen and follow the presentation conversation in this activity. Play the tape.

2 Aim: to practise reading to understand text organisation.

- Ask the students to read the conversation and to put it in the right order. Remind them of the model they listened to and read in activity 1.
- Ask the students to check their answers in pairs,

Answers

1	Maria	What's your job, Hillary?
2	Hillary	I'm a secretary. What's your job, Maria?
3	Maria	I'm a teacher.

- Play the tape and ask the students to listen and check their answers.

GRAMMAR AND FUNCTIONS

1 Aim: to present the use of the indefinite article.

- Ask the students to read the information in the grammar and functions box and then to do the exercises. They may like to do this activity in writing or with the whole class.

- Explain that in English you always use the indefinite article when you talk about jobs, and that an is used when the following noun begins with a vowel.

Answers
1 a 2 a 3 an 4 an 5 a 6 a

2 Aim: to practise using the present simple form of the first and third person singular of *be*.

- The students were presented with these structures in Lesson 1.

Answers
1 *'s* 2 *'s* 3 *'m* 4 *'s*

3 Aim: to practise using the present simple form of the first and third person singular of *be*.

Answers

Hashimi What's your job, Yildiz?
Yildiz I'm a student. What's your job, Hashimi?
Hashimi I'm an engineer.

4 Aim: to practise talking about jobs.

- This is the first time the students use the target language in a communicative context. Ask the students to answer the questions for themselves.

- Ask the students to go round asking and answering questions about their jobs. They can change jobs each time.

READING AND SPEAKING

1 Aim: to practise reading for main ideas.

- Ask the students to read the sentences and to match them with the photos.

Answers
1 - b
2 - c
3 - d
4 - a

2 Aim: to check comprehension.

- Explain that the sentences in activity 1 are true. Ask the students to read the conversations and to correct the false information. They can do this on their own and then they should check their answers with another student.

- Make sure everyone has corrected the false information.

Answers

Hello, what's your name?
I'm Philip. What's your name?
I'm Mel. What's your job?
I'm a doctor. What's your job, Mel?
I'm a waiter.

Hello, what's your name?
I'm Angie. What's your name?
I'm Jacqueline. What's your job?
I'm a student. What's your job, Jacqueline?
I'm a teacher.

3 Aim: to practise using the target language.

- Ask the students to work in pairs and to act out the correct conversations.

- Ask two or three pairs to perform their role play to the whole class.

4 Aim: to practise using the target language.

- Ask the students to think of other jobs, real or ideal, which they would like to know the English for. Ask them to act out similar conversations using these jobs.

- You may like to ask the students to write out these conversations for homework.

LISTENING

1 Listen and read.

JOSÉ What's your job, Pete?
PETÉ I'm a journalist. What's your job, José?
JOSÉ I'm a doctor.

2 Number the sentences in the right order.

☐ Hillary I'm a secretary. What's your job, Maria?
☐ Maria I'm a teacher.
☐ Maria What's your job, Hillary?

Now listen and check.

GRAMMAR AND FUNCTIONS

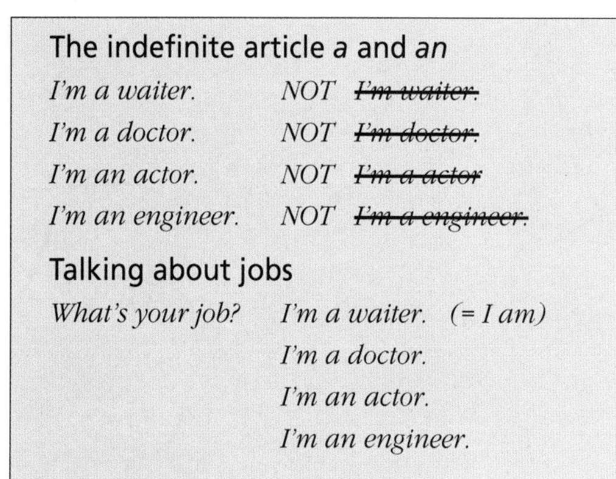

The indefinite article *a* and *an*

I'm a waiter.	*NOT ~~I'm waiter.~~*
I'm a doctor.	*NOT ~~I'm doctor.~~*
I'm an actor.	*NOT ~~I'm a actor~~*
I'm an engineer.	*NOT ~~I'm a engineer.~~*

Talking about jobs

What's your job?	*I'm a waiter. (= I am)*
	I'm a doctor.
	I'm an actor.
	I'm an engineer.

1 Write *a* or *an*.

1 I'm ____ doctor. 4 I'm ____ actor.
2 I'm ____ student. 5 I'm ____ journalist.
3 I'm ____ engineer. 6 I'm ____ waiter.

2 Write *'s* or *'m*.

1 What ____ your job? 3 I ____ a doctor.
2 What ____ your name? 4 My name ____ Bob.

3 Complete.

Hashimi What's ____ job, Yıldız?
Yıldız I'm a student. ____ your job, Hashimi?
Hashimi I'm ____ engineer.

4 Answer the questions.

1 What's your name?
2 What's your job?

READING AND SPEAKING

1 Match the sentences with the photos.

a Hello, I'm Jacqueline. I'm a teacher.
b Hello, I'm Philip. I'm a doctor.
c Hello, I'm Angie. I'm a student.
d Hello, I'm Mel. I'm a waiter.

2 The sentences in 1 are true. Correct the conversations below.

Hello, what's your name?
Hello, I'm Philip. What's your name?
I'm Mel. What's your job?
I'm a student. What's your job, Mel?
I'm a doctor.

Hello, what's your name?
Hello, I'm Angie. What's your name?
I'm Jacqueline. What's your job?
I'm a teacher. What's your job, Jacqueline?
I'm a doctor.

3 Work in pairs and act out the correct conversations.

4 Work in pairs and act out your own conversations.

3 How are you?

Greeting people; asking for and saying telephone numbers

VOCABULARY AND SOUNDS

1 Listen and repeat.

0 zero (oh)	1 one	2 two	
3 three	4 four	5 five	6 six
7 seven	8 eight	9 nine	10 ten

2 Say.

2 6 9 3 1 8 4
7 10 5 6 3 1

Now listen and check.

3 Complete.

tw_	o_ _	s_ _	ei_ _ _	th_ _ _
se_ _ _	fi_ _	fo_ _	te_	n_ _ _

4 Work in pairs. Say and write numbers.

Student A: (Say) *two*
Student B: (Write) *2*

5 Listen to these telephone numbers.

(tele)phone number

01223 589933 0171 454523
00 44 1 865 774356 01227 654398

6 Say these telephone numbers.

0175 348900 01456 88466
0378 015030 0161 778 4598

Now listen and check. As you listen, repeat the numbers.

LISTENING AND READING

1 Listen and read the conversations.

A FRANK Hello, Sarah. How are you?
SARAH Hello, Frank. I'm fine, thanks. How are you?
FRANK I'm very well, thank you.

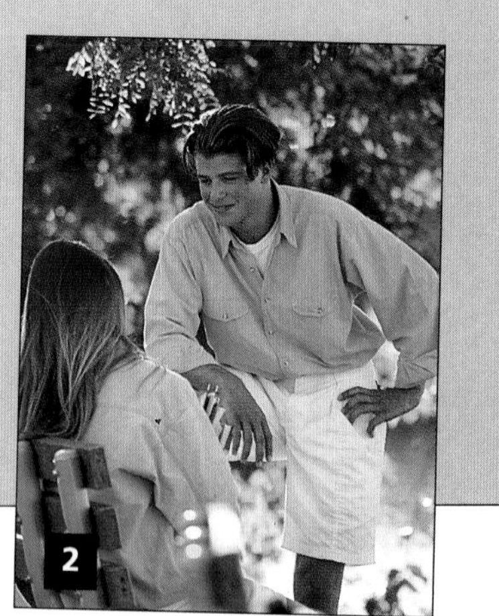

B MIKE What's your telephone number, Sue?
SUE 0171 589 3245. What's your telephone number, Mike?
MIKE 01993 453298.

2 Number the sentences in the right order.

A
- ☐ I'm fine, thanks.
- ☐ Hello, Michiko. I'm very well, thanks. How are you?
- ☐ Hello, Joan. How are you?

B
- ☐ 01967 328123.
- ☐ Goodbye.
- ☐ 0134 521 3987. What's your telephone number, Pete?
- ☐ Kate, what's your telephone number, please?
- ☐ Thank you. Goodbye, Pete.

Now listen and check.

3

GENERAL COMMENTS

Numbers

One of the most important lexical sets is numbers. The numbers 1 - 10 are presented in this lesson, numbers 11 - 20 in Lesson 6 and 21 - 100 in Lesson 7. You may feel that you need to have some extra practice at this stage. You can find some extra activities for numbers in the Resource Pack and in the Practice Book, or they will be easy for you to create yourself, using the model suggested in the Student's Book.

Pairwork

It may be that students have not done pair work in any other school subject. You may like to explain that doing pair work creates more opportunities for them to practise speaking. Furthermore, it's often more reassuring to practise a foreign language in a pair or in a small group rather than in front of the whole class. Perhaps most important, pair work is used as one of a number of techniques, the variety of which will contribute to the motivation of the students.

VOCABULARY AND SOUNDS

1 Aim: to present the numbers 1 to 10.

- Play the tape and ask the students to repeat the numbers. They may like to do this several times, on their own or in chorus.

2 Aim: to practise saying the numbers 1 to 10.

- Ask the students to say the numbers which the figures represent.
- Play the tape and ask them to listen and check.
- You may like to continue this activity by writing numbers in random order on the board, and asking students to say what they are.

3 Aim: to practise recognising the numbers 1 to 10 as words.

- Ask the students to complete the numbers with suitable missing letters.

Answers

two	one	six	eight	three
seven	five	four	ten	nine

4 Aim: to practise saying and recognising the numbers 1 to 10.

- Ask the students to work in pairs. One student should say a number, the other should write it down. You can give an example by dictating a series of numbers and for one student to write them on the board.

5 Aim: to present the words in the vocabulary box; to present telephone numbers.

- Write a telephone number on the board and ask them how they say it in their country. If the digits are pronounced in pairs, link like this: 0‿1 2‿2 3‿4 7‿6. Explain that telephone numbers in English are said digit by digit, and not, as in some countries, in pairs of digits.
- Play the tape and ask the students to listen to the telephone numbers.

6 Aim: to practise saying telephone numbers.

- Ask two or three students to say the telephone numbers to the whole class.
- Play the tape so the students can listen and check.
- Ask the students to practise saying the telephone numbers in pairs.

LISTENING AND READING

1 Aim: to present the target structures; to practise reading for main ideas.

- Ask the students to listen and look for clues which will help them match the conversation with the right picture.
- When they have done the matching activity, ask them how they came to the right answer.

Answer
Conversation A: Photo 1
Conversation B: Photo 2

2 Aim: to present the pronunciation of the conversations; to focus on text organisation.

- Ask the students to put the sentences in the correct order. Ask them to listen and check their answers.

Answers

1 Hello, Joan, how are you?
2 Hello, Michiko, I'm very well, thanks. How are you?
3 I'm fine thanks.

1 Kate, what's your telephone number, please?
2 0134 521 3987. What's your phone number, Pete?
3 01967 328123.
4 Thank you. Goodbye, Pete.
5 Goodbye.

FUNCTIONS

1 Aim: to focus on word order; to practise using the target structures.

- Ask the students to read the information in the functions box and then to do the exercises. You may like to ask them to do the exercises in writing or orally with the whole class.

● Explain that the words all belong to a single sentence but are in the wrong order. Check that they use suitable punctuation. Point out that *thanks* is an informal version of *thank you.*

● You may wish to point out that the question *How are you?* does not require a detailed answer!

Answers
1 Hello, how are you?
2 I'm fine, thank you.
3 I'm very well, thanks.
4 What's your telephone number, please?

2 Aim: to practise using the target structures; to focus on text organisation.
● Ask the students to read and complete the dialogue.

Answers
1 b 2 a

3 Aim: to practise using the target structures.
● Ask the students to complete the dialogue.

Answers
Hello, Pete, how are you?
Hello, Geoff. I'm fine/well, thanks. How are you?
I'm very well, thank you.

4 Aim: to practise using the target structures.
● Ask the students to work in pairs and to practise using the target language.

● Ask the students to go round the class practising the conversation.

5 Aim: to practise writing numbers.
● Ask the students to write the numbers in full. Tell them that it would be rare to do this in real life, but the activity is designed to check they have acquired the first ten numbers in English.

Answers
oh one two three three three four five
oh one seven eight six five four three three two
oh one seven seven eight three four five six
oh one two two three five six seven six five

READING AND SPEAKING

1 Aim: to practise saying telephone numbers.
● Ask the students to say the number aloud.

2 Aim: to practise recognising and saying telephone numbers.
● Ask the students to work in pairs. Student A says a number, Student B has to recognise the number and say the name.

3 Aim: to practise asking and saying telephone numbers.
● Ask students to go round asking and saying their names, jobs and telephone numbers. They should make a chart of each other's information.

FUNCTIONS

Greeting people

How are you? I'm fine, thanks. (= I am fine.)

How are you? I'm very well, thank you. (= I am very well.)

Asking for and saying telephone numbers

What's your telephone number, please?

Oh one seven one eight three seven seven two.

Remember! You say *oh* for *0* in telephone numbers.

1 Put the words in the right order and make sentences.

1 are you how hello?
2 you fine thank I'm
3 thanks very I'm well
4 your what's number please telephone ?

2 Read and complete.

a I'm very well, thank you.
b Hello, Val. How are you?

Hello, Henry.
(1) ____
I'm fine, thanks. How are you?
(2) ____

3 Complete.

____, Pete, how are ____?
Hello, Geoff. I'm ____, thanks. How ____ you?
____ very well, ____ you.

4 Work in pairs. Ask and say.

Hello, (name), how are you?
Hello, (name). I'm fine, thanks. How are you?
I'm very well, thank you.

5 Write in words.

0123 3345 01778 3456
01786 54332 01223 56765
Oh one two three, three three four five

READING AND SPEAKING

1 Read and say the numbers.

NAME	TELEPHONE NUMBER
Tim Clark	0161 524 3345
Will Bush	01557 345877
Dan Ford	01287 890992
Anna Green	0181 227 4567
Graham White	01821 778 2695
Jane Smith	00 44 1873 456789

2 Work in pairs.

Student A: Say a number.
Student B: Say the name.
Student A: 0181 227 4567.
Student B: Anna Green.

3 Ask and answer with other students. Complete the chart.

What's your name?
What's your job?
What's your telephone number?

Name	Job	Telephone number
Bertrand	*Student*	*91 23 78 45 67*

4 Are you James Bond?

Asking and saying names; spelling

VOCABULARY AND SOUNDS

1 Listen and repeat.

a b c d e f g h i j k l m n
o p q r s t u v w x y z

A B C D E F G H I J K L M N
O P Q R S T U V W X Y Z

2 Listen and repeat.

/eɪ/	/iː/	/e/	/aɪ/
A H J K	B C D E G P T V	F L M N X Z	I

/əʊ/	/uː/	/ɑː/
O	Q U	R

3 Listen and repeat.

spell how How do you spell ... ?

How do you spell James? How do you spell Bond?

How do you spell your name?

4 Work in pairs. Ask and say how you spell the names.

Francesca Yıldız Keiko Xavier Maria

How do you spell Francesca? F-R-A-N-C-E-S-C-A

5 Work in pairs.

Student A: Turn to Communication activity 1 on page 92.

Student B: Turn to Communication activity 15 on page 94.

LISTENING AND SPEAKING

1 Listen and read.

MAN 1	Are you Count Dracula?
MAN 2	Yes, I am.
MAN 1	Thank you. Are you Cleopatra?
WOMAN 1	Yes, I am.
MAN 1	Thank you. Are you Sylvester Stallone?
MAN 3	No, I'm not.
MAN 1	Oh! Are you Frank Sinatra?
MAN 3	No, I'm not. I'm Bond – James Bond.
MAN 1	Ah ha! Mr Bond, thank you very much. Are you Frankenstein?
WOMAN 2	No, I'm not. I'm Morticia.
MAN 1	Morticia. How do you spell Morticia, please?
WOMAN 2	M-O-R-T-I-C-I-A.
MAN 1	Ah, yes, Morticia. Thank you very much.
WOMAN 2	Thank you.

2 Work in pairs. Act out the conversation in 1.

4

GENERAL COMMENTS

GRAMMAR AND FUNCTIONS

Although the target language of asking and saying names in this lesson is described as a function, grammatically it represents the next step in the coverage of the present simple of the verb *be*. So far, What's *your name/phone number?* and *I'm a* ..., has been covered, and in this lesson *yes/no* questions for first and second person singular are presented.

VOCABULARY AND SOUNDS

1 Aim: to present the pronunciation of the English alphabet.

- Write the English alphabet on the board. Tell the students that there are twenty-six letters in the English alphabet. Ask them how many letters there are in their alphabet. If their alphabet is in Roman script, ask them to compare the letters of their alphabet with those of English. Are there any extra letters in English? Are there any extra letters in the students' alphabet(s)?

- Play the tape and ask the students to listen and repeat. Point to the letters on the board as you hear them.

2 Aim: to focus on the sounds of the English alphabet.

- Explain that the there are several similar vowel sounds in the letters of the English alphabet. Play the tape and ask the students to listen and repeat the sounds.

3 Aim: to practise the pronunciation of the target structures.

- Play the tape and ask students to repeat the phrases. Do this with the whole class and with individual students.

4 Aim: to practise pronouncing the target language.

- Explain what the words *spell* means. Spell your name and several students' names.

- Ask the students to work in pairs. Ask them to ask and say how you spell the names.

5 Aim: to practise spelling names.

- This is the first Communication activity, in which students work in pairs, and exchange information to be found in different places in the Communication activities section at the back of the book. This creates between the two students a fundamental concept in communicative teaching, the *information gap*, in which one student knows something the other student doesn't know, and vice versa. Make sure everyone knows whether they are Student A or Student B, and that they should not look at or read the other student's task/information. Show them where the Communication activities are (at the back of the book from page 92) and ask them to read their instructions.

- Ask the students to work in pairs. Explain the instructions to them.

LISTENING AND SPEAKING

1 Aim: to practise saying the target language.

- This activity is designed to encourage the students to manipulate the target structures in a relaxed way. Ask them to listen and repeat the sentences.

2 Aim: to practise saying the target language.

- Ask the students to work in pairs and to role play the conversation.

FUNCTIONS

1 Aim: to focus on the target language.

- Ask the students to read the information in the functions box and then to do the exercises. You may like to ask them to do the exercises in writing or orally with the whole class.
- Ask the students to do this on their own and then to check their answers in pairs.

Answers
Are you Philip?
Yes, I am. Are you Michael?
No, I'm not.
What's your name?
My name's Oonagh.
How do you spell Oonagh?
Oonagh.

- Point out that as a reply, there is no contraction in Yes, I am.

2 Aim: to focus on word order.

- Ask the students to put the words in the right order and make sentences.

Answers
1 Are you Yildiz?
2 No, I'm not.
3 What's your name?
4 My name's Chris.
5 Are you Thomas?
6 Yes, I am.

3 Aim: to practise using the target language.

- Ask the students to ask and say names, and how they spell them.
- When they're ready, ask the students to find a new partner and to continue the activity.

LISTENING AND SPEAKING

1 Aim: to practise using the target language.

- Ask the students to listen and take dictation of the spelling of the names below.
- Ask the students to match the names with the photos.

Answers
1 James Bond
2 Cleopatra
3 Dracula
4 Frankenstein
5 Rambo

2 Aim: to practise using the target language; to practise speaking.

- Ask the students to choose a character and to act out the conversation shown.

3 Aim: to practise using the target language; to practise speaking.

- Mime two or three jobs and elicit the target structure, *Are you ...?*
- Ask the students to work in groups of three or four and explain the instructions to them. They should read their own Communication activity and then be prepared to mime the job described. Each student has two jobs. The other students in the group should try to guess the job using *Are you ...?*

4 Aim: to practise using the target language; to practise speaking.

- Ask the students to act out the conversations and find out who all the people are and what they do.

Answers

Henry Schwarzkopf	doctor
Fiona Pink	teacher
Dave Dingle	student
Mike Handy	engineer
Fifi Lamour	actress
Tom James	singer
Frank Fearless	actor
Adam Hackett	journalist

FUNCTIONS

Asking and saying names

Are you Count Dracula? *Yes, I am.* NOT ~~*Yes, I'm*~~
Are you Frank Sinatra? *No, I'm not. (= No, I am not.)*

Spelling

How do you spell your name? *M-O-R-T-I-C-I-A.*

1 Complete.

Are ___ Philip?
Yes, I ____. Are you Michael?
No, ____ not.
What___ your ____?
My ____ Oonagh.
How do you ____ Oonagh?
O-O-N-A-G-H.

2 Put the words in the right order and make sentences.

1 you Yildiz are?
2 I'm no not.
3 your name what's?
4 Chris my name's.
5 you are Thomas?
6 yes am I.

3 Work in pairs. Ask and say.

Are you Marco?
No, I'm not. I'm (name). Are you (name)?
Yes, I am.
How do you spell (name)?
(Spell your name).

LISTENING AND SPEAKING

1 Listen and take dictation.

Now match the names and the photos.

2 Choose a character. Work in pairs and act out the conversation.

Are you Rambo? *No, I'm not.*
Are you James Bond? *Yes, I am.*

3 Work in groups of four.

Student A: Turn to Communication activity 2 on page 92.
Student B: Turn to Communication activity 16 on page 95.
Student C: Turn to Communication activity 26 on page 97.
Student D: Turn to Communication activity 40 on page 100.

4 Work together and ask questions to find out who the other students are and what their jobs are.

Name	Henry Schwarzkopf Fiona Pink Dave Dingle Mike Handy Fifi Lamour Tom James Frank Fearless Adam Hackett
Job	actress doctor teacher singer student actor journalist engineer

Are you Henry Schwarzkopf? *No, I'm not.*
Are you an actress? *Yes, I am.*

The first person to find out all the names and the jobs is the winner.

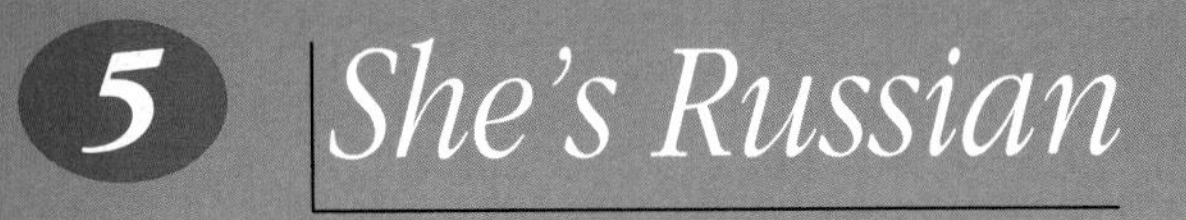

5 *She's Russian*

Saying where people are from; saying what nationality people are

VOCABULARY AND SOUNDS

1 Match the correct countries with the photos.

the United States of America Britain Turkey Italy Brazil Russia Japan Thailand

2 Listen and repeat.

Thailand the United States of America
Britain Turkey Italy Brazil Russia Japan

3 Count the syllables.

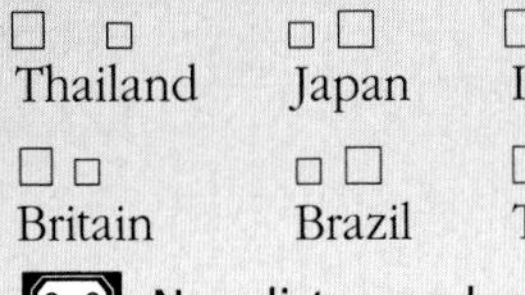

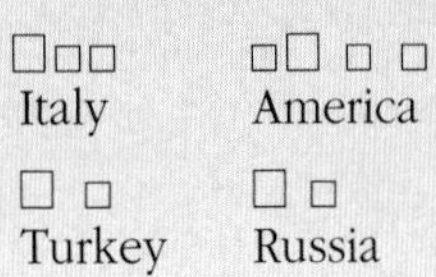

Thailand Japan Italy America
Britain Brazil Turkey Russia

Now listen and repeat.

4 Read.

country nationality

Britain is a *country*. British is a *nationality*.

5 Match *country* and *nationality*.

American Japanese Italian Brazilian Thai British Turkish Russian

American – the USA

Now listen and check. As you listen, repeat the words.

6 Write your country and nationality.

LISTENING AND READING

1 Listen and read.

A Steve Forrest is a doctor. He's British and he's from London.

B Henry Fuller is American. He's a waiter and he's from New York.

C Silvia Soares is from Rio. She's Brazilian and she's a student.

5

GENERAL COMMENTS

Be

This lesson is the next in the sequence of lessons presenting the verb *be* and focuses on the third person singular forms. You may decide you want to revise what the students have already learned. Write the main information from the functions/grammar boxes in Lessons 1 to 4 on the board.

Countries

As with jobs, the most important countries for students to learn are their own and those of their neighbours. Exceptionally, therefore, the words in the vocabulary box are to be seen as examples rather than target vocabulary. However, it will be useful if they can learn these countries as well. With stronger groups of learners, you may like to write the names of other countries on the board and to draw attention to the similarity of the name in English with the name in the students' own language(s).

VOCABULARY AND SOUNDS

1 Aim: to present the names of countries in the vocabulary box.

- Explain that the pictures show some well-known sights. Ask the students to look at the list of countries and to choose names for each picture.

Answer
Picture 1 - Japan
Picture 2 - Russia

2 Aim: to present the pronunciation of countries.

- Play the tape and ask the students to repeat the words they hear.

- Now that they can pronounce the names of countries, ask the students to check their answers to 1 in pairs.

3 Aim: to focus on syllable stress in words.

- Explain what a syllable is by writing a few words for countries on the board, saying them aloud, and underlining/numbering each syllable.

- Say the countries aloud and ask the students to count the syllables.

- Play the tape and ask the students to listen and repeat.

4 Aim: to present the words in the vocabulary box.

- The explanatory sentences in this activity are designed to illustrate the meaning of *nationality* and *country*.

5 Aim: to present the words in the vocabulary box

- Ask the students to look at the words in the Vocabulary box and match *country* with *nationality*.

- Play the tape and ask the students to listen and check. Ask them to repeat the words.

6 Aim: to check students know their own country and nationality.

- Tell the students what nationality they are and what country they come from. Write these words on the board. Do the same for neighbouring countries.

- Ask the students to copy their country and nationality.

- It may be useful at this stage to revise the language taught so far which they can use to describe themselves, in the form of a chart. Ask them to complete this chart as much as they can. Within the next few lessons they will be able to complete all of it. It will also help them to do *Listening and reading* activity 3.

  Name
  Job
  Country
  Nationality
  From
  Married
  Age

LISTENING AND READING

1 Aim: to present the pronunciation of the target structures.

- Ask the students to listen and to follow the descriptions.

2 Aim: to practise reading for main ideas.

- Ask the students to complete the chart with the information from activity 1.

- Ask the students to check their answers in pairs.

Answers

Name	Steve Forrest	Henry Fuller	Silvia Soares
Nationality	British	American	Brazilian
Job	doctor	waiter	student
From	London	New York	Rio

3 Aim: to practise listening for word recognition.

- If you have done the activity in *Vocabulary and sounds* activity 5, then your students may find this activity quite easy to do.

- Ask the students to read the paragraphs.

- Explain that you're going to play the tape of what they can read in this activity. Some of the information they hear is different from what they read. As they listen, they should underline anything which is different from what they hear.

Answers
"Hello, I'm Olga Maintz. I'm a secretary. I'm Russian and I'm from Moscow."
"Hi! I'm Mustafa Polat. I'm Turkish and I'm an actor. I'm from Ankara."
"Hello! I'm Patrizio Giuliani. I'm from Rome. I'm Italian and I'm a teacher."

4 Aim: to check the answers to activity 3.
● Ask the students to complete the remainder of the chart with the information they heard in activity 3.

Olga Maintz	Mustafa Polat	Patrizio Giuliano
Russian	Turkish	Italian
engineer	teacher	actor
St Petersburg	Istanbul	Venice

FUNCTIONS

1 Aim: to focus on word order.
● Ask the students to read the information in the functions box and then to do the exercises. You may like to ask them to do the exercises in writing or orally with the whole class.

● Ask the students to put the words in the correct order.

Answers
1 He's French and he's from Paris.
2 She's Italian and she's from Rome.
3 He's Thai and he's a teacher.
4 I'm an actor and I'm from London.
5 I'm Russian and I'm a doctor.
6 You're a secretary and you're from New York.

2 Aim: to practise writing the target structures.
● Ask the students to write out their *Listening and reading* activity 3 in full.

Answers
Olga Maintz is an engineer. She's Russian and she's from St Petersburg.
Mustafa Polat is Turkish and he's a teacher. He's from Istanbul.
Patrizio Giuliani is from Venice. He's Italian and he's an actor.

3 Aim: to practise using the target structures.
● Do this activity with one or two students to show them how to do it.

● Ask the students to work in pairs and to ask and say where they're from and what nationality they are. When they've finished, they should work with another student.

WRITING AND SPEAKING

1 Aim: to practise writing; to practise using the target language.
● Ask the students to complete the chart about these well-known people, and then to write sentences. You might like to check these sentences in groups, or as a class, to see that everyone has the correct information.

Answers
1 Pele is Brazilian. He's from Brazil.
2 Princess Diana is British. She's from Britain.
3 Pavarotti is Italian. He's from Italy.
4 Cher is American. She's from the USA.

2 Aim: to practise reading; to practise using the target language.
● Ask the students to do this activity in groups of three. Ask the students to look at the Communication activities and to read and remember the information.

3 Aim: to check the students' answers.
● You will find this activity works best if you tell them to start by giving the information which includes the names first.

● Ask the students to work together and use the information they have memorised to complete the chart.

Name	Terry Crystal	Maria Agnelli	Misha Godonov
Nationality	American	Italian	Russian
Job	actor	secretary	singer
From	Los Angeles	Naples	St Petersburg

● You may like to check the answers with the whole class.

● You may like to ask your students to write paragraphs about the people in activity 3 for homework.

2 Complete.

Name	*Steve Forrest*					
Nationality						
Job						
From						

3 Listen and underline anything which is different.

'Hello, I'm Olga Maintz. I'm a secretary. I'm Russian and I'm from Moscow.'

'Hi! I'm Mustafa Polat. I'm Turkish and I'm an actor. I'm from Ankara.'

'Hello! I'm Patrizio Giuliani. I'm from Rome. I'm Italian and I'm a teacher.'

4 Complete the chart with the information you hear in 3.

FUNCTIONS

Saying where people are from

I'm from Bangkok. (= I am)
He's from London. (= he is)
You're from Rome. (= you are)
She's from Rio. (= she is)

Saying what nationality people are

I'm Thai. *He's British.*
You're Italian. *She's Brazilian.*

1 Put the words in the right order and make sentences.

1 from Paris he's French and he's
2 Italian she's from Rome she's and
3 he's and teacher Thai he's a
4 I'm and actor from London an I'm
5 a Russian and I'm doctor I'm
6 you're from a you're secretary and New York

2 Write your answers to *Listening and reading* activity 3.

Olga Maintz is a secretary. She's ...

3

3 Work in pairs.

Student A: Say where you're from.

Student B: Say what nationality Student A is.

I'm from Rome. *You're Italian.*

WRITING AND SPEAKING

1 Complete the chart and write sentences.

Person	Nationality	Country
Pele	Brazilian	Brazil
Diana, Princess of Wales		
Pavarotti		
Cher		

Pele is Brazilian. He's from Brazil.

2 Work in groups of three.

Student A: Turn to Communication activity 3 on page 92.

Student B: Turn to Communication activity 10 on page 93.

Student C: Turn to Communication activity 22 on page 96.

3 Work together and complete the chart.

Name	Nationality	Job	From

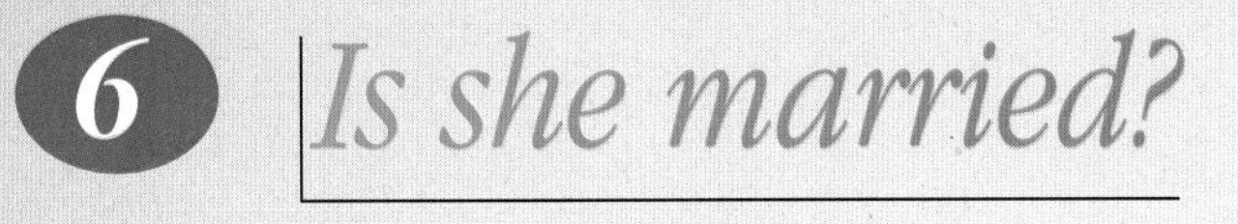

6 Is she married?

Yes/no questions and short answers

VOCABULARY AND SOUNDS

1 Listen and repeat.

11	eleven	16	sixteen
12	twelve	17	seventeen
13	thirteen	18	eighteen
14	fourteen	19	nineteen
15	fifteen	20	twenty

2 Say.

11 14 18 13 20 19 15
16 11 17 12 18 20

Now listen and check.

3 Listen and tick.

1 ☐	6 ☐	11 ☐	16 ☐
2 ☐	7 ☐	12 ☐	17 ☐
3 ☐	8 ☐	13 ☐	18 ☐
4 ☐	9 ☐	14 ☐	19 ☐
5 ☐	10 ☐	15 ☐	20 ☐

4 Now play *Numbers Bingo*.

Numbers Bingo

1 Complete the chart with numbers from 1 – 20
2 Work in groups of four or five. One of you says numbers from 1 – 20.
3 Tick (✔) the numbers in your chart if they are there.
4 Are there five ticks (✔) in a line? Yes? Say *Bingo*!

5		13		8
	7			
			12	

5 Complete Shirley Smith's card with these words.

name married nationality job address age

LISTENING AND WRITING

1 Listen and read.

Is Shirley Smith from Kenton?
Yes, she is.
Is she married?
No, she isn't. She's sixteen.
Is she a student?
Yes, she is.
And she's British?
Yes.

2 Number the sentences in the right order.

☐ And is he British?
☐ No, he isn't. He's American.
☐ Is Ken Stanwell from Kenton?
☐ Yes, he is.
☐ Is he married?
☐ Yes, he is.
☐ No, he isn't. He's seventeen.
☐ Is he a student?

Now listen and check.

3 Copy and complete the Membership card for Ken Stanwell.

6

GENERAL COMMENTS

Numbers

Numbers belong to a type of language known as fixed systems. These are lexical sets which pose no conceptual problem because they have direct equivalents in most other language. They are treated as vocabulary items in *Reward* and this lesson focuses on 11 - 20. Although these numbers are easy to understand, they may take time to learn as the number system only begins to follow a predictable pattern after 20.

VOCABULARY AND SOUNDS

1 Aim: to present the pronunciation of numbers 11 to 20.

● Write the numbers 11 to 20 on the board. Point to each number in turn and say it in English.

● Ask the students to listen and repeat the numbers as you play the tape.

● Point to numbers in turn and ask the class to say the number in chorus. Ask individual students to say what the numbers are.

2 Aim: to practise numbers 11 to 20.

● Ask the students to say the numbers they see on the page.

● Play the tape and ask the students to listen and check.

3 Aim: to focus on recognition of numbers.

● Ask the students to listen and to tick the numbers they hear. Play the tape.

Answers

1 ☑	6 ☑	11 ☐	16 ☐
2 ☑	7 ☐	12 ☐	17 ☑
3 ☐	8 ☐	13 ☑	18 ☑
4 ☐	9 ☑	14 ☑	19 ☐
5 ☑	10 ☐	15 ☐	20 ☑

4 Aim: to practise recognising numbers.

● Hearing and writing down numbers is difficult in a foreign language. This game is designed to give some intermediary practice before asking the students to do this. Explain that **Bingo** is a game which is played in Britain. The idea is that each player has a card with different numbers on it. Someone calls out numbers and if a player has the number on their card, they tick it. If a player has three or four numbers in a row, they call *Bingo*!

● Ask the students to complete the chart with numbers 1 to 20. Put the students in groups of 4 or 5. Ask one student to call out numbers from 1 to 20 in any order. Make sure the students tick the numbers as they are said. The first student to get four numbers in a line - vertical, horizontal or diagonal, is the winner.

● You could act as the number caller to start with as an example to the class. You may find that the game works better if you give out lists of numbers from 1 to 20 for the callers to use and cross off the numbers as they call them out.

5 Aim: to present the words in the vocabulary box.

● Say the words aloud and ask the students to repeat them. Explain that the words are often seen in documents, such as forms, identity cards etc. Ask them to look at the Membership card and to decide where the words go. They will recognise some of the words.

● Ask the students to check their answers in pairs.

● Check the answers with the whole class.

Answers

1 name	2 address	3 married
4 age	5 job	6 nationality

● You may wish to ask them to write their personal details by the words, and to work in pairs and ask and answer questions about each other. Check the questions they will need to ask first.

LISTENING AND WRITING

1 Aim: to present the target language.

● Ask the students to listen and read the conversation. Point out that the conversation refers to the person featured on the Membership card.

● Play the tape.

2 Aim: to practise using the target language; to focus on text organisation.

● This activity gives the students further exposure to the target language without asking them to manipulate the structure for the moment. Ask them to number the sentences in the right order.

Answers

7 And is he British?
8 No, he isn't. He's American.
1 Is Ken Stanwell from Kenton?
2 Yes, he is.
3 Is he married?
6 Yes, he is.
4 No, he isn't, He's seventeen.
5 Is he a student?

● Play the tape and ask the students to listen and check.

3 Aim: to practise writing.

● Ask the students to use the personal information about Ken Stanwell in activity 2 to complete his Membership card.

Answers

1 Name	Ken Stanwell
2 Address	Kenton.
3 Married	Single ☑
4 Age	17
5 Job	Student
6 Nationality	American

GRAMMAR

1 Aim: to focus on the target structures.

● Ask the students to read the information in the grammar box and then to do the exercises. You may like to ask the students to do the exercises in writing, or orally with the whole class.

● Make sure that everyone understand that the short answers do not use the contracted forms in the affirmative.

Answers
1e 2a 3f 4b 5c 6d 7g

2 Aim: to practise using the target structures.

● Ask the students to work in pairs and to act out the conversations in *Listening and writing* activities 1 and 2.

● Ask two or three pairs to perform the conversations to the whole class.

● Ask the students to act out conversations using information about someone in the class.

● Ask two or three pairs to act out these conversations to the whole class.

3 Aim: to practise using the target structures.

● [tape] Play the tape and ask the students to put a tick by the people who are married.

Answers
Jane ✓ Anna ✗ Sema ✗ Kazuo ✓ Steve ✓

4 Aim: to practise using the target structures.

● Ask the students to match the two parts of the exchanges.

Answers
1a 2c 3d 4c 5b

5 Aim: to practise using the target structures.

● Ask the students to work in pairs and to check their answers.

6 Aim: to focus on possible mistakes.

● Ask the students to tick the correct answer or question.

Answers
1b 2a 3a 4a

● Discuss why these answers are correct.

SPEAKING AND LISTENING

1 Aim: to practise speaking; to practise using the target structures.

● Ask the students questions about various members of the class, and elicit a correct short answer. Ask them to write 6 questions about another student.

● Ask the students to work in pairs and to continue asking and answering questions about people in the class. You may like to turn this into a game, in which each correct answer scores a point.

2 Aim: to practise speaking and listening.

● Ask the students to work alone and to think about their answers to the questions.

● You may like to check their answers with the whole class.

● [tape] Play the tape and ask the students to listen and check.

Answers

1 ✗	6 ✓/✗	11 ✗	16 ✗
2 ✓	7 ✗	12 ✓	17 ✗
3 ✓	8 ✗	13 ✗	18 ✓
4 ✓	9 ✓	14 ✓	19 ✗
5 ✓	10 ✓	15 ✗	20 ✓/✗

GRAMMAR

Yes/no questions and short answers		
Are you Italian?	*Yes, I am.*	*No, I'm not.*
Is he from Rome?	*Yes, he is.*	*No, he isn't.*
Is she married?	*Yes, she is.*	*No, she isn't.*
Is your name Dave?	*Yes, it is.*	*No, it isn't.*

1 Match the questions and answers.

1 Are you English? — a Yes, he is.
2 Is Ken Stanwell from Kenton? — b Yes, she is.
3 Is Ken Stanwell married? — c No, she isn't.
4 Is Shirley Smith from Kenton? — d Yes, it is.
5 Is Shirley Smith married? — e No, I'm not.
6 Is a Fiat Panda Italian? — f No, he isn't.
7 Is a Mercedes Brazilian? — g No, it isn't.

2 Work in pairs and act out the conversations in *Listening and writing* activities 1 and 2.

3 Listen and put a tick (✔) or a cross (✘).

	Jane	Anna	Sema	Kazuo	Steve
Married	✔	✘			

4 Match the questions and answers.

1 Is Jane married? — a Yes, she is.
2 Is Kazuo married? — b No, she isn't.
3 Is Anna married? — c Yes, he is.
4 Is Steve married? — d No, she isn't.
5 Is Sema married?

5 Work in pairs. Check 4.

Is Jane married? *Yes, she is.*
Is Anna married? *No, she isn't.*

6 Tick (✔) the correct sentence.

1 Are you married? a Yes, I'm. b Yes, I am.
2 Is she a secretary? a Yes, she is. b Yes, she's.
3 Is he from Rio? a Yes, he is. b Yes, it is.
4 a Is she Japanese? No, she isn't.
b Are she Japanese? No, she isn't.

SPEAKING AND LISTENING

1 Work in pairs. Write six questions about another student and ask and answer.

Is Kazuo Japanese? *Yes, he is./No, he isn't.*

Now check your answers.

Are you Japanese, Kazuo? *Yes, I am.*

2 Work in pairs. Ask and answer.

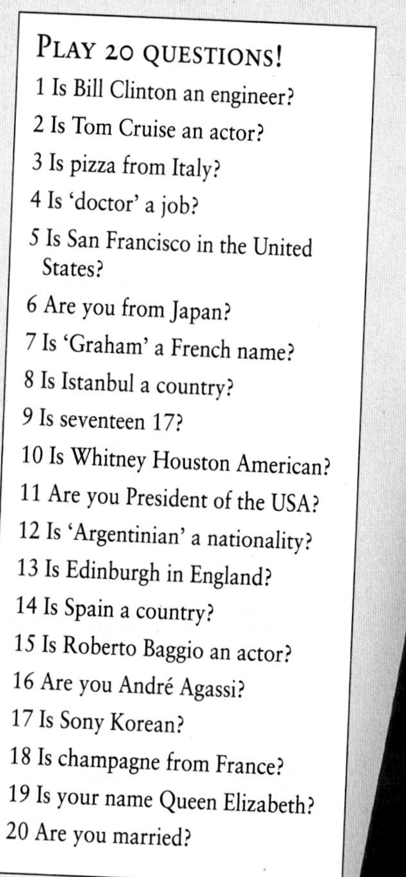

PLAY 20 QUESTIONS!

1 Is Bill Clinton an engineer?
2 Is Tom Cruise an actor?
3 Is pizza from Italy?
4 Is 'doctor' a job?
5 Is San Francisco in the United States?
6 Are you from Japan?
7 Is 'Graham' a French name?
8 Is Istanbul a country?
9 Is seventeen 17?
10 Is Whitney Houston American?
11 Are you President of the USA?
12 Is 'Argentinian' a nationality?
13 Is Edinburgh in England?
14 Is Spain a country?
15 Is Roberto Baggio an actor?
16 Are you André Agassi?
17 Is Sony Korean?
18 Is champagne from France?
19 Is your name Queen Elizabeth?
20 Are you married?

Now listen and check.

7 How old is he?

Asking and saying how old people are; present simple (review)

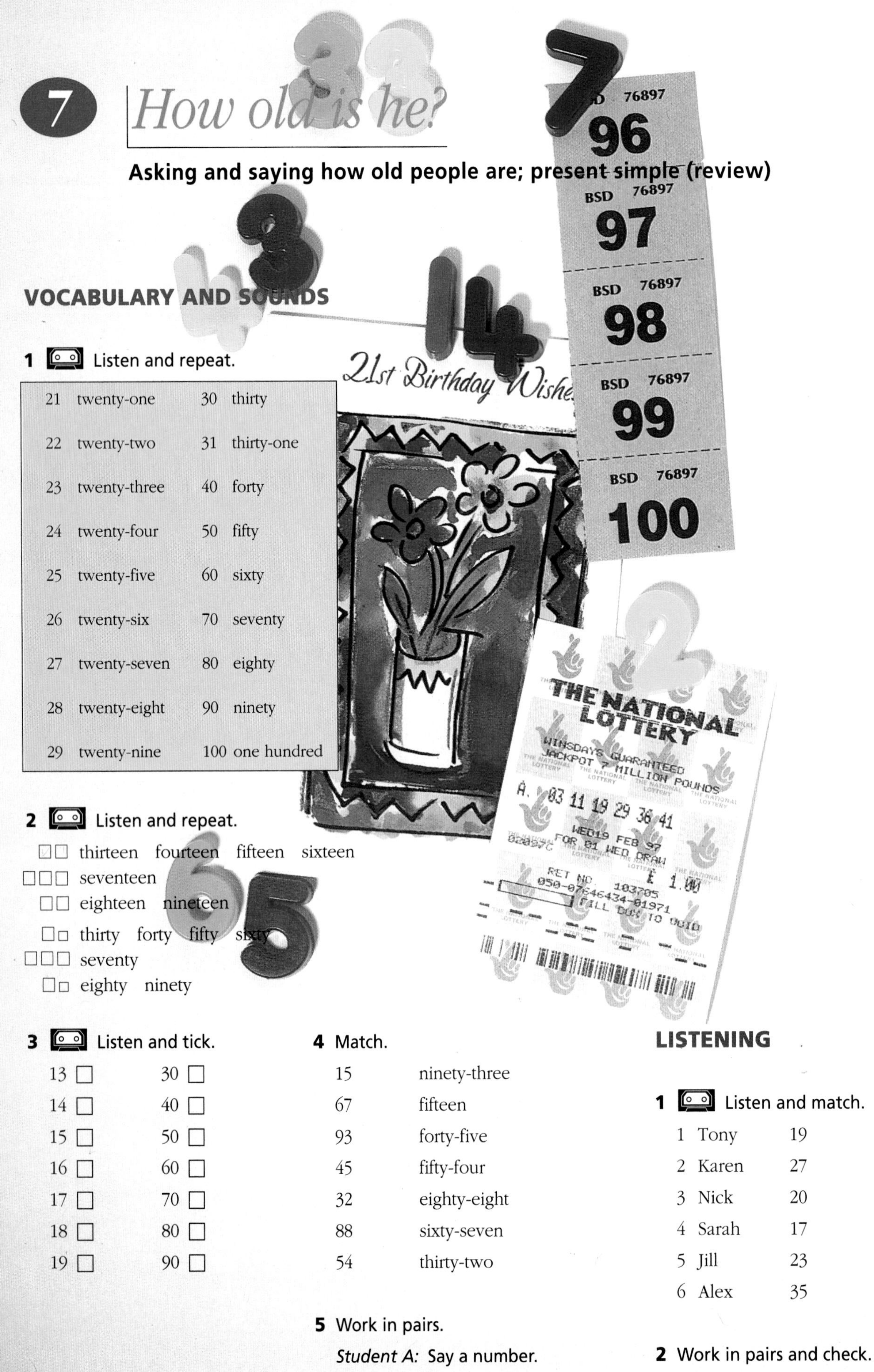

VOCABULARY AND SOUNDS

1 Listen and repeat.

21	twenty-one	30	thirty
22	twenty-two	31	thirty-one
23	twenty-three	40	forty
24	twenty-four	50	fifty
25	twenty-five	60	sixty
26	twenty-six	70	seventy
27	twenty-seven	80	eighty
28	twenty-eight	90	ninety
29	twenty-nine	100	one hundred

2 Listen and repeat.

□□ thirteen fourteen fifteen sixteen
□□□ seventeen
□□ eighteen nineteen
□□ thirty forty fifty sixty
□□□ seventy
□□ eighty ninety

3 Listen and tick.

13 □	30 □
14 □	40 □
15 □	50 □
16 □	60 □
17 □	70 □
18 □	80 □
19 □	90 □

4 Match.

15	ninety-three
67	fifteen
93	forty-five
45	fifty-four
32	eighty-eight
88	sixty-seven
54	thirty-two

5 Work in pairs.

Student A: Say a number.

Student B: Point to the photo.

LISTENING

1 Listen and match.

1 Tony	19
2 Karen	27
3 Nick	20
4 Sarah	17
5 Jill	23
6 Alex	35

2 Work in pairs and check.

How old is Tony? He's twenty.

7

GENERAL COMMENTS

Numbers

This lesson completes the presentation of numbers. Make sure everyone understands the phonetic difference between *thirteen* and *thirty*, *fourteen* and *forty* etc.

Socio-cultural training

As the introduction mentioned, an important syllabus strand in the *Reward* series is socio-cultural training, which is encouraging the students to develop an awareness that other cultures have different attitudes, beliefs, traditions and customs and that behaviour in one culture is not necessarily transferable to another. There is not a great deal of socio-cultural training that can be done at this level in the course. However, there is an opportunity in this lesson to discuss whether it is appropriate to ask people their age in the students' culture(s). In many cultures in the West, it is not considered polite to ask an adult how old they are unless they are in very specific circumstances, such as at the doctor's, for an identity card etc. In certain cultures in the East it is more acceptable to talk about people's age. Old age is highly respected as an indication of wisdom, and ascertaining someone's age may be necessary to find out which form of address is appropriate. If you can have this kind of discussion, even if it's in the students' own language, you will be able to begin the process of socio-cultural training,

VOCABULARY AND SOUNDS

1 Aim: to present the pronunciation of numbers 21 – 100.

- Write the numbers in the box on the board and say them aloud.

- Play the tape and ask the students to repeat the numbers in the box.

- Point to numbers on the board and ask the class to say them aloud in chorus. Then ask individual students to say them aloud.

2 Aim: to focus on the number of syllables.

- Say the numbers slowly and ask the students to repeat them.

- Play the tape and ask the students to repeat the numbers.

3 Aim: to focus on the distinction between *thirteen* and *thirty*.

- Ask the students to listen and tick the numbers they hear. Play the tape.

Answers

13 ✓	30
14	40 ✓
15	50 ✓
16 ✓	60
17 ✓	70
18	80 ✓
19 ✓	90

4 Aim: to practise matching numbers and words.

- Ask the students to match the numbers on the left with their word forms on the right.

Answers

15 fifteen
67 sixty-seven
93 ninety-three
45 forty-five
32 thirty-two
88 eighty-eight
54 fifty-four

5 Aim: to practise saying and recognising numbers.

- Ask the students to look at the photos and to point to the one which shows the number you say. Say numbers in the photos.

- Ask the students to continue this activity in pairs.

LISTENING

1 Aim: to practise recognising numbers.

- Tell the students that they are going to hear some people talking about ages. Play the tape and ask them to match the name of the person with their age.

Answers

1 Tony 20	2 Karen 27	3 Nick 19
4 Sarah 23	5 Jill 35	6 Alex 17

2 Aim: to practise speaking.

- Write the structure *How is he? How old is she?* on the board and say it aloud. Ask the students to say it aloud in chorus.

- Ask the students to check their answers to activity 1 in pairs.

GRAMMAR AND FUNCTIONS

1 Aim: to focus on punctuation; to focus on the target structures.

- Ask the students to read the information in the grammar and functions box and then to do the exercises. You may like to ask the students to do the exercises in writing or orally with the whole class.

- This activity can be done with students working alone and then checking their answers in pairs, or with students writing on the board.

Answers

1 How old are you?	4 She's twenty-three.
2 How old is she?	5 He's thirty-five
3 How old is he?	6 I'm twenty-two.

2 Aim: to focus on the target structures.

- Ask the students to match the questions and answers in activity 1.

Answers
1 - 6
2 - 4
3 - 5

3 Aim: to practise *yes/no* questions.

- This activity begins to revise aspects of the present simple of *be* which have been covered in preceding lessons.

Answers
1 - e 2 - d 3 - a 4 - b 5 - c 6 - a

4 Aim: to practice using the target structures.

- Ask the students to work in pairs and to check their answers to activity 3.

5 Aim: to practise using the target structures.

- Ask the students to ask and say what the age is of other members of the class.

LISTENING AND WRITING

1 Aim: to practise listening.

- Explain that the students are going to hear people in the photos talking. As they listen they should put the number of the person by their photo.

Answers

1 - Ella	2 - Maria	3 - Carlos
4 - Erol	5 - Anant	6 - Miki

2 Aim: to practise speaking.

- Ask the students to work in pairs. Ask student A to talk about one of the people and ask student B to listen and decides who Student A is talking about.

3 Aim: to practise writing.

- Bring old magazines into the classroom and ask students to choose someone famous, and to cut out photos of him or her and to write sentences describing them.

- Ask the students to stick the photos onto large sheets of paper and to write the sentences by the photos. They should then put the photos up on the wall so everyone can see them.

4 Aim: to revise vocabulary.

- Since this lesson reviews the presentation of the verb *be* so far, it may be useful to revise the vocabulary of jobs and nationalities.

Answers
jobs doctor engineer teacher journalist waiter singer secretary student actor actress
nationalities American Japanese Italian Brazilian Thai British Turkish Russian

- Ask the students if they can think of any more jobs and nationalities which they know. Make sure everyone knows what their own jobs and nationalities are!

5 Aim: to revise vocabulary.

- Ask the students to work in pairs and select words they know in Lessons 1-7 to translate into their own language(s).

- This activity will work best in a monolingual class.

GRAMMAR AND FUNCTIONS

Asking and saying how old people are

How old are you?	*I'm thirty-five.*
	I'm thirty-five years old.
How old is he?	*He's nineteen.*
How old is she?	*She's twenty-seven.*

Present simple (review)

Affirmative	Negatives	Questions
I'm	*I'm not*	*Am I?*
you're	*you aren't*	*Are you?*
he's	*he isn't*	*Is he?*
she's	*she isn't*	*Is she?*
it's	*it isn't*	*Is it?*

1 Punctuate and write questions and answers.

1 how old are you
2 how old is she
3 how old is he
4 shes twentythree
5 hes thirtyfive
6 im twentytwo.

1 How old are you?

2 Match the questions and answers in 1.

How old are you? *I'm twenty-two.*

3 Match the questions and answers.

1 Is Tony fifty-two?	a Yes, he is.
2 Is Karen thirty-five?	b No, she isn't. She's twenty-three.
3 Is Nick nineteen?	c No, she isn't. She's thirty-five.
4 Is Sarah nineteen?	d No, she isn't. She's twenty-seven.
5 Is Jill eighty-nine?	e No, he isn't. He's twenty.
6 Is Alex seventeen?	

4 Work in pairs. Check 3.

Is Tony fifty-two? *No, he isn't.*

5 Ask and answer about the ages of students in the class.

Is Marco thirty? *Yes, he is./No, he isn't.*

LISTENING AND WRITING

1 Listen and match the name with the picture.

Ella Miki Maria Erol Carlos Anant

1 – Ella

2 Work in pairs.

Student A: Talk about the people in the pictures.

Student B: Point to the correct picture.

She isn't married. She's 42.
She's an actress. She's American.

3 Make a poster of someone famous. Write sentences about:

– job
– where he or she's from
– nationality
– if he or she is married
– how old he or she is

4 Look at the vocabulary boxes in lessons 1–7. Count the words you know.

5 Work in pairs and check your answers.

Student A: Say words you know in lessons 1–7.

Student B: Translate the words Student A says.

8 His favourite car is a Porsche

Who **and** ***what*****; possessive adjectives:** ***my, your, his, her***

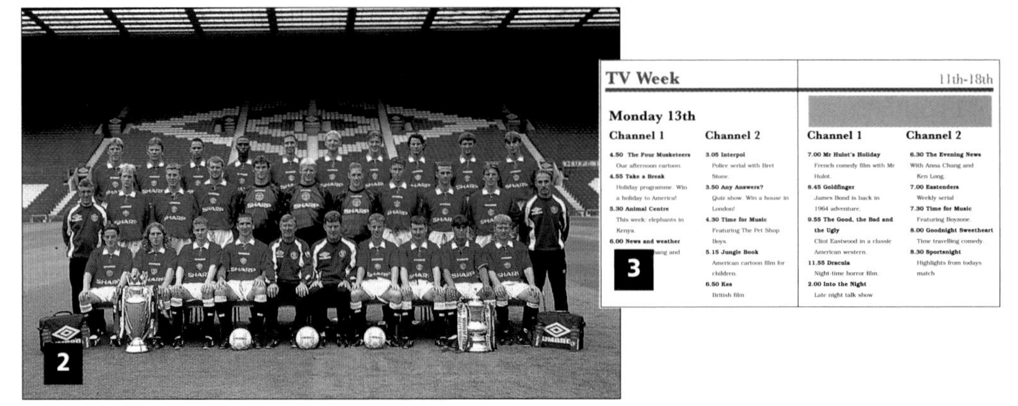

TV Week 11th-18th

Monday 13th

Channel 1

4.50 The Four Musketeers Our afternoon cartoon.
4.55 Take a Break Holiday programme. Win a holiday to America!
5.30 Animal Centre This week: elephants in Kenya.
6.00 News and weather ...hang and

Channel 2

3.05 Interpol Police serial with Bret Stone.
3.50 Any Answers? Quiz show. Win a house in London!
4.30 Time for Music Featuring The Pet Shop Boys.
5.15 Jungle Book American cartoon film for children.
6.50 Kes British film.

Channel 1

7.00 Mr Hulot's Holiday French comedy film with Mr Hulot.
8.45 Goldfinger James Bond is back in 1964 adventure.
9.55 The Good, the Bad and the Ugly Clint Eastwood in a classic American western.
11.55 Dracula Night-time horror film.
2.00 Into the Night Late night talk show.

Channel 2

6.30 The Evening News With Anna Chang and Ken Long.
7.00 Eastenders Weekly serial.
7.30 Time for Music Featuring Boyzone.
8.00 Goodnight Sweetheart Time travelling comedy.
8.30 Sportsnight Highlights from todays match

VOCABULARY AND SOUNDS

1 Match the words with the photos.

group politician football team TV programme TV presenter car

1 car

2 Listen and check. As you listen, repeat the words.

3 Listen and repeat.

favourite

singer favourite your favourite singer
Who's your favourite singer?

car favourite your favourite car
What's your favourite car?

actor favourite your favourite actor
Who's your favourite actor?

group favourite your favourite group
What's your favourite group?

READING AND LISTENING

1 Read and answer *Favourite people ... Favourite things.*

Favourite people ... Favourite things

Who's your favourite	singer?
	actor?
	politician?
	actress?
What's your favourite	car?
	group?
	football team?
	TV programme?

2 Read and listen.

Samantha Alton is a secretary. She's twenty and she's from Birmingham. Her favourite singer is Paul Young and her favourite actor is Sylvester Stallone. Her favourite group is U2 and her favourite TV programme is The Clothes Show.

Bill Henderson is a student. He's American and he's from Los Angeles. His favourite politician is Bill Clinton and his favourite actress is Sharon Stone. His favourite car is a Mercedes and his favourite American football team is the Chicago Bears.

3 Write the questions to Samantha and Bill's answers.

Samantha: Who's your favourite singer/actor?
What's your favourite ...?

8

GENERAL COMMENTS

Topics

Textbooks are not always able to present the most up-to-date topics because they are written some time, often years, before they are used in class. Events and personalities connected with certain topics, such as fashion, popular music and sport events may quickly recede into the past. But the textbook can create the opportunity for students to talk about favourite people and things and to personalise it so that the subjects become more student-centred. This is the intention of this lesson.

VOCABULARY AND SOUNDS

1 Aim: to present the words in the vocabulary box.

- It's likely the students will recognise some of these words, so ask them to say the meaning of any they know.
- Ask the students to say which of the words they see in the photos.

2 Aim: to present the pronunciation of the words in the box.

- [cassette] Ask the students to listen and repeat the words.
- Write the words on the board, point to them in turn and ask the students to say the words aloud.

3 Aim: to present the word in the vocabulary box; to present the pronunciation of the target structures.

- [cassette] Ask the students to listen and repeat the word in the box and the sentences. Use back chaining to build up the full sentences.
- [cassette] Ask several students to say the sentences, and then play the tape again.

READING AND LISTENING

1 Aim: to present the target structures.

- Ask the students to read the questions and to think about their answers.

2 Aim: to practise reading and listening.

- [cassette] Ask the students to listen and follow the text.
- You may like to use the paragraphs for some reading aloud practice. Ask the students to read the passages through to themselves. Then ask three or four students to read the passages aloud.

3 Aim: to practise writing the target structures; to practise reading for specific information.

- This activity will encourage the students to read the passages again more carefully and to think of the questions which the interviewer asked Samantha and Bill.

Answers

Samantha: Who's your favourite singer?
Who's your favourite actor?
What's your favourite group?
What's your favourite TV programme?

Bill: Who's your favourite politician?
Who's your favourite actress?
What's your favourite car?
What's your favourite American football team?

- Make sure everyone understands that you use *who* for people and *what* for things.

GRAMMAR

1 Aim: to focus on questions with *who, what.*

- Ask the students to read the information in the grammar box and then to do the exercises. You may like to ask them to do the exercises in writing or orally with the whole class.
- Ask the students to complete the sentences.
- Check this exercise with the whole class.

Answers

1 Who 2 What 3 What 4 What 5 Who 6 What

2 Aim: to focus on possessive adjectives.

- Ask the students to complete the chart.

Answers

I	my
you	your
he	his
she	her

3 Aim: to practise using possessive adjectives.

- Ask the students to write questions using the possessive adjectives *his/her*.

Answers

1 What's his favourite American football team?
2 Who's her favourite actor?
3 What's her favourite group?
4 Who's his favourite actress?

4 Aim: to practise using possessive adjectives; to practise reading for specific information.

- Ask the students to write full answers to the questions in 3. To do so, they will have to look back at the passages and look for the answers to the specific questions.

Answers

1 His favourite American football team is the Chicago bears.
2 Her favourite actor is Sylvester Stallone.
3 Her favourite group is U2.
4 His favourite actress is Sharon Stone.

WRITING AND LISTENING

1 Aim: to practise writing the target structures.

● Ask the students to imagine that these five pieces of information are answers. Ask them to write the questions.

> **Answers**
> 1 What's your favourite car?
> 2 Who's your favourite actor?
> 3 What's your favourite football team?
> 4 What's your favourite group?
> 5 Who's your favourite singer?

2 Aim: to practise listening for main ideas.

● Explain that they are going to hear Max and Sally talking about their favourite things. Ask them to listen and decide which question the two speakers are answering.

> **Answers**
> 1 M 2 S 3 M 4 M 5 S

3 Aim: to check comprehension; to practise speaking.

● Ask the students to check their answers in pairs.

4 Aim: to practise speaking.

● Ask the students to work in pairs and to talk about their favourite people and things.

● When they have finished, they can go round and talk to new partners.

5 Aim: to practise speaking.

● Ask the students to report back to the whole class what their partners said about their favourite people and things.

● You may like to ask the students to write a short account of their partner's favourite people and things.

GRAMMAR

Who and what

Who's your favourite singer?
Who's your favourite teacher?
What's your favourite car?
What's your favourite TV programme?

Possessive adjectives

	my		*My*	
What's	*your*	*name?*	*Your*	*name's Pat.*
	his		*His*	
	her		*Her*	

1 Complete with *who* or *what*.

1 _______ is your teacher?
2 _______ is your name?
3 _______ is your favourite country?
4 _______ is your address?
5 _______ is fifteen?
6 _______ is your job?

2 Complete.

I	my
you	
he	
she	

3 Write questions using *his/her.*

Samantha's favourite singer
Who's her favourite singer?
Bill's favourite car
What's his favourite car?

1 Bill's favourite American football team
____
2 Samantha's favourite actor
____
3 Samantha's favourite group
____
4 Bill's favourite actress
____

4 Write full answers to the questions in 3.

Samantha: Her favourite singer is Paul Young.
Bill: His favourite car is a Mercedes.

WRITING AND LISTENING

1 Here are some answers. Write the questions.

1 a Porsche ☐
2 Arnold Schwarzenegger ☐
3 Manchester United ☐
4 the Beatles ☐
5 Diana Ross ☐

1 What's your favourite car?

2 Listen to Max and Sally talking about their favourite people and things. Write M for Max and S for Sally by the answers in 1.

3 Work in pairs and check your answers.

His favourite car is a Porsche.
Her favourite actor is ...

4 Work in pairs. Talk about your favourite people and favourite things.

Who's your favourite singer? *Diana Ross.*

5 Tell the rest of the class about your partner's favourite people and things.

His/Her favourite singer is Diana Ross.

9 We're twins

Present simple: *we're, you're, they're*; plurals

VOCABULARY AND SOUNDS

1 Match the sentences with the photos.

friend twin neighbour

a 'We're friends.'
b 'We're neighbours.'
c 'We're twins.'

2 Match singular and plural words.

brother sister boy girl man woman

sisters boys girls women brothers men

3 Match the sentences with the photos in 1.

a 'They're girls.' b 'They're men.'
c 'They're women.' d 'They're brothers.'

4 Listen and repeat.

/z/ friends neighbours boys girls brothers sisters twins

READING AND LISTENING

1 Read and complete.

JANE Are you twins?
NICK Yes we are. I'm Nick.
DAVE And I'm Dave.
JANE Are you from London?
NICK/DAVE (1) ____ . We're from Manchester.
JANE How old are you?
NICK/DAVE (2) ____ .
JANE What are your jobs?
NICK/DAVE (3) ____ .
JANE What's your favourite football team?
NICK/DAVE (4) ____ .

a We're twenty-three.
b Manchester United.
c No, we aren't.
d We're students.

2 Work in pairs and check your answers.
Now listen and check.

3 Read the conversation and correct any information which is wrong.

PAUL Who are they?
JANE They're ... er Steve and Dick.
PAUL Are they from London?
JANE No, they're from, er, ... Liverpool.
PAUL And how old are they?
JANE They're eighteen. They're actors.
Now listen and check.

9

GENERAL COMMENTS

Plurals

This is the first of the lessons on plurality in nouns and in verbs. As far the nouns are concerned, explain that most plurals are formed with the addition of *-s*, but that there are a number of irregular plurals. As far as verbs are concerned, this may be a suitable occasion to explain that there is no difference in form between *you* in the singular and *you* in the plural. Furthermore, English has no distinction between a polite and an informal *you*, which students may find strange and even be uncomfortable about.

VOCABULARY AND SOUNDS

1 Aim: to present the first person plural form of *be* and regular plural nouns.

- Ask the students to match the sentences with the photos.
- Say the sentences aloud and ask the students to repeat them in chorus or individually.

> **Answers**
> 1 - c 2 - a 3 - b

2 Aim: to present the words in the vocabulary box; to focus on the form of regular plural nouns.

- Ask the students to match the singular and plural words. Tell the students that it's a good idea to note down any irregular plural forms.

> **Answers**
> brother - brothers sister - sisters boy - boys
> girl - girls man - men woman - women

- Say the words aloud and ask the students to repeat them. Make sure they pronounce woman /wʊmən/ and women /wɪmɪn/.

3 Aim: to practise using the words in the vocabulary box.

- Explain that some of the sentences can be used more than once.

> **Answers**
> a - 2/3 b - 1 c - 2/3 d - 1

4 Aim: to practise the /z/ pronunciation of most regular plural nouns.

- Play the tape and ask the students to repeat the words.

READING AND LISTENING

1 Aim: to present the target structures; to practise reading for text organisation.

- Ask the students to read the conversation and to decide where the sentences go.

> **Answers**
> 1c 2a 3d 4b

2 Aim: to check comprehension; to practise listening for specific information.

- Ask the students to check their answers in pairs.
- Ask the students to listen and check their answers to activity 1. Play the tape.

3 Aim: to read for specific information.

- This activity will involve some careful reading. Explain that there are some mistakes in the conversation. Ask the students to read it and underline anything which is not correct. Ask them to correct the wrong information.

> **Answer**
> **Frank** Who are they?
> **Jane** They're ... er ... Steve and Dick.
> **Frank** Are they from London?
> **Jane** No, they're from ... er ... Liverpool.
> **Frank** And how old are they?
> **Jane** They're eighteen. They're actors.
>
> **Correct information**
> Dave and Nick
> Manchester
> twenty-three
> students

- Play the tape and ask the students to listen and check their versions.

GRAMMAR

1 Aim: to focus on the affirmative form of the present simple of *be*.

● Ask the students to read the information in the grammar box and then to do the exercises. You may like to ask the students to do the exercises in writing or orally with the whole class.

● This activity represents a review of the different forms in the affirmative of the verb *be*. Check everyone uses suitable contractions.

Answers
1 're 2 're 3 'm 4 's 5 're 6 're

2 Aim: to focus on the affirmative and negative forms of the third person plural of *be*.

● Ask the students to correct the sentence in *Reading and listening* activity 3. This will involve both affirmative and negative forms of *be*.

Answers
1 They aren't Steve and Nick. They're Dave and Nick.
2 They aren't from Liverpool. They're from Manchester.
3 They aren't eighteen. They're twenty-three.
3 They aren't actors. They're students.

3 Aim: to focus on affirmative and negative forms of the first person plural of *be*.

● Ask the students to work in pairs and to write sentences which are true for them.

● Ask several pairs to read out their answers and correct them with the whole class.

4 Aim: to focus on affirmative and negative forms of the third person plural of *be*.

● Ask the students to work with new pairs and to talk about their answers to 3.

● Ask the students to report back to their original partners and to report back on what the second partner talked about.

5 Aim: to focus on the formation of plurals.

● Ask the students to say how most plurals are formed.

Answer
By adding *s* to the noun.

6 Aim: to focus on possible mistakes.

● Tell the students that in each pair of phrases/sentences, there is a mistake. Ask the students to tick the correct phrase or sentence.

Answers
1b 2a 3a 4a 5b 6b

READING AND WRITING

1 Aim: to practise reading for specific information; to practise writing.

● Ask the students to read the passages and to complete the chart.

Answers

Names	Kasem and Ladda
Nationality	Thai
From	Chiang Mai
Age	16/17

2 Aim: to practise speaking.

● Ask the students to complete the chart with information about themselves in pairs.

3 Aim: to practise speaking.

● Ask the students to work with someone they have a lot in common with. Encourage them to work with people other than their usual partners. Ask them to tell the class what they have in common.

GRAMMAR

Present simple: *we're, you're, they're*

we're	*(= we are)*	*we aren't*	*(= we are not)*
you're	*(= you are)*	*you aren't*	*(= you are not)*
they're	*(= they are)*	*they aren't*	*(= they are not)*

Plurals

Singular	Plural
brother	*brother**s***
sister	*sister**s***
boy	*boy**s***
girl	*girl**s***
BUT	
woman	*women*
man	*men*

1 Complete with *'m*, *'s* or *'re*.

1 We ____ doctors.
2 They ____ from Manchester.
3 I ____ British.
4 He ____ a student.
5 We ____ fine, thank you.
6 They ____ French.

2 Correct the information in *Reading and listening* activity 3.

They aren't Steve and Dick.
They're Dave and Nick.

3 Work in pairs. Write true sentences with *'re* or *aren't* .

1 We ____ students.
2 We ____ British.
3 We ____ from Bangkok.
4 We ____ seventeen.
5 We ____ friends.
6 We ____ neighbours.

4 Work with another pair and tell them your answers to 3. Then tell the class about each other.

They're students.

They aren't British.

5 Answer the question.

How do you form most plurals?

6 Tick (✔) the correct phrase or sentence.

1 a Two student. b Two students.
2 a Three books. b Three book.
3 a A football team. b A football teams.
4 a My favourite car is a Porsche.
b My favourite cars is a Porsche.
5 a They're doctor. b They're doctors.
6 a We're neighbour. b We're neighbours.

READING AND WRITING

1 Read and complete the chart.

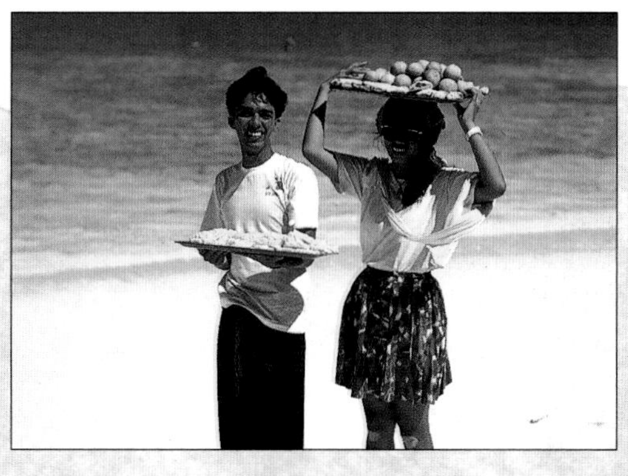

'We're Kasem and Ladda. We're friends. We're Thai and we're from Chiang Mai. We aren't married. We're seventeen and sixteen.'

Names	Kasem and Ladda	Students A and B
Nationality		
From		
Age		

2 Work in pairs. Complete the chart.

We're Kemal and Erol.

We're Turkish.

3 Find someone you have a lot in common with. Tell the class.

We're sixteen. We're from Italy...

10 What are these?

Asking and saying what things are; *this, that, these* and *those*

VOCABULARY AND SOUNDS

1 Listen and repeat.

pen books cassettes clock umbrella
watch wallet glasses bag keys

2 Listen and number.

1 - cassettes

3 Work in pairs. Look at the picture. Point and check.

One They're cassettes.

Now listen and check.

4 Read and listen.

/e/ pen cassette French ten

/ɒ/ clock watch wallet doctor

/ɪ/ this is six

Now say the words.

LISTENING AND SPEAKING

1 Listen and read. Point to the objects.

A What's this?
It's a watch.

B What are these?
They're glasses.

C What's that?
It's an umbrella.

D What are those?
They're books.

2 Ask and say what things are in the classroom.

10

GENERAL COMMENTS

Progress

The students have now completed the nine lessons in which the present simple of *be* is presented, and the next few lessons present structures which use *be* but which have a slightly different focus. You may want to ask the students if they feel they're making progress. They can spend a few minutes looking back over the lessons they have covered. Remind them about the function of the grammar and vocabulary boxes: they can be used to remind the students quickly of the language which has been covered so far. Point out that every lesson recycles what has already been taught and builds on it with new structures and vocabulary. This lesson is more of a vocabulary lesson, presenting some important words to be used in the classroom.

VOCABULARY AND SOUNDS

1 Aim: to present the pronunciation of the words in the vocabulary box.

- Ask the students to listen and repeat the words in the box.

2 Aim: to present the meaning of the words in the vocabulary box.

- [tape] Explain that the students are going to hear the words in the box in a certain order, and they should number the words as they hear them. Ask the students to number the items in the illustration to show the meaning of the word. Play the tape.

Answers

1 - cassettes
2 - glasses
3 - wallet
4 - pen
5 - clock
6 - umbrella
7 - keys
8 - book
9 - watch
10 - bag

3 Aim: to check comprehension.

- Ask the students to work in pairs and to check their answers to 2. They should point at each object illustrated and say what it is.

- [tape] Check this activity with the whole class.

4 Aim: to practise the pronunciation of /e/, /ɒ/ and /ɪ/.

- Write the words on the board and say them aloud.

- [tape] Play the tape and ask the students to listen and point to the words.

- Ask the student to say the words aloud.

- Point to the words on the board in random order and ask the whole class to repeat them. Continue with individual students.

LISTENING AND SPEAKING

1 Aim: to present *this, that, these* and *those.*

- The distinction between these words is one of distance and number.

- Ask the students to match the exchanges with the objects shown in the illustration.

- [tape] Play the tape and ask the students to listen and point.

- Explain that you use *this* for a singular object which is close, *that* for a singular object which is distant, *these* for plural objects which are close, and *those* for plural objects which are distant.

2 Aim: to practise using *this, that, these* and *those.*

- Write up the target structures *What's this? What's that? What are these? What are those?*

- Ask several students what various objects in the classroom are.

- Ask the students to work in pairs and to continue asking and saying what things are. You may like to use this activity to teach some important items of vocabulary which *Reward* Starter has not yet covered, but which are useful to you immediately.

FUNCTIONS

1 Aim: to practise using *this, that, these* and *those.*

- Ask the students to look at the information in the functions box and then to do the exercises.

- Communication activity: Ask the students to decide who is Student A and who is Student B, and then to follow their separate instructions. Student A has the words for some of the items in the illustration. Student B has the words for the other items.

2 Aim: to practise using *this, that, these* and *those.*

- Ask the students to work together again and to say what the objects are.

VOCABULARY AND SPEAKING

1 Aim: to present the words in the vocabulary box; to focus on loan words, cognates and international words.

- Explain that there are many words in English which are like words in the students' own language(s). Ask them if they recognise any of the words in the box. How many are words in the students' language(s)?

- Explain also that English has borrowed many words from other languages, such as *pizza*. Are there any words which English has borrowed from the students' language(s)?

2 Aim: to revise the words in Lessons 1 to 10.

- The students have already played Number Bingo in Lesson 6. This is the same game except that the chart is filled with words and not numbers. Ask them to fill the chart with words taken only from the vocabulary boxes in Lesson 1 to 10.

- Ask students to work in groups of 4 or 5. Give one student in each group a list of 30+ words from Lessons 1 to 10. The student with the list calls out the words randomly from the list (ticking off those he/she calls out) and the other students cross through the words in their charts. When a student has ticked off five words in a row - horizontally, vertically or diagonally - he/she is the winner.

FUNCTIONS

Asking and saying what things are

What's this?	*It's a watch.*
What's that?	*It's an umbrella.*
What are these?	*They're glasses.*
What are those?	*They're books.*

1 Work in pairs.

Student A: Turn to Communication activity 4 on page 92.

Student B: Turn to Communication activity 17 on page 95.

2 Work in pairs. Ask and say what's in the picture below.

What's this? It's a football.

What's that? It's a television.

VOCABULARY AND SPEAKING

1 Translate. How many words are similar to your language?

sandwich television pizza theatre
football telephone coffee cinema tennis
taxi bus burger video

2 Play *Word Bingo*.

Word Bingo

1 Complete the chart with words from Lessons 1 – 10.

2 Work in groups of four or five. One of you says words from lessons 1 – 10.

3 Tick (✔) the words in your chart if they are there.

4 Are there five ticks (✔) in a line? Yes? Say *Bingo*!

telephone				
		group		
			football	
				American
	teacher			

Progress check 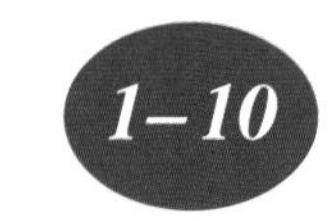

1–10

VOCABULARY

1 Put the words from Lessons 1 – 10 under the following headings: *nationalities, countries, jobs, numbers, family, classroom language.*

Nationalities: American

American ask correct sister doctor English fifteen forty journalist brother Japan listen one read student teacher Thai Turkey twenty-four

2 Write more words in the columns in 1.

3 Look at the pictures and complete the crossword with classroom words.

	1			c				
2				l				
			3	a				
				4 s	a	y		
				5 s				
			6	r				
			7 l	o	o	k		
			8 p	o	i	n	t	
		9		m				

4 Look at the words in Lessons 1 to 10 again. Choose words which are useful to you and write them in your *Wordbank* in the Practice Book.

1

2

3

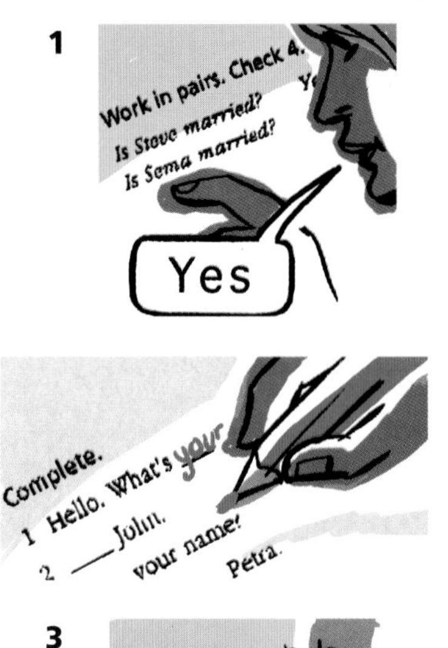

5

9

GRAMMAR

1 Match the questions and answers.

1 What's your name?
2 How are you?
3 Are they from London?
4 What's this?
5 Who's your favourite actor?
6 Is she nineteen?
7 What are these?
8 How old are you?
9 What's his job?
10 Are you married?

a No, they aren't.
b They're glasses.
c Sylvester Stallone.
d No, I'm not.
e My name's Steve.
f He's a teacher.
g Fine thanks, how are you?
h Twenty-seven.
i It's a book.
j Yes, she is.

2 Punctuate.

1 whats her name
2 im very well
3 how do you spell book
4 is this a book
5 my names frank
6 where are you from
7 im from acapulco in mexico
8 no it isnt

1 What's her name?

Progress check 1–10

You can work through this Progress check in the order shown, or concentrate on areas which may have caused difficulty in Lessons 1 to 10. You can also let the students choose the activities which they would like or feel the need to do.

VOCABULARY

1 Aim: to revise words presented in the vocabulary boxes in lessons 1 to 10.

● You may like to explain that categorising vocabulary is a good way to reinforce the vocabulary acquisition process. The more vocabulary the students acquire the more useful it becomes. It's also a good way of recording new words. Sometimes words can be recorded according to their topic; on other occasions, it can be more personalised, such as words which are useful to the student, words which sound nice, words which look like words in their own language, etc.

Answers

nationalities	American English Thai
countries	Japan Turkey
jobs	doctor journalist student teacher
numbers	fifteen forty one twenty-four
family	sister brother
classroom	ask correct listen read student teacher

2 Aim: to revise words presented in the vocabulary boxes in lessons 1 to 10.

● Ask the students to look back at the words in the vocabulary boxes in Lessons 1 to 10 and to choose four or five more words for each category.

3 Aim: to revise the classroom language presented on pages 2 and 3.

● Ask the students to look at the illustrations and decide what word they show. The number corresponds to the illustration.

Answers
1 - check
2 - complete
3 - match
5 - spell
6 - order
9 - number

4 Aim: to develop good learner training skills.

● Ask the students to look at the words they have learned in Lessons 1–10 and to write down ones which are useful to them in their *Wordbank* in the Practice Book.

GRAMMAR

1 Aim: to revise question forms and answers.

Answers
1e 2g 3a 4i 5c 6j 7b 8h 9f 10d

2 Aim: to revise punctuation.

Answers
1 What's her name?
2 I'm very well.
3 How do you spell *book?*
4 Is this a book?
5 My name's Frank.
6 Where are you from?
7 I'm from Acapulco in Mexico.
8 No, it isn't.

3 Aim: to revise possible mistakes.

Answers
1a 2a 3b 4a 5a 6a

4 Aim: to revise *yes/no* questions and short answers.

1 Is he your brother? Yes, he is.
2 What are those? They're glasses.
3 Are you English? Yes, we are.
4 Are they French? Yes, they are.

SOUNDS

1 Aim: to revise the pronunciation of /æ/, /e/ and /ɑɪ/.

- Play the tape and ask the students to listen and repeat the sounds. If these phonemes exist in your students' own language(s), there's no need to spend more time than necessary.

2 Aim: to revise stress in words.

- Ask the students to remember on which syllable the stress in these words fall.
- Play the tape and ask the students to underline the stressed syllables.

Answers

Turkey Japan Thailand England
seven eleven thirty eighteen hundred
cassette umbrella telephone

3 Aim: to revise stressed words in sentences.

- Tell the students that the words which a speaker stresses are the words which the speaker considers to be important in a sentence. Encourage them to listen to the stressed words in English.
- Play the tape and ask the students to repeat the sentences. Make sure they stress the words which are underlined.
- Ask the students to repeat the sentences again.
- Play the tape one more time.

READING AND LISTENING

1 Aim: to practise reading for text organisation.

- The songs in *Reward* Starter are included above all for entertainment. It's important to use the students' interest in listening to British and American songs as a source of motivation. It's also important to expose them to as much authentic English as soon as possible, and to make them realise that even if they don't understand every word, they can understand the general sense.
- Ask the students to read the Bill Hailey song and to decide where the sentences go.

Answers

1e 2c 3d 4a 5b

2 Aim; to practise listening for specific information; to listen for pleasure.

- Although this activity involves listening and checking, it's main aim is to listen and enjoy the song.
- Play the song and ask the students to follow it in their books.
- You may want to explain a few words, but it's essential not to explain the meaning of every word. The students must be trained to realise that they will not understand every word when they listen to authentic English. Suggest that you'll explain the meaning of, say, six words and that they must choose them carefully. After a few sessions restricting the number of words you explain, they will stop asking for further explanation.

3 Tick (✔) the correct sentence.

1 a He's English. ☐
  b His English. ☐
2 a His name's Frank. ☐
  b He's name's Frank. ☐
3 a What's you're name? ☐
  b What's your name? ☐
4 Are you married?
  a Yes, I am. ☐
  b Yes, I'm. ☐
5 a They're from Mexico. ☐
  b Their from Mexico. ☐
6 a We're English. ☐
  b Where English. ☐

4 Complete.

1 Is ____ your brother? Yes, he ____.
2 What ____ those? They ____ glasses.
3 Are you English? Yes, we ____.
4 Are ____ French? Yes, they ____.

SOUNDS

1 Listen and repeat.

/æ/ thank taxi actor American
/e/ telephone pen umbrella eleven
/aɪ/ five nine ninety my United

2 Listen and underline the stressed syllable.

Turkey Japan Thailand England seven eleven thirty eighteen hundred cassette umbrella telephone

3 Listen and repeat.

1 What's your name? 3 How old are you?
2 Are you from London? 4 What's your job?

READING AND LISTENING

1 Read the words of the song *Rock around the clock* by Bill Hailey and the Comets. Decide where these sentences go.

a eight, nine, ten, eleven, too
b twelve
c two, three and four,
d five and six and seven
e Five, six, seven o'clock, eight o'clock rock

One, two, three o'clock, four o'clock rock,
(1) ____
Nine, ten, eleven o'clock, twelve o'clock rock,
We're gonna rock around the clock tonight.
Put your glad rags on and join me hon'
We'll have some fun when the clock strikes one,
Chorus
We're gonna rock around the clock tonight
We're gonna rock, rock, rock til broad daylight
We're gonna rock, gonna rock around the clock tonight.
When the clock strikes (2) ____
If the band slows down, we'll yell for more
Chorus
When the chimes ring (3) ____
We'll be rockin' up in seventh heaven.
Chorus
When it's (4) ____
I'll be going strong and so will you,
Chorus
When the clock strikes (5) ____, we'll cool off, then
Start a rocking round the clock again.
Chorus

2 Listen and check.

11 How much are they?

Talking about prices; position of adjectives; the definite article *the*

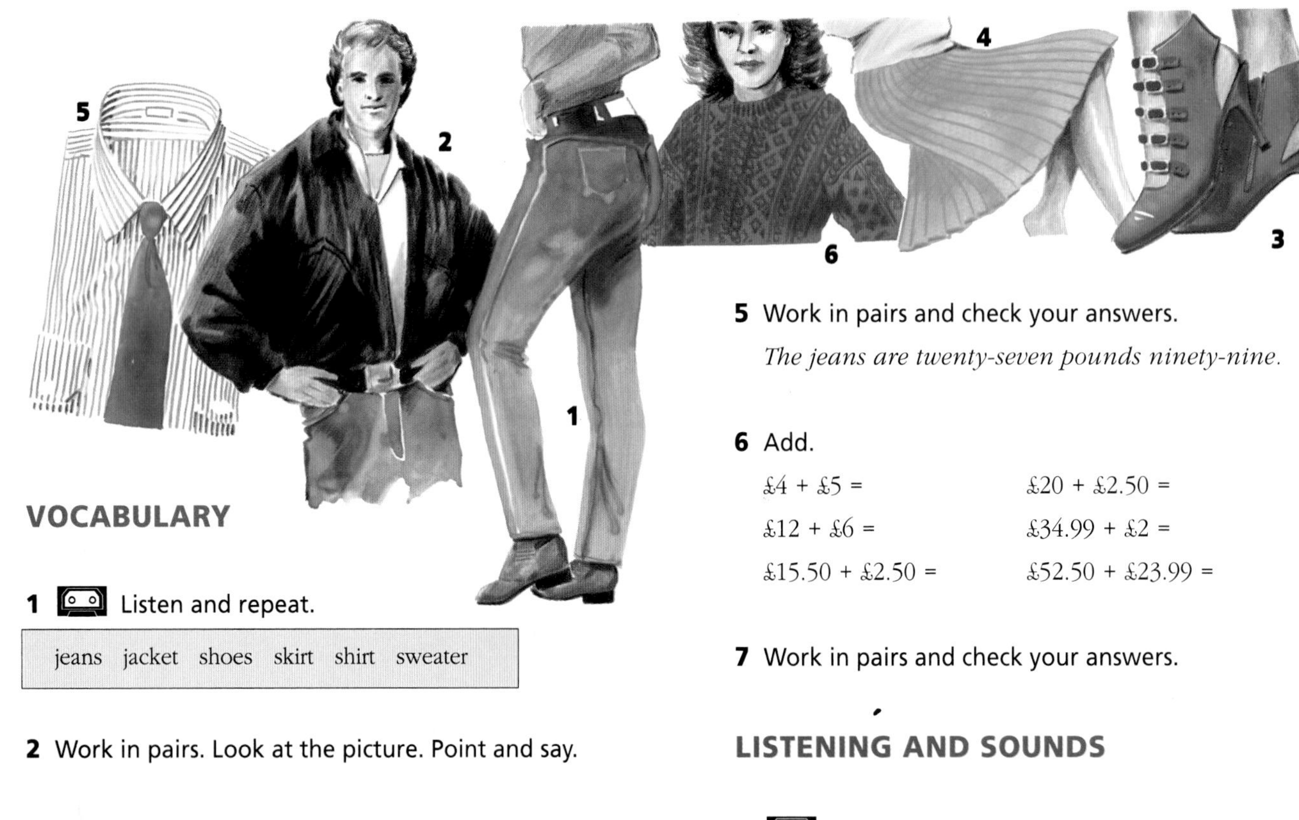

VOCABULARY

1 Listen and repeat.

jeans jacket shoes skirt shirt sweater

2 Work in pairs. Look at the picture. Point and say.

3 Match the words in the box with the colours below.

black blue white red green

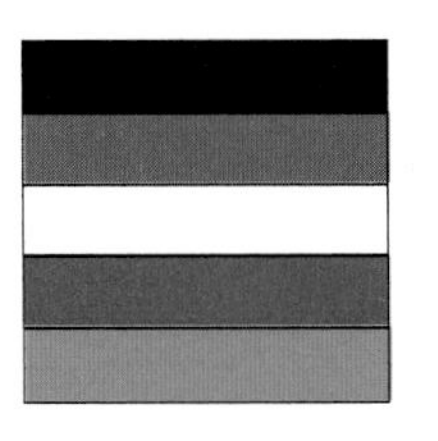

4 Listen and match the clothes and the prices.

pound pence

Twelve pounds fifty pence = £12.50

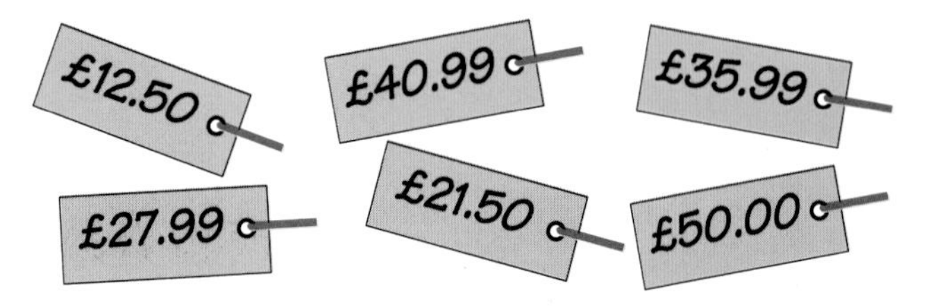

5 Work in pairs and check your answers.

The jeans are twenty-seven pounds ninety-nine.

6 Add.

£4 + £5 =
£12 + £6 =
£15.50 + £2.50 =
£20 + £2.50 =
£34.99 + £2 =
£52.50 + £23.99 =

7 Work in pairs and check your answers.

LISTENING AND SOUNDS

1 Listen and underline anything which is different.

CUSTOMER How much are these red shoes?
ASSISTANT They're £27.50.
CUSTOMER And how much is that white sweater?
ASSISTANT It's £15.
CUSTOMER How much is this black jacket?
ASSISTANT It's £50.
CUSTOMER How much are these blue jeans?
ASSISTANT They're £35.99.

2 Work in pairs and correct the conversation.
Now listen again and check.

3 Listen and repeat.

How much is this black jacket?
It's fifty pounds.
How much are these blue jeans?
They're thirty-five, ninety-nine.

11

GENERAL COMMENTS

Adjectives

This is the first time adjectives have been presented in *Reward* Starter. It's important to point out that most adjectives can go in two positions: after the verb *be* and before the noun. Some very common adjectives can only go after the verb *be*, for example *asleep, ill*. However, this type of adjective is avoided until a later stage.

VOCABULARY

1 Aim: to present the words in the vocabulary box.

- The words in the boxes, here and below, represent the barest minimum of words for clothes and colours. It's a good idea to ask the students to suggest two or three extra words for clothes and colours which they particularly require during the course of the lesson, and add them to the list of productive vocabulary.

- Ask the students to listen and repeat the words as you play the tape.

- Ask the students to work in pairs, to look at the pictures, point to and say the corresponding word.

2 Aim: to present the words in the vocabulary box.

- Ask the students to work in pairs, to look at the pictures, point to and say the corresponding word.

3 Aim: to present the words in the vocabulary box.

- Say the words aloud and ask the students to repeat them.

- Explain to the students that the colour of the boxes in the chart corresponds to the word for the colour. Ask them to do this activity on their own and then to check it in pairs.

4 Aim: to present the words in the vocabulary box; to check comprehension.

- Say the words aloud and ask students to repeat them.

- Ask the students to guess how much the clothes in the illustration cost.

- Ask the students to listen and match the prices and the clothes. Play the tape.

Answers
1 - £27.99 2 - £50 3 - £40.99
4 - £35.99 5 - £12.50 6 - £21.50

5 Aim: to practise using the new vocabulary; to practise speaking.

- Ask the students to work in pairs and to check their answers to activity 4.

6 Aim: to practise using numbers and prices.

- The students will have already covered numbers in earlier lessons, but they may still find them difficult to say. Ask them to do this activity alone. In the next activity, they will have the opportunity of checking their answers in pairs.

7 Aim: to practise using numbers and prices; to practise speaking.

- Ask the student to check their answers to activity 5 in pairs. Then check the answers with the whole class. Make sure everyone is using numbers and prices correctly.

Answers
£9 £22.50
£18 £36.99
£18 £76.49

- Write a few more prices on the board, and ask the students to say them aloud.

LISTENING AND SOUNDS

1 Aim: to practise listening for specific information; to present the target structures.

- This activity will encourage some very careful listening. Explain to the students that they will hear a conversation which is slightly different from what they read. They should listen and underline anything which is different from what they hear. Play the tape.

Answers

Customer	How much are these red shoes?
Assistant	They're £27.50.
Customer	And how much is that white sweater?
Assistant	It's £15.
Customer	How much is this black jacket?
Assistant	It's £50.
Customer	How much are these blue jeans?
Assistant	They're £35.99.

2 Aim: to practise speaking.

- Ask the students to work together and to correct the conversation with the information they heard.

- Play the tape again and ask the students to listen and check.

3 Aim: to practise pronouncing the target structures.

- Ask the students to listen and repeat the sentences shown.

- Say some similar sentences and ask the students to repeat them.

FUNCTIONS AND GRAMMAR

1 Aim: to practise using *how much is it/are they?*

- Ask the students to read the information in the functions and grammar box and then to do the exercises.

- Make sure everyone understands that *How much is it?* goes with singular items and *How much are they?* goes with plural items.

Answers
a - 1 b - 2

2 Aim: to practise using the target structures; to practise speaking.

- Ask the students to act out the corrected conversation they heard in *Listening and sounds* activity 1.

3 Aim: to practise using the target structures; to practise speaking.

- Explain to the students that they are going to ask and answer questions about the items in the illustration. Student A will have information that Student B doesn't have.

- Ask the students to decide who in each pair is Student A and who is Student B. Ask them to follow the instructions.

- Check the answers with the whole class.

4 Aim: to focus on possible mistakes.

- Ask the students to tick the correct sentence.

Answers
1 b 2 a 3 a

- Check the answers with the whole class. Explain why the sentences are wrong. (When an adjective goes with a noun, it goes before not after it.)

LISTENING AND SPEAKING

1 Aim: to practise using the target structures.

- Explain to the students that the prices of internationally known products are often used to illustrate the relative wealth of a nation's economy. Ask them if they know what the products are.

2 Aim: to practise listening.

- Say the prices aloud and ask the students to repeat them.

- Ask the students to listen and put the letter corresponding to the correct price in the *BRITAIN* column of the chart. Play the tape.

Answers
Big Mac - £2 Levi jeans - £30
Nike trainers - £40 Cola - £0.35

- Ask the students to work in pairs and to check their answers.

- Check the answers with the whole class.

3 Aim: to practise speaking.

- Ask the students to compare the prices of the items in Britain with their price in the students' own country(ies).

FUNCTIONS AND GRAMMAR

Talking about prices

How much is this black jacket?
It's fifty pounds. (£50)
How much are these blue jeans?
They're thirty-five, ninety-nine. (£35.99)

Position of adjectives

the blue jacket
the black jeans
the white sweater
NOT ~~the jacket blue~~
NOT ~~the jeans black~~
NOT ~~the sweater white~~

The definite article *the*

How much are the red shoes?

1 Match the sentence with the picture.

a How much are they?
b How much is it?

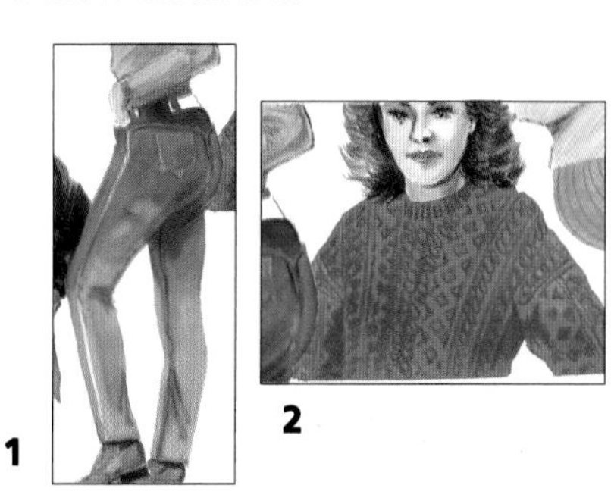

2 Work in pairs. Act out the conversation in *Listening and sounds* activity 1.

3 Work in pairs.

Student A: Turn to Communication activity 5 on page 92.

Student B: Turn to Communication activity 18 on page 95.

4 Tick (✔) the correct sentence.

1 a How much are the shoes black?
  b How much are the black shoes?

2 a How much is the white shirt?
  b How much is the shirt white?

3 a How much is the green sweater?
  b How much are the green sweater?

LISTENING AND SPEAKING

1 Say what the objects in the photo are.

2 Listen and complete the chart.

a £30 b £0.35 c £3.50 d £2
e £10 f £40 g £5.99

	Britain	Your country
Big Mac		
Levi jeans		
Nike trainers		
Cola		

Now work in pairs and check your answers.

How much is a Big Mac in Britain?
It's …

3 Complete the column with prices for your country. Work in pairs and ask and answer.

How much is a Big Mac in Thailand?
It's ….

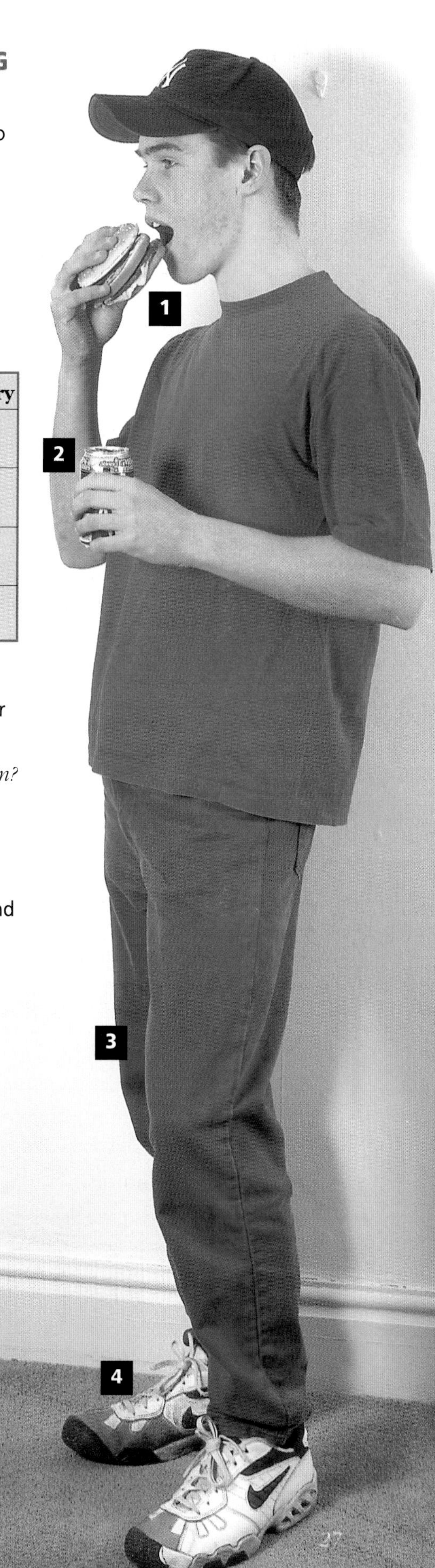

12 Where are Jane's keys?

Prepositions of place: *in, on, under*; possessive *'s*

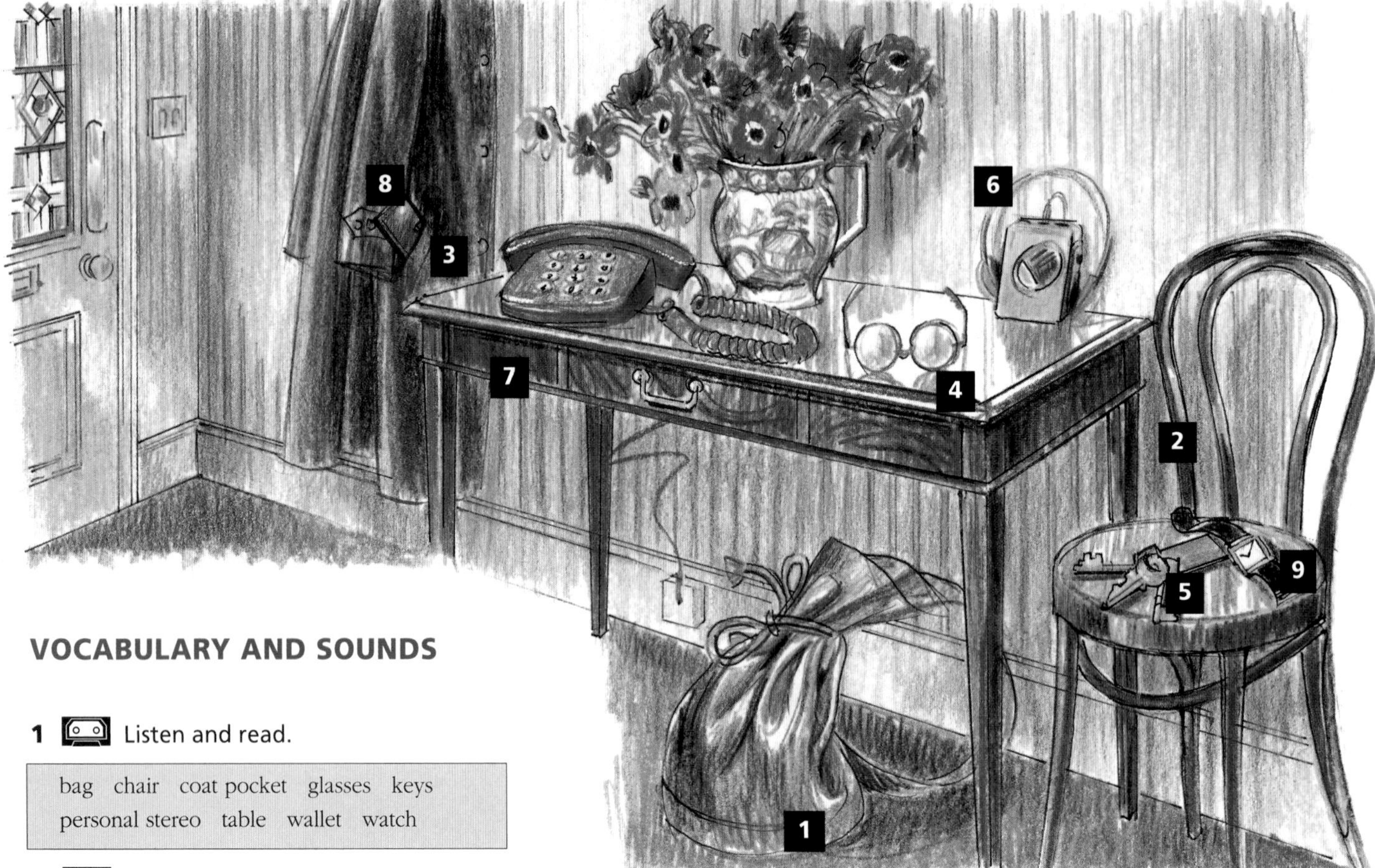

VOCABULARY AND SOUNDS

1 Listen and read.

bag chair coat pocket glasses keys personal stereo table wallet watch

Now listen and repeat.

2 Work in pairs. Look at the picture. Ask and say the words you know.

What's this?

It's a chair. And what are these?

They're keys.

LISTENING

1 Listen and match.

Jane	bag
Graham	glasses
Frank	keys
Joely	personal stereo
Nicola	watch
Tom	wallet

12

GENERAL COMMENTS

Possessive 's

The possessive 's is a very common structure in English. The position of the apostrophe 's depends on whether the noun is singular or plural, and if plural, whether it is a regular or irregular plural. Not surprisingly, many students make mistakes in their written work. Remind yourself, and your students if necessary, that even native speakers have difficulty in knowing where to put the apostrophe. You may like to know that the so-called intrusive apostrophe is also quite common among native speakers, in which an apostrophe is used for straightforward plurals. Quite often, specific shops are referred to using the apostrophe 's but without a following noun: *baker's, grocer's, chemist's*. The missing word is, of course, *shop*, but it's common to leave it out.

Prepositions of place

This is the first lesson on prepositions of place. You may need to illustrate the meaning of these prepositions with objects in the classroom. This may be easier to do than doing a book-based lesson.

VOCABULARY AND SOUNDS

1 Aim: to present the pronunciation of the words in the vocabulary box.

- Ask the students to listen and read the words in the box. Then ask them to listen and repeat.

- Say the numbers in the picture to the class. Students give you the name of the object.

2 Aim: to present the meaning of the words in the vocabulary box.

- Ask the students to work together again and to ask and say what the items in the illustration are.

LISTENING

1 Aim: to prepare for the presentation of the possessive '*s*; to practise listening.

- Ask the students to listen and to find out who the items belong to. They should draw a line matching the name and the item.

- Tell the students not to be worried about the prepositions of place in the conversation for the moment.

Answers
Jane - keys Graham - wallet Frank - watch
Joely - bag Nicola - glasses Tom - personal stereo

- Ask the students to check their answers with each other.

2 Aim: to check comprehension; to present the possessive *'s*.

- Ask the students to match the phrase with the relevant illustration.

Answers
a - 5 b - 8 c - 9 d - 1 e - 4 f - 6

3 Aim: to present prepositions of place.

- Ask the students to match the item, the preposition and the place.

Answers
bag - under table
glasses - on table
keys - on chair
personal stereo - on table
watch - on chair
wallet - in coat pocket

- Play the tape again and ask the students to listen and check their answers.

4 Aim: to practise using prepositions of place; to practise using the possessive *'s*.

- Explain to the students that some of these sentences are wrong. Ask them to read the sentences and to compare them with the matching exercise they did in activity 3.

- They will be able to check this activity in *Grammar 1*.

GRAMMAR

1 Aim: to practice using prepositions of place.

- Ask the students to read the information in the grammar box and then to do the exercises.
- Ask the students to check their answers to *Listening* activity 4.

Answers
1, 3, 4, 6, 8, 9

- Check the answers to this activity with the whole class.

2 Aim: to practise using prepositions of place.

- Ask the students to look at the wrong sentences in *Listening* activity 4 and then to correct them in writing.
- Ask students to come up to the board in turn and to write corrected sentences.

3 Aim: to focus on the target structures.

- Ask the students to complete the conversations.

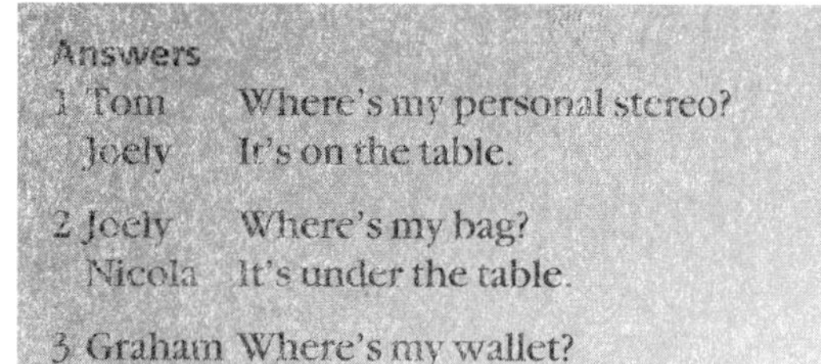
Answers

1 Tom — Where's my personal stereo?
Joely — It's on the table.

2 Joely — Where's my bag?
Nicola — It's under the table.

3 Graham — Where's my wallet?
Jane — It's in your coat pocket.

- Play the tape and ask the students to check their answers.

4 Aim: to practise using the target structures.

- Ask the students to look at activity 3 again and to write sentences.
- Additionally, ask them to look at the illustration again and to write 2 true sentences and 2 false sentences. When they're ready, they should swap sentences and find their partner's two false sentences.

5 Aim: to focus on possible mistakes.

- You may like to do this activity quickly with the whole class.

Answers
1a 2a 3b 4b

SPEAKING AND WRITING

1 Aim: to practise using the target structures; to practise speaking; to practise writing.

- Ask the students to work in pairs and to decide who is Student A and who is Student B. They should then follow the instructions.
- Ask the students to look at the photo and to write sentences describing where objects are.

Possible answers
The book is on the table./The glasses are on the television.

2 Aim: to practise using the target structures; to practise speaking.

- Choose three students to go out of the room. Move six objects in the classroom, such as a bag on a chair, a chair on a table – ask the students for suggestions.
- Bring the three students back into the room. Ask them where things are now.

2 Match with the correct object in the picture.

a Jane's keys	d Joely's bag
b Graham's wallet	e Nicola's glasses
c Frank's watch	f Tom's personal stereo

3 Match.

bag		
glasses	in	chair
keys	on	table
personal stereo	under	coat pocket
watch		
wallet		

Now listen and check 2 and 3.

4 Tick (✔) the correct sentences.

1 Frank's watch is on the chair. ☐
2 Graham's wallet is on the table. ☐
3 Joely's bag is under the table. ☐
4 Tom's personal stereo is on the table. ☐
5 Nicola's glasses are under the chair. ☐
6 Jane's keys are on the chair. ☐
7 Nicola's glasses are in her coat pocket. ☐
8 Graham's wallet is in his coat pocket. ☐
9 Nicola's glasses are on the table. ☐
10 Frank's watch is under the table. ☐

GRAMMAR

Prepositions of place: *in, on, under*
Jane's keys are ***on*** *the chair.*
Graham's wallet is ***in*** *his coat pocket.*
Joely's bag is ***under*** *the table.*

Possessive *'s*
*Jane***'s** *keys = the keys of Jane.*
*Graham***'s** *wallet = the wallet of Graham.*
*Joely***'s** *bag = the bag of Joely.*

1 Work in pairs and check your answers to *Listening* activity 4.

2 Look at *Listening* activity 4 and correct the wrong sentences.
2 Graham's wallet is in his coat pocket.

3 Complete.

1 **TOM** ____'s my personal stereo?
JOELY ____ on the table.

2 **JOELY** Where's ____ bag?
NICOLA It's under ____ table.

3 **GRAHAM** Where ____ my wallet?
JANE It's in ____ coat pocket.

Now listen and check.

4 Look at 3 and write sentences.
Tom's personal stereo is on the table.

5 Tick (✔) the correct sentence.

1 a Anna's watch is in her coat pocket.
b Anna is watch is in her coat pocket.

2 a Where's Graham's wallet?
b Where's is Graham's wallet?

3 a Jane's keys on the table.
b Jane's keys are on the table.

4 a Nicola's glasses in her coat pocket.
b Nicola's glasses are in her coat pocket.

SPEAKING AND WRITING

1 Work in pairs.
Student A: Turn to Communication activity 7 on page 92.
Student B: Turn to Communication activity 19 on page 95.

Now write sentences describing the picture you completed.
The bag is under the table.

2 Choose three students and ask them to leave the classroom. Move six objects and ask the three students to say what is different.
Maria's bag is under the table.

Have got; possessive adjectives: _our, your, their_

READING AND VOCABULARY

1 Read and match the texts with the photos.

A Hello, my name's Maria and this is my husband Carlo. We've got three children. Our daughter's name is Laura and she's four. Our sons are Pablo and Octavio. Pablo is twelve and Octavio is ten.

B Hello, I'm Carlos. I'm twelve. This is my family. I've got two sisters and one brother. My father's name is Javier. He's forty. My mother's name is Victoria. She's thirty-five. My sisters' names are Luisa and Teresa. They're eight and ten. My brother's name is Juan. He's five.

C Hello, I'm Mehmet and this is my wife Sema. We've got two daughters, Leyla and Serap.

2 Complete.

husband wife mother father son(s) daughter(s) brother(s) sister(s) children

1 My _____ is Carlo.
2 Our _____ is Laura.
3 Our _____ are Pablo and Octavio.
4 Our _____ are Laura, Pablo and Octavio.
5 My _____ is Javier.
6 My _____ is Victoria.
7 My _____ are Luisa and Teresa.
8 My _____ is Juan.
9 My _____ is Sema.
10 My _____ are Leyla and Serap.

3 Complete the columns in the chart with names.

	husband	wife	father	mother	son (s)	daughter (s)	sister (s)	brother (s)
Maria								
Carlos								
Mehmet								

14 She's got fair hair and blue eyes

Talking about appearance and character; *has got*

READING AND VOCABULARY

1 Listen and repeat.

hair eyes fair dark red blue brown black green

2 Write the words in the correct group.

hair – fair red ...

eyes – blue ...

3 Listen and repeat.

good-looking friendly pretty nice quiet tall short

Now translate the words.

4 Put the words in 2 and 3 in two groups.

***Appearance** – good-looking . . .*

***Character** – friendly . . .*

5 Think about people you know and choose words to describe them. Now work in pairs and talk about these people.

quite very

My brother's tall and quite good-looking. He's very friendly.

LISTENING AND READING

1 Listen and read.

JILL Hey Sarah! We've got a new neighbour. His name's Mike.

SARAH What's he like?

JILL He's got dark hair and brown eyes. He's very good-looking and very friendly.

SARAH Dark hair, brown eyes, good-looking and friendly! How old is he?

JILL I don't know. Twenty, twenty-one.

SARAH Has he got a brother?

JILL I don't know.

2 Decide where these sentences go.

a She's got dark hair and green eyes.

b Yes, she has.

c What's she like?

d She's nice, but very quiet.

MIKE Hey! Simon! We've got a very pretty neighbour.

SIMON Really? What's her name?

MIKE Jill.

SIMON (1) ____

MIKE (2) ____ She's very pretty.

SIMON Green eyes! Has she got a friend?

MIKE (3) ____

SIMON What's she like?

MIKE (4) ____

LISTENING AND SPEAKING

1 Listen and read.

INTERVIEWER Are you married, Maria?

MARIA Yes, I am. My husband's name is Carlo.

INTERVIEWER Have you got any children?

MARIA Yes, we have. We've got three children. Our daughter's name is Laura, and our sons' names are Pablo and Octavio.

INTERVIEWER How old are they?

MARIA They're twelve, ten, and four.

2 Decide where these sentences go.

a Paolo, Giovanni, and Patrizia.

b No, I haven't.

c Yes, I have. I've got two brothers and one sister.

d Yes I am.

Are you married, Marco?

(1) _____.

Have you got any children?

(2) _____.

Have you got any brothers or sisters?

(3) _____.

What are their names?

(4) _____.

Now listen and check.

GRAMMAR

Possessive adjectives

Our *daughter is Laura.*

Your *brothers are Pablo and Octavio.*

Their *names are Laura, Pablo and Octavio.*

Have got

Have you got any brothers and sisters?

Yes, I have. I've got two brothers and one sister.

Have you got any children?

No, I haven't.

1 Answer the questions.

Is *our* the possessive adjective for *we, you* or *they*?

Is *their* the possessive adjective for *we, you* or *they*?

2 Complete.

I – *my* he – ____ we – ____

you – ____ she – ____ they – ____

3 Tick (✔) the correct sentence.

1 a Are they're names Carla and Patrizia?
b Are their names Carla and Patrizia?

2 a Our son is seven.
b We're son is seven.

3 a Their son's name is Enrique.
b They're sons name Enrique.

4 Complete.

1 Have you ____ any brothers or sisters?

2 Yes, I ____. I ____ got two brothers.

3 ____ you got any children?

4 No, I ____.

SOUNDS AND SPEAKING

1 Listen and repeat.

/ə/ husband mother father daughter brother sister

2 Complete the *You* line with names of members of your family.

	husband	wife	mother	father
You				
Your partner				
	son	daughter	brother	sister
You				
Your partner				

3 Work in pairs. Talk about your families. Ask and say what their names are. Complete the chart.

Have you got any brothers or sisters?

What are their names?

Are you married?

What's your wife's name?

3 Aim: to focus on possible mistakes.

● Explain to the students that it is very common to mix up *they're* and *their*. Even native speakers make this mistake in writing. Point out, however, that in speaking, the mistake is not noticeable as the two words are pronounced the same way. In any case, there is very little confusion created by the mistake. But in the interests of accuracy, it's important to draw attention to the potential error.

Answers
1 b 2 a 3 a

4 Aim: to focus on *have got*.

● Ask the students to do this activity and then to check it in pairs.

Answers
1 got 2 have 've 3 Have 4 haven't

SOUNDS AND SPEAKING

1 Aim: to focus on the pronunciation of /ə/.

● All the words for members of the family have the unstressed *schwa* phoneme. Play the tape and ask the students to listen and repeat the words.

● Ask the students to say the words aloud. Check they do not stress the /ə/ sound.

2 Aim: to prepare for speaking.

● Ask the students to complete the *You* line with names of members of their family.

3 Aim: to practise speaking.

● Ask the students to work in pairs and to talk about their families. Ask them to complete the other line for their partner.

● Ask two or three students to talk about their families to the whole class.

● You may like to ask the students to write a full description of their family for homework. They can use the passages in *Reading and vocabulary* 1 as models.

13

GENERAL COMMENTS

Has/have got

This lesson presents *have got* and Lesson 14 presents *has got.* This is a common structure in British English and used when you talk about facilities, possessions or relationships. You don't use it in the past tense.

Possessive adjectives

The students will already have seen the possessive adjectives for the first, second and third person singular in earlier lessons. This lesson on the family introduces first, second and third person plural possessive adjectives.

READING AND VOCABULARY

1 Aim: to practise reading for main ideas; to present possessive adjectives and *have got.*

- Ask the students to read the passages and to match them with the photos.

Answers
A - 2 B - 1 C - 3

- Check the answers with the whole class.

2 Aim: to present the words in the vocabulary box.

- The students should remember some of these words from earlier lessons, so this should be mostly revision.
- Say the words aloud and ask the students to repeat them.
- Ask the students to complete the sentences with words from the box.

Answers
1 husband 2 daughter 3 sons 4 children
5 father 6 mother 7 sisters 8 brother
9 wife 10 daughters

- Point out that *children* is the irregular plural of *child*.

3 Aim: to check comprehension; to provide an opportunity for a second reading.

- Ask the students to read the passages again and to complete the chart.

	husband	wife	father	mother	son(s)	daughter(s)	sister(s)	brother (s)
Maria	Carlo				Pablo, Octavio	Laura		
Carlos			Javier	Victoria			Luisa, Teresa	Juan
Mehmet		Sema				Leyla, Serap		

LISTENING AND SPEAKING

1 Aim: to present the pronunciation of the target structures.

- Ask the students to listen and follow the conversation. Play the tape.

2 Aim: to focus on text organisation; to practise listening for specific information.

- The conversation in 1 acts as a model for this activity. Ask them to decide where the sentences should go.
- Correct this activity with the whole class before you play the tape.

Answers
1d 2b 3c 4a

GRAMMAR

1 Aim: to focus on possessive adjectives.

- Ask the students to read the information in the grammar box and then to do the exercises.
- Do this activity with the whole class.

Answers
our - we their - they

2 Aim: to focus on possessive adjectives.

- Ask the students to complete the pairs.

Answers
I - my, you - your, he - his, she - her, we - our, they - their

14

GENERAL COMMENTS

Appearance

Some students may be sensitive about their appearance. Others may prefer not to talk about their appearance for religious reasons. The language and activities presented in this lesson are carefully chosen not to cause offence to anyone.

Has got

This is the second of two lessons on *have got.* In this lesson, the third person singular form is presented. Remember that it's often used to describe family, possessions, relationships and appearance.

READING AND VOCABULARY

1 Aim: to present the words in the vocabulary box.

- Play the tape and ask the students to repeat the words in the box.
- Check that everyone understand the words in the box.

2 Aim: to categorise the words in the vocabulary box.

- Ask the students to categorise the adjectives according to the nouns they go with.

> Answers
> hair – fair red brown black
> eyes – blue brown green

- Explain that you usually only have red eyes when you're tired!
- Ask the students to say what colour eyes and hair they've got.
  I've got black hair and brown eyes.

3 Aim: to present the words in the vocabulary box.

- Play the tape and ask the students to repeat the words in the box.
- Check that everyone understands the words in the box.
- Ask the students to translate the words into their own language(s).

4 Aim: to categorise the words in the vocabulary box.

- Ask the students to put the words from the vocabulary boxes under the appropriate headings.

> Answers
> appearance – good-looking, pretty, (quiet), tall, (quiet), short
> character – friendly, nice

5 Aim: to practise using the vocabulary.

- Ask the students to work in pairs and to describe people they know, friends and family.
- Ask two or three students to describe someone to the whole class.

LISTENING AND READING

1 Aim: to focus on the use of *has got.*

- Ask the students to listen and read the conversation. Ask them who they think Jill and Sarah might be – friends, work colleagues.
- Play the tape again.

2 Aim: to focus on text organisation; to practise listening for specific information.

- The conversation in 1 acts as a model for this activity. Ask the students to decide where the sentences go.

> Answers
> 1c 2a 3b 4d

- You'll correct this activity in *Grammar and functions* activity 3.

GRAMMAR AND FUNCTIONS

1 Aim: to focus on *has/have got.*

- Ask the students to read the information in the grammar and functions box and then to do the exercises.
- Ask the students to think about which person *has* and *have got* go with. Do this activity with the whole class.

> Answer
> has got – he, she, it
> have got – we, you, they

2 Aim: to focus on *has/have got.*

- This is a chart completion activity to make quite sure that the students have grasped the form of the structure.

Answers

I've		
we've		
you've		
they've	got	fair hair
he's		
she's		
it's		

3 Aim: to check the answers to *Listening and reading* activity 2.

- Ask the students to work in pairs and to check their answers to *Listening and reading* activity 2.

4 Aim: to practise using the target structures.

- Ask the students to write a description of someone they know. As well as writing about appearance, the students should write about age, job etc., and include as much information as possible.

5 Aim: to practise using the target structures.

- In pairs ask student A to describe another student in the class. Student B tries to say who it is.

READING AND SPEAKING

1 Aim: to practise reading for main ideas.

- Find out if there is anyone in your class who uses *E-mail* (electronic mail or messages sent by computer via the Internet).

- The text represents a summary of the main ideas of the E-mail message. Ask the students to read the message and to complete the chart.

Answers

Brad: 27, dark hair/blue eyes, doctor
Joe: 25, brother, engineer
Bill: 23, dark hair/brown eyes, brother, student
Judy: 17, sister, student

2 Aim: to practise speaking and reading.

- Ask the students to decide who is Student A and who is student B. They should then follow the instructions. Each has the same reply from Sue, but with different information missing. They should ask and answer questions to complete the message.

3 Aim: to practise speaking.

- The students will now be able to complete the chart for Sue.

Name	Sue
Job	teacher
Nationality	English/British
Age	23
Appearance	dark hair, brown eyes
Family information	Mother: Pippa, teacher Father: Henry, doctor, blue eyes, no hair Brother: James, engineer, 22, fair hair Sister: Sarah, 11, fair hair, blue eyes

WRITING

1 Aim: to practise writing.

- Ask the students to copy and complete the chart for themselves and their families.

2 Aim: to practise writing.

- Ask the students to use the messages as models to write a paragraph describing themselves and their families.

- You may like to ask the students to do this activity for homework.

GRAMMAR AND FUNCTIONS

Talking about appearance and character.
What's he like? What's she like?
He's got dark hair and green eyes. He's very good looking.
She's got fair hair and blue eyes. She's pretty.
She's nice, but very quiet.

1 Answer the questions.

Do you use *has got* with *we, you, they* or with *he, she, it?*

Do you use *have got* with *we, you, they* or with *he, she, it?*

2 Complete.

I	____		
we	____		
you	____		
they	____	got	fair hair.
he	____		
she	____		
it	____		

3 Work in pairs and check your answers to *Listening and reading* activity 2.

4 Write a description of someone you know. Say:

– what colour hair he/she's got
– what colour eyes he/she's got
– what he/she's like

Bruno has got dark hair and brown eyes. He's tall. He's quite quiet but nice.

5 Work in pairs.
Student A: Choose somebody in your class and describe them.
Student B: Say who it is.

She's got dark hair and brown eyes. She's got a red bag.

Is it Yıldız?

Yes!

READING AND SPEAKING

1 Read this part of an E-mail and complete the chart.

```
Dear Sue,
Hi, I'm Brad Summers from Chicago. I'm a doctor.
I'm 27 and I've got dark hair and blue eyes.
I've got two brothers, Joe and Bill, and a
sister, Judy. Joe is 25 and he's an engineer.
Bill's 23 and he's at college. Judy's 17 and
she's at school . . .
```

Name	Age	Appearance	Relation	Job
Brad	27			
Joe		"		
Bill		dark hair/ brown eyes	brother	student
Judy		"		

2 Work in pairs.

Student A: Turn to Communication activity 8 on page 93.

Student B: Turn to Communication activity 20 on page 96.

Sue		dark hair/ brown eyes		
Pippa	51	"		teacher
Henry	55		father	
James				
Sarah				

3 Work in pairs. Complete the chart for Sue.

WRITING

1 Copy and complete the chart above for you and your family.

2 Write a paragraph describing yourself and your family.

15 Stand up!

Imperatives

VOCABULARY AND LISTENING

1 Listen and repeat.

window door book light cassette player pen bag coat

2 Work in pairs. Look at the picture. Point and say. Use all the words from 1.

3 Match the instructions with the people in the picture.

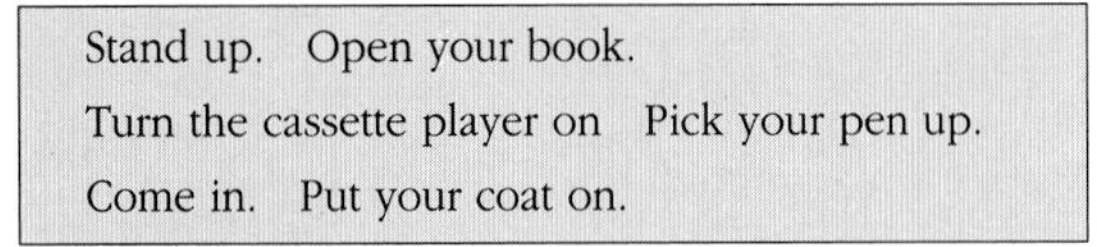

Stand up. Open your book.
Turn the cassette player on Pick your pen up.
Come in. Put your coat on.

1 – Stand up

4 Match the instruction with its opposite.

Sit down. Close your book. Turn the cassette player off. Put your pen down. Go out. Take your coat off.

Stand up – sit down

5 Make instructions with these verbs and the words in 1.

open close turn on turn off pick up put down

Open the window. Open the door.

6 Think about what you do when you start your English class. Number the instructions in 3 and 4.

1 – Come in. 2 – Take your coat off.

 Now listen and check.

7 Match the sentences with the pictures.

a Don't talk! b Don't look! c Don't listen!

15

GENERAL COMMENTS

Classroom language

The focus of this lesson is the language used most often in the classroom, instructions and imperatives. At the beginning of *Reward Starter*, you will remember there were two pages of useful instructional language, with which little work could be done. It wasn't suitable to begin a new course with a lesson actively presenting this language, but it would certainly be appropriate to check that the students have understood and are using it now. You may need to point out that while it is entirely appropriate for instructions in the classroom to be given using imperatives, other contexts are likely to require a more polite, less direct form of expression.

VOCABULARY AND LISTENING

1 Aim: to present the words in the vocabulary box.

- The students will already have come across some of these words. They have been selected because they are most likely to be present in the classroom, so if this is the case, point to them in the classroom.

- Ask the students to listen to the tape and repeat the words.

2 Aim: to identify the words in the vocabulary box.

- Ask the students to work in pairs and point to the items in the illustration which correspond to the words in the box.

3 Aim: to present the words in the vocabulary box.

- Some of the words in the box (stand up, turn on, pick up, come in, put on) are phrasal verbs. It would be quite inappropriate at this level to spend any time on this complex area of grammar, but the students may, on occasions, find the particles at the end of the phrase, difficult to deal with. Explain that the grammatical point is a hard one to manipulate and will be dealt with later in the course.

- Ask the students to match the instructions and the drawings.

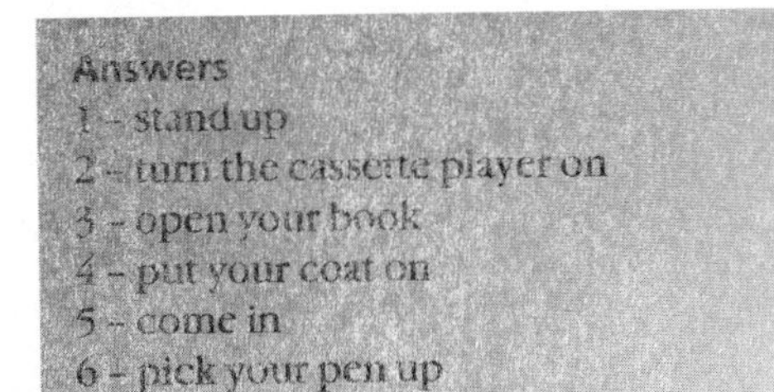
Answers
1 – stand up
2 – turn the cassette player on
3 – open your book
4 – put your coat on
5 – come in
6 – pick your pen up

4 Aim: Match the words with their opposites.

- Ask the students to match the instructions in this activity with their opposites in activity 3.

Answers
Sit down – stand up
Close your book – open your book
Open the door – close the door
Turn the cassette player off – turn the cassette player on
Put your pen down – pick your pen up
Go out – come in
Take your coat off – put your coat on

- Check this activity with the whole class.

5 Aim: to practise using the words in the vocabulary boxes.

- Explain that the verbs and nouns can be combined in different ways to make new instructions. Ask the students to find out how many instructions they can make with the verbs and nouns.

Possible answers

open, close	window door book bag
turn on/off	light cassette player
pick up, put down	book cassette player
	pen bag coat
put on take off	coat

6 Aim: to practise using the new words.

- Ask the students to think about the things they do when they start their English lesson. Ask them to number the instructions in 3 and 4.

Possible answers
Come in. Take your coat off
Sit down Open your book Pick your pen up
Turn the cassette player on

- Play the tape and ask students to check their answers.

7 Aim: to present the negative imperative.

- Ask the students to match the instruction with the illustration.

Answers
a – 3
b – 1
c – 2

SOUNDS AND SPEAKING

1 Aim: to present the phoneme /əʊ/.

- This phoneme is particularly hard for many students to pronounce correctly. Play the cassette and ask the students to repeat the words.

- Ask the students to read the words aloud, and correct their pronunciation if necessary.

2 Aim: to focus on word stress in sentences.

- Ask the students to listen and follow the sentences.

- Point out that some key words are stressed in these instructions while the less important words are not.

3 Aim: to practise listening.

- Ask the students to listen to the instructions and to act accordingly.

4 Aim: to practise speaking.

- Ask the students to work in pairs. Student A should give Student B instructions, and Student B should follow them. If the classroom allows you to do so, ask them to stand up and to use all the space available.

- Ask the students to change round when they're ready.

GRAMMAR

1 Aim: to focus on the use of imperatives in instructions.

- Ask the students to read the information in the grammar box and then to do the exercises.
- Explain that the imperative is simply the infinitive form of the verb but without *to*.

- Ask the students to write out the instructions.

Answers
1 - Turn off the cassette player./Turn the cassette player off. 2 - Sit down. 3 - Open the window. 4 - Close the door. 5 - Switch on the light./Switch the light on. 6 - Close your eyes.

2 Aim: to revise vocabulary.

- These words were all presented on the first two teaching pages of *Reward* Starter. Check everyone understands them by asking the students to translate them into their own language(s).

READING AND WRITING

1 Aim: to practise reading for main ideas.

- Explain that some of the instructions in the *Students' Charter* are wrong or not applicable to your class. Ask the students to read it and to decide which ones are true for their class.

2 Aim: to check comprehension.

- Ask the students to work in pairs and to check their answers. Do they both agree on the true instructions?

3 Aim: to practise writing.

- Ask the students to rewrite the wrong instructions. They should either use the opposite verb, or use *don't* + infinitive, or, with instructions beginning with *don't*, leave out the *don't*.

- Check the students' answers with the whole class.

4 Aim: to practise writing.

- Ask the students to write more instructions. Encourage them to be as inventive or humorous as they like.

- You may like to ask the students to do this activity for homework.

SOUNDS AND SPEAKING

1 Listen and repeat.

/əʊ/ don't close open coat

2 Listen and read.

Stand up.	Sit down.
Open your book.	Close your book.
Don't talk!	Don't look!
Pick your bag up.	Put your pen down.

3 Listen and follow the instructions.

4 Work in pairs. Give your partner instructions.

Close your book.

GRAMMAR

Imperatives

Infinitive	Imperative	Negative imperative
look	*look*	*Don't look (= do not look)*
read	*read*	*Don't read*
write	*write*	*Don't write*
listen	*listen*	*Don't listen*

1 Look at the pictures below and write instructions.

2 Translate these words.

read listen write underline number match correct

READING AND WRITING

1 Read *The Students' Charter*. Which instructions are true for your English class?

The Students' Charter

- ☐ Don't speak English.
- ☐ Don't read in class.
- ☐ Put your bags under your chair.
- ☐ Do your homework.
- ☐ Say please and thank you.
- ☐ Don't talk to other students.
- ☐ Listen to your personal stereo.
- ☐ Stand up when your teacher speaks to you.
- ☐ Look out of the window.

2 Work in pairs and check your answers.

3 Correct the wrong instructions.

4 Write some more instructions for your classroom or your school.

Don't speak Turkish.

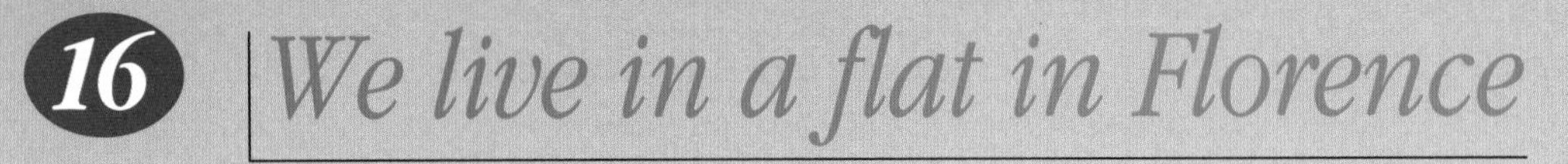

16 We live in a flat in Florence

Present simple: regular verbs *I, we, you, they*; prepositions of place *in, to*

VOCABULARY AND SOUNDS

1 Listen and repeat.

flat house office shop school

live work go

2 Listen and repeat.

/æ/ flat match thank
/aʊ/ house how
/ɒ/ office shop clock
/uː/ school two student
/ɪ/ live tick six
/ɜː/ work turn Turkey

3 Listen and repeat.

live in a flat
live in a house

work in an office
work in a shop

go to school
go to work

READING AND LISTENING

1 Match the sentences with the photos.

A I live in a flat in Florence.
B I work in an office in Tokyo.
C We go to school in Istanbul.

1

2

3

2 Listen and read.

Hello, I'm Anna. I'm from Italy and I'm twenty-five. I'm a secretary and I work in an office. My husband's name is Bruno and we live in a flat in Florence. My mother's name is Francesca and my father's name is Alberto. My sister's name is Paola and she's sixteen. They live in a house in Fiesole.

3 Match the sentences with the photos in 1.

☐ Hello, I'm Kazuo.
☐ Hello, I'm Erol.
☐ I'm from Japan and I'm thirty-five.
☐ I'm from Turkey and I'm sixteen.
☐ I'm a student.
☐ I'm a journalist and I work in an office in Tokyo.
☐ My sister's name is Belma and we go to school in Istanbul.
☐ My wife's name is Michiko and we live in a flat in Ichikawa.
☐ We live with our parents in a flat in Galata.
☐ We've got two children.
☐ My father is an engineer and my mother is a secretary.
☐ Our son's name is Koji and our daughter's name is Miki.
☐ They work in an office in Beyoglu.
☐ They go to school in Funabashi.

Now listen and check your answers.

16

GENERAL COMMENTS

Present simple of verbs other than *be*

The progression of the early stages of *Reward* Starter is designed to be a gentle as possible, with only one or two structures being taught in each lesson. So far, the language covered has been the verb *be* with all its variations using prepositions and adjectives, and imperatives. Lesson 16 is the first lesson in which other verbs are presented in the present simple. Nevertheless, the progression of this presentation is slow and carefully considered, starting with the forms of the verb which are the same for all persons and are the same as the infinitive, and going on to third person singular, negatives, *yes/no* questions and short answers and *wh-* questions. It is hoped that this relatively light load of new structures is most appropriate for real beginners of English.

VOCABULARY AND SOUNDS

1 Aim: to present the words in the vocabulary box.

- Ask the students to listen and repeat the words.

2 Aim: to practise the pronunciation of /æ/, /aʊ/, /ɒ/, /uː/, /ɪ/, and /ɜː/.

- If your students' language(s) contain(s) any of these phonemes, you may want to spend less time on this activity. Remember also that most mistakes of pronunciation come from stress and intonation pattern and not individual phonemes.

- Play the tape and ask the students to repeat the words.

3 Aim: to present new phrases.

- Ask the students to listen to the tape and repeat the phrases.

READING AND LISTENING

1 Aim: to present the first person singular present simple of regular verbs.

- Ask the students to match the sentences with the photos.

> Answers
> A – 3 B – 2 C – 1

2 Aim: to present the first person, singular and plural, and third person plural of regular verbs; to practise reading and listening.

- Explain to the students that the reading text refers to photo 3. Ask the students to listen to the tape and read the passage.

- When they're ready, ask the students to underline all the verbs.

- Ask the students to tell you the verbs and write them on the board. As they tell you the verbs, ask for the spelling. This is designed to draw attention to the similarity of endings with those of the infinitives.

3 Aim: to focus on text organisation.

- This reading activity focuses on the internal coherence of the paragraphs. The sentences form two paragraphs, corresponding to photos 1 and 2 above.

> Answers
>
> **Photo 1**
> Hello, I'm Erol.
> I'm from Turkey and I'm sixteen.
> I'm a student.
> My sister's name is Belma and we go to school in Istanbul.
> We live with our parents in a flat in Galata.
> My father is an engineer and my mother is a secretary.
> They work in an office in Beyoglu.
>
> **Photo 2**
> Hello, I'm Kazuo.
> I'm from Japan and I'm thirty-five.
> I'm a journalist and I work in an office in Tokyo.
> My wife's name is Michiko and we live in a flat in Ichikawa.
> We've got two children.
> Our son's name is Koji and our daughter's name is Miki.
> They go to school in Funabashi.

- Ask your students to listen and check their answers. Play the tape.

GRAMMAR

1 Aim: to focus on the form of the first person, singular and plural, and third person plural of regular verbs.

- Ask the students to read the information in the grammar box, and ask them to do the exercises.

- Ask the students to complete the sentences.

Answers
1 live 2 work 3 go 4 live
5 work 6 go 7 work 8 go 9 live

- Draw attention to the similarity of form between the different persons.

2 Aim: to focus on word order.

- Ask the students to write the words in the correct order and to form sentences.

Answers
1 I go to school in Paris.
2 We go to school in New York.
3 We live in a flat in Venice.
4 I work in an office in Tokyo.
5 We live in a house in Rio.
6 I work in an office.

3 Aim: to focus on prepositions of place.

- Ask the students to complete the sentences. Point out that *to* is used when there is an idea of movement towards a place.

Answers
1 in 2 in 3 to/in 4 in/in 5 in/in 6 to/in

READING AND WRITING

1 Aim: to practise reading; to practise using the target structures.

- Ask the students to read *What's my name?* and to guess who's speaking. At the time of writing this course the answer is Bill Clinton. You may have to change the answer in future years.

Answer
Bill Clinton

2 Aim: to practise writing; to practise using the target structures.

- This activity is designed to consolidate the presentation and practice of the structures taught in this lesson. Ask the students to think of someone famous and to write sentences about them. You may like to ask the students to do this in pairs.

- When they're ready, ask the students to exchange their sentences with another pair and to guess who is speaking.

3 Aim: to practise writing; to practise using the target structures.

- Ask the students to write a paragraph about where they live, work and/or go to school.

- You may like to ask the students to do this activity for homework.

GRAMMAR

Present simple: regular verbs *I, we, you, they*

I	
We	*live*
You	
They	

Prepositions of place

In	*I work **in** an office **in** Tokyo. I live **in** a flat **in** Florence.*
To	*I go **to** school.*

1 Complete.

1 I ____ in a flat in Paris.
2 I ____ in an office in London.
3 We ____ to school in New York.
4 They ____ in a flat in Paris.
5 We ____ in an office in London.
6 I ____ to school in New York.
7 They ____ in an office in London.
8 They ____ to school in New York.
9 We ____ in a flat in Paris.

2 Put the words in the right order and make sentences.

1 school Paris in I to go
2 school we go to New York in
3 live flat we in in a Venice
4 work I office Tokyo in an in
5 we live in a in Rio house
6 I in an office work

1 I go to school in Paris.

3 Complete.

1 We live in a house ____ Buenos Aires.
2 I work ____ a shop in Istanbul.
3 I go ____ school ____ Lyon.
4 They work ____ an office ____ Seoul.
5 We work ____ a shop ____ London.
6 They go ____ school ____ Athens.

READING AND WRITING

1 Read and answer *What's my name?*

What's my name?

1 I'm from the USA.
2 I live in Washington.
3 I live with my wife and daughter.
4 I work in the USA and around the world.
5 We live in the White House.
6 I'm President of the USA.
7 My name's ________________.

2 Write sentences about someone famous. Use *I* and *we*.

I live in Buckingham Palace.

I live with my husband and my dogs.

Now work in pairs and play *What's my name.*

3 Write a paragraph about where you live.

Hello, I'm Marcella. I'm from Argentina and I'm twenty. I live in Rosario with my father and mother ...

17 What's the time?

Telling the time (1); present simple: *have*; prepositions of time: *at, in*

SPEAKING AND VOCABULARY

1 Listen and repeat.

o'clock

What's the time?

A It's eight o'clock.

B It's eleven o'clock.

C It's ten o'clock.

2 Match the sentences in 1 with the correct time.

3 Work in pairs. Ask and answer about the times.

What's the time? It's 10.00.

4 Listen and tick (✔).

1 a 3 o'clock ☐ b 5 o'clock ☐
2 a 7 o'clock ☐ b 11 o'clock ☐
3 a 6 o'clock ☐ b 9 o'clock ☐
4 a 12 o'clock ☐ b 1 o'clock ☐

5 Listen and repeat.

have breakfast have lunch have dinner

morning afternoon evening

6 Complete sentences about you.

1 I have breakfast at ____ in the ____.
2 I have lunch at ____ in the ____.
3 I have ____ at ____ in the evening.

7 Look and read.

am pm

Seven o'clock in the morning = 7am
One o'clock in the afternoon = 1pm
Seven o'clock in the evening = 7pm

Now rewrite these times with *am* or *pm*.

1 Four o'clock in the morning.
2 Two o'clock in the morning.
3 Eleven o'clock in the evening.
4 Three o'clock in the afternoon.

LISTENING AND READING

1 Listen and read. Say which country you see in the photo.

'In Britain, we have breakfast at about 8 am. Lunch is at 1pm and dinner is at 6 pm.'

'In Spain, we have breakfast at 7am and lunch at 2 or 3 pm. Dinner is at 10 pm.'

'In Thailand we have breakfast at 6 am and lunch at 11 am. Dinner is at about 6 pm.'

17

GENERAL COMMENTS

Telling the time

This lesson is the first of two in which telling the time is presented. Although the learning load is shared – Lesson 17 presents the hours, Lesson 20 presents the half and quarter hours – it may still be too much for real beginners to manage successfully. You may decide you need to supplement the work with material from the Practice Book, the Resource Pack, and from other sources. It may even be appropriate to leave the subject and return to it at regular intervals using your own material.

Socio-cultural training

One aspect of socio-cultural training is to make the students aware of differences between cultures without necessarily modifying one's own cultural behaviour. A good example of this is the subject covered in this lesson, the time people in different countries have certain meals. Remember, however, that another aspect of this kind of training is to encourage cultural self-awareness, so take the opportunity to explore major cultural differences between the countries presented and that of your students, as well as the more personal differences between families and individuals.

SPEAKING AND VOCABULARY

1 Aim: to present the target structure.

- Ask the students to listen and repeat the sentences as you play the tape.

- Ask the students to repeat the sentences in chorus, then individually.

2 Aim: to present the target structure.

- Ask the students to say what the time is in their own language.

- Ask the students to count from one to twelve in English.

- Ask the students to match the sentences with the clocks.

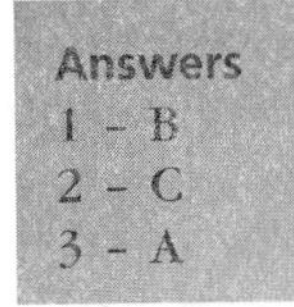

Answers
1 – B
2 – C
3 – A

- Explain that in most everyday situations in English, the twelve-hour clock is used, and not the twenty-four clock. However, the twenty-four hour clock is often used for timetables, especially for trains and planes.

3 Aim: to practise saying the time.

- You may find it easier to do this activity on the board. Draw the clocks (11, 10, 8 and 4 o'clock) quickly on the board.

- Ask the students to look at the clocks and say what the times are.

- Check everyone can say what the times are.

- You may like to draw some other clocks on the board and to continue this practice activity in pairs.

4 Aim: to practise recognising the time.

- Explain that the tape you're going to play contains four radio extracts in which the time is mentioned. Ask the students to listen and tick the times they hear.

Answers
1 3 o'clock 2 11 o'clock 3 6 o'clock 4 1 o'clock

5 Aim: to present the words in the vocabulary box.

- Explain that the words in the first box are *have* + *meal*, and in the second are times of the day. The word *night* is not presented because it requires the preposition of time *at*, while the other times of the day require *in*. You may nevertheless want to teach it.

- Ask the students to listen and repeat the words.

6 Aim: to present the preposition of time *in*; to practise using the new words.

- Ask the students to complete the sentences so that they're true for them.

- Ask the students to work in pairs and to compare the times they have different meals.

- Find out who has the earliest breakfast and the latest dinner.

7 Aim: to present the abbreviations in the vocabulary box.

- Explain that because English uses the 12 hour clock, there needs to be an expression to indicate whether someone is referring to morning or afternoon/evening. *am* is an abbreviation for the Latin expression *ante meridian* (before midday) and *pm* for *post meridian* (after midday). The abbreviations are used in both formal and informal spoken and written English, and are much more common than references to times in the 24 hour clock.

- Ask the students to rewrite the times with *am* or *pm*.

Answers
1 4 am 2 2 am 3 11 pm 4 3 pm

LISTENING AND READING

1 Aim: to practise reading for main ideas.

- Ask the students to listen to the tape and to read the text. Ask them to say which country they see in the photograph.

Answer
Spain

2 **Aim: to check comprehension.**
- Ask the students to check their answer to activity 1 in pairs.
- Check the answer to activity 1 with the whole class.
- Ask the students if the times of the meals mentioned are very different from the times they have the same meals. Are they surprised by this information? What would be the advantages and disadvantages of eating at these times?

3 **Aim: to practise listening for specific information.**
- Ask the students to work in groups of three. Explain that each group will listen to the same tape, but each student will listen for different information.
- Ask the students to follow their instructions. At this stage they work on their own.

4 **Aim: to practise speaking; to check comprehension.**
- Ask the students to work together and to complete the chart with the information they listened for.

	breakfast	lunch	dinner
Russia	7 o'clock	12 o'clock	6 o'clock
Hong Kong	7 o'clock	1 o'clock	8 o'clock
Mexico	8 o'clock	2 or 3 o'clock	8 or 9 o'clock

FUNCTIONS AND GRAMMAR

1 **Aim: to practise recognising the time.**
- Ask the students to read the information in the functions and grammar box and then to do the exercises.
- Ask the students to read and complete the sentences.

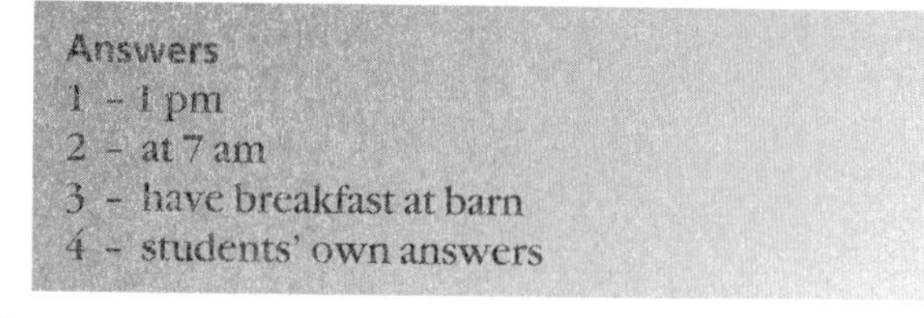
Answers
1 – 1 pm
2 – at 7 am
3 – have breakfast at barn
4 – students' own answers

2 **Aim: to focus on possible mistakes.**
- Ask the students to do this activity on their own and then to check it with another student.
- Check the answers with the whole class.

Answers
1 – a 2 – a 3 – b 4 – a

3 **Aim: to focus on prepositions of time *at, in*.**
- Do this activity with the whole class.

Answers
1 at/in 2 at/in 3 at/in

- Remind them that you use *at* for times of the day and *in* for clock times.

SPEAKING

1 **Aim: to practise speaking; to practise using the target structures.**
- Ask the students to look at the map of time zones in pairs and talk about what time it is in different cities around the world.

2 **Aim: to practise speaking; to practise using the target structures.**
- Ask the students to talk about the times people in the class have breakfast, lunch and dinner. Ask them to complete the chart.
- You may like to ask the students to write sentences describing the chart for homework.

2 Work in pairs and check your answer to 1.

3 Work in groups of three.

Student A: Turn to Communication 9 on page 93.

Student B: Turn to Communication 21 on page 96.

Student C: Turn to Communication 27 on page 97.

4 Work together and complete the chart.

speaker	country	breakfast	lunch	dinner
1				
2				
3				

FUNCTIONS AND GRAMMAR

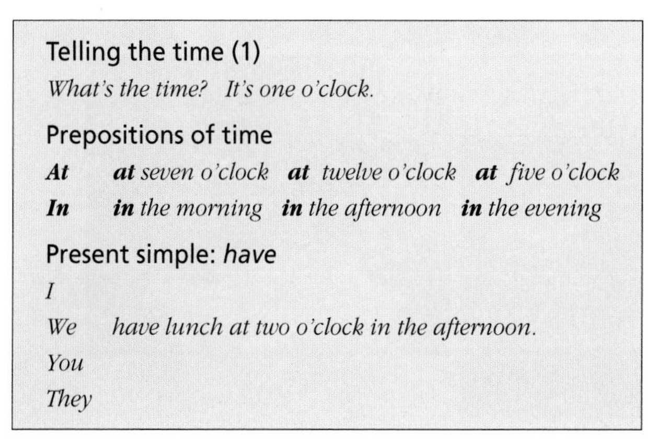

Telling the time (1)

What's the time? It's one o'clock.

Prepositions of time

At	***at** seven o'clock*	***at** twelve o'clock*	***at** five o'clock*
In	***in** the morning*	***in** the afternoon*	***in** the evening*

Present simple: *have*

I
We *have lunch at two o'clock in the afternoon.*
You
They

1 Write.

1 In Britain they have breakfast at eight o'clock in the morning. They have lunch at _____.

2 In Spain they have breakfast _____.

3 In Thailand they _____.

4 In my country, we _____.

2 Tick (✔) the correct sentence.

1 a What's the time? b What the time?

2 a Seven o'clock. b It seven o'clock.

3 a I'm breakfast at eight o'clock.
b I have breakfast at eight o'clock.

4 a We have lunch at one o'clock.
b We have lunch one o'clock.

3 Complete.

1 We have breakfast ____ seven o'clock ____ the morning.

2 I have lunch ____ one o'clock ____ the afternoon.

3 They have dinner ____ nine o'clock ____ the evening.

SPEAKING

1 Work in pairs. Look at the map below. It's twelve o'clock in London. Ask and say.

What's the time in New York?

It's seven o'clock in the morning. What's the time in Hong Kong?

It's eight o'clock in the evening.

2 Find out what time people in your class have breakfast, lunch and dinner.

Name	Nationality	breakfast	lunch	dinner
Marco	Italian	8 am	1-3 pm	8 pm

In Italy, they have breakfast at 8 ...

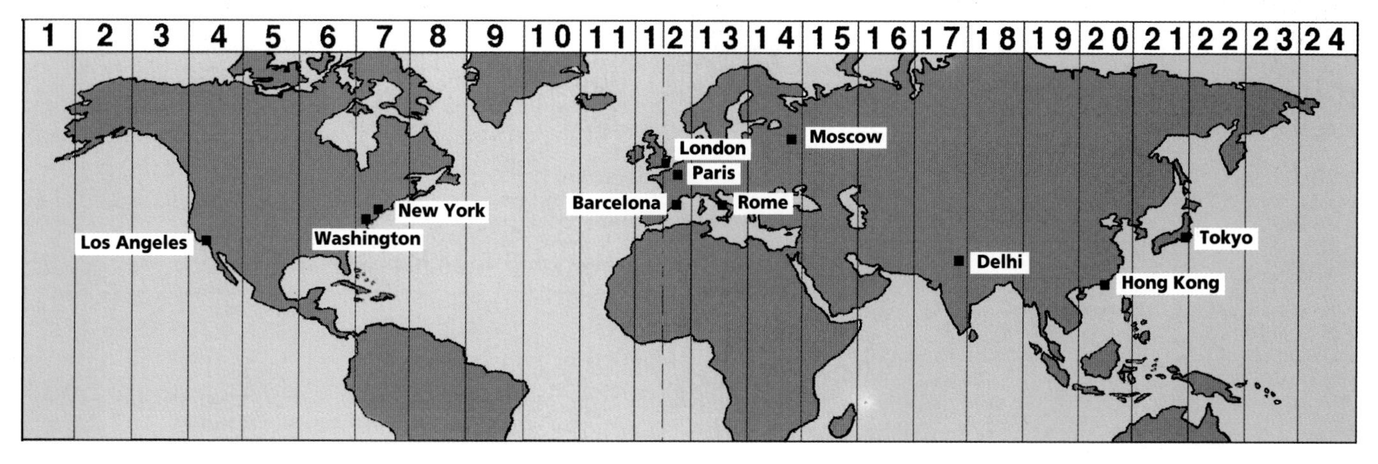

18 I don't like Monday mornings

Present simple: negatives; preposition of time: *on*

VOCABULARY AND SOUNDS

1 Listen and repeat.

Monday	Tuesday	Wednesday	
Thursday	Friday	Saturday	Sunday

2 Complete.

1 Today is ____.

2 Tomorrow is ____.

3 Listen and repeat.

on Monday
on Tuesday
on Wednesday
on Thursday

on Monday morning
on Tuesday afternoon
on Wednesday evening

in the morning
in the afternoon
in the evening

4 Match the verbs with the photos.

watch television	go to the cinema	
see friends	go shopping	write letters
go for a walk		

5 Match.

listen to	a newspaper
read	a letter
write	homework
correct	music
	a book

listen to music, ...

LISTENING AND READING

1 Listen and read.

Hello! My name's Fiona and I'm a teacher. I work in a school in the mornings and in the afternoons from Monday to Friday. In the evenings I watch television, listen to music, read, or write letters. In Britain we don't work at the weekend, so on Saturdays I go shopping in the morning or in the afternoon, and, in the evening, I go to the cinema or see friends. I don't live with my family so on Sunday morning I go to their house. We have Sunday lunch and then my father and brother watch the football on television. My sister and I don't like football so we go for a walk with Mum on Sunday afternoon. On Sunday evening, I correct my students' homework. I go to bed at 9 and get up at 7.30 am. I don't like Monday mornings!

18

GENERAL COMMENTS

Revision

Although this lesson does not have times of the day as its main focus, it nevertheless recycles the language presented in Lesson 17. By now, it should be clear that each lesson recycles and builds on the language taught in earlier lessons. For this reason, all the language taught is productive and there is no assumption that the students have come to the English lesson with anything they have learnt outside the classroom. The Progress checks are designed to contribute to the whole process of recycling and revision.

VOCABULARY AND SOUNDS

1 Aim: to present the words in the vocabulary box.

- Explain that the words in the box are the days of the week in English. Ask the students to listen and repeat the words.

2 Aim: to check comprehension.

- To make sure the students have understood the words, ask them to complete the sentences. You can ask them what day yesterday was in their own language – they don't yet know the word *was*.

- Ask the students to say what day of the week other occasions are, such as birthdays, main religious festivals, the national day etc.

3 Aim: to practise the pronunciation of expressions of time.

- Point out that *on* is the preposition used with days of the week. Ask them to say what preposition is used with times of the day (*in the morning* etc.) and clock times (*at one o'clock* etc.).

- Play the tape and ask the students to listen and repeat the expressions of time.

4 Aim: to present the expressions in the vocabulary box.

- Explain that the words in the vocabulary box are fixed expressions to describe everyday activities. Point out that, for example, they are made up from a verb and a noun. They have already come across some of the verbs in Lesson 16.

- Ask the students to match the expressions with the illustrations.

Answers

1 – watch TV 2 – go to the cinema 3 – go shopping
4 – write letters 5 – go for a walk 6 – see friends

5 Aim: to focus on verbs and nouns which go together.

- This is another collocation activity with some very common words and expressions which often go together. Ask the students to work in pairs and to think of possible combinations of the words. Explain that there may be more than one combination possible.

Answers

listen to	music
read	a newspaper a letter a book
write	a letter a book
correct	homework

LISTENING AND READING

1 Aim: to focus on the pronunciation of the target language.

- Ask the students to listen and follow the passage.

- You may like to use the passage for some reading aloud practice.

2 Aim: to practise reading for specific information; to provide an opportunity for a second reading.

- This is probably the longest passage in the book so far. The level of the language is carefully graded, and has already been presented both in the *Vocabulary and sounds* section as well as elsewhere in the book. However, there may be some words which your students will have forgotten. It's important for you to work out your strategy on developing reading skills. You can either explain every word, and improve their vocabulary work at the expense of their reading skill, or you develop the skills to deal with unfamiliar words, which will be far more helpful for the students in the long term. At the very least, if there are some vocabulary difficulties, find out if other students can explain, translate, mime or illustrate in some other way, the meaning of the word.

- Ask the students to read the passage again and to complete the chart.

	Morning	Afternoon	Evening
Monday – Friday	work	work	watch TV, listen to music, read, or write letters
Saturday	go shopping	go shopping	go to the cinema, see friends
Sunday	go to parents' house	have lunch, go for a walk	correct homework, go to bed

GRAMMAR

1 Aim: to focus on the negative of the present simple.

- Ask the students to read the information in the grammar box and then to do the exercises.
- Explain that the auxiliary *do* is used in present simple questions and negatives. The students have already seen *don't* in negative imperatives in Lesson 15.
- Ask the students to complete the sentences.

> Answers
> 1 don't 2 live 3 don't 4 don't 5 go 6 like

2 Aim: to focus on prepositions of time.

- Ask the students to complete the sentences with a preposition of time.

> Answers
> 1 on 2 On 3 in 4 In 5 On 6 on

3 Aim: to practise using the negative of the present simple.

- Ask the students to tick the sentences which are true for them and correct the false ones.

WRITING AND SPEAKING

1 Aim: to prepare for writing.

- Ask the students to copy the chart in *Listening and reading* activity 2 and complete it with information about their daily routines.

2 Aim: to prepare for writing.

- Ask the students to do this activity orally in pairs. Student A says a day and Student B says what he/she does on that day.

3 Aim: to practise writing.

- Ask the students to write sentences describing their daily routine. They should use the information they wrote in the chart and the passage in *Listening and reading* activity 1 to help them.
- For correction, you can either ask the students to read their sentences aloud, or collect their work and correct it later.

2 Write what Fiona does.

	Morning	Afternoon	Evening
Monday → Friday			
Saturday			
Sunday			

GRAMMAR

Present simple: negatives

I
We *don't (= do not) like Monday mornings.*
You
They

Preposition of time

on *Monday* ***on*** *Tuesday* ***on*** *Wednesday*
on *Monday morning* ***on*** *Tuesday afternoon*
on *Wednesday evening*

1 Complete.

1 We're students. We ____ work in an office.
2 I live in London. I don't ____ in Paris.
3 They ____ have breakfast at seven o'clock. They have breakfast at eight.
4 We ____ watch television on Saturday. We go to the cinema.
5 I ___ shopping on Saturday. I don't go shopping on Sunday.
6 I don't like tennis. I ____ football.

2 Complete.

1 I don't work ____ Saturday and Sunday.
2 ____ Sunday morning, I read the newspaper.
3 We don't watch television ____ the morning.
4 ____ the evening I write letters.
5 ____ Saturday afternoon they play football.
6 We see friends ____ Saturday.

3 Tick (✔) the sentences which are true for you. Correct the false ones.

1 I like Monday mornings.
2 We work on Sunday.
3 My parents live in France.
4 I go to the cinema on Monday morning.
5 We go shopping on Thursday evening.
6 My friends play football on Wednesday.

1 I don't like Monday mornings.

WRITING AND SPEAKING

1 Copy the chart in *Listening and reading* activity 2 and complete it for you.

2 Work in pairs.

Student A: Say a day.

Student B: Say what you do.

3 Write a paragraph about what you do during the week.

I go to school/work from Monday to Friday. On Monday evening, I ...

19 Do you like running?

Yes/no questions and short answers

VOCABULARY AND SOUNDS

1 Listen and repeat.

football tennis volleyball table tennis skiing
running basketball gymnastics swimming
baseball sailing

2 Say the words you know.

3 Work in pairs.

Student A: Turn to Communication activity 11 on page 93.

Student B: Turn to Communication activity 23 on page 96.

4 Complete.

team sport individual sport

team sport *football …*
individual sport *tennis …*

5 Write the words in 1 under these headings: *I like* and *I don't like.*

like

I like: football, tennis…
I don't like: badminton, skiing…

LISTENING AND WRITING

1 Listen and read.

DAVE Do you like swimming?
JACK Yes, I do. I like swimming very much.
DAVE Do you like running?
JACK No, I don't.

2 Complete.

TIM Do you ____ gymnastics, Gwen?
GWEN Yes, I ____. I like gymnastics very much.
TIM ____ you like basketball?
GWEN ____, I don't.

3 Number the sentences in the right order.

☐ Alison No, I don't.
☐ James Do you like skiing?
☐ James Do you like volleyball, Alison?
☐ Alison Yes, I do. I like volleyball very much.

Now listen and check 2 and 3.

19

GENERAL COMMENTS

Sport

Sport is one of the most popular topics in the language classroom, but it has certain disadvantages. It is usually more popular with boys/men than with girls/women. Furthermore, its real interest value comes from the immediacy of the sporting occasion, which can never be reproduced in the textbook. Nevertheless, it is possible for the textbook to create the opportunity for some motivated work on a popular topic.

Yes/no questions and short answers

The students will have done some work on *yes/no* questions and short answers with the verb *be* in Lesson 4, so the concept will not be new to them. These are complicated structures and you may need to take plenty of time to help the students manipulate them successfully. Extra practice is, as usual, provided in the Resource Pack and the Practice Book.

VOCABULARY AND SOUNDS

1 Aim: to present the pronunciation of the words in the vocabulary box.

- Words for sports are very common cognates in different languages, so it is to be expected that none of these words will be very difficult to learn.
- Play the tape and ask the students to repeat them as they listen.

2 Aim: to present the meaning of the words in the vocabulary box.

- Ask the students to say the words they know.

3 Aim: to present the meaning of the words in the vocabulary box.

- Ask the students to work in pairs and to decide who is Student A and who is Student B. They should then follow their instructions. Student A should mime his/her sports for Student B to guess. Then Student B should mime and Student A guess.

4 Aim: to reinforce the acquisition of new words.

- This categorisation activity is designed to reinforce the acquisition of the new words presented in this lesson. Ask the students to categorise the words according to whether they are team or individual sports.

Answers
team sport: football volleyball basketball baseball
individual sport: tennis table tennis skiing running gymnastics swimming sailing

5 Aim: to reinforce the acquisition of new words.

- This is a further activity to reinforce the acquisition of new words. Ask the students to think about the sports they like and don't like.
- Ask the students to list the sports under the headings *I like* or *I don't like* and then work in pairs and talk about their likes and dislikes.

LISTENING AND WRITING

1 Aim: to present the target structures.

- Ask the students to listen and read the conversation. Play the tape.

2 Aim: to focus on the target structures.

- Ask the students to look at the conversation in *Listening and Writing* activity 1 and to complete the conversation in this activity.

Answers

Tim	Do you like gymnastics, Gwen?
Gwen	Yes, I do. I like gymnastics very much.
Tim	Do you like baseball?
Gwen	No, I don't.

3 Aim: to focus on the target structures; to focus on text organisation.

- This activity focuses on the logical organisation of a text. Ask the students to read the conversation and to number it in the right order. Once again they can use the conversation in *Listening and Writing* activity 1 to help them.

Answers

1 James	Do you like volleyball Alison?
2 Alison	Yes, I do. I like volleyball very much.
3 James	Do you like skiing?
4 Alison	No, I don't

- Ask the students to listen and check their answers to 2 and 3. Play the tape.

4 Aim: to check comprehension.

- Ask the students to complete the chart by putting a tick beside the sports Jack, Gwen and Alison like and a cross beside the sports they don't like.

Answers

	Jack	Gwen	Alison
football			
tennis			
volleyball			✓
table tennis			
skiing			✗
running	✗		
basketball		✗	
gymnastics		✓	
swimming	✓		

GRAMMAR

1 Aim: to focus on possible mistakes.

- Ask the student to read the information in the grammar box and then to do the exercises.
- Point out that the auxiliary in the short answer is the same as the auxiliary in the *yes/no* question. *Yes/no* questions with the verb *be* don't use an auxiliary; other *yes/no* questions use *do*.
- Ask the students to do this activity in pairs.

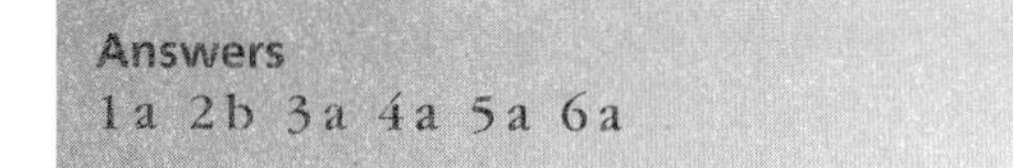

Answers
1a 2b 3a 4a 5a 6a

2 Aim: to practise writing questions.

- Ask the students to use the words to write five questions of their own.
- Ask three or four students to read out some of their questions.

3 Aim: to practise speaking; to practise using the target language.

- Ask the students to work in pairs and to ask and answer the questions.

4 Aim: to practise using the target language.

- Ask the students to work alone and write short answers to these questions. Make sure they use *Yes, I do* or *No, I don't*.

5 Aim: to practise speaking.

- Ask the students to work in pairs and to act out the conversations in *Listening and writing* activities 2 and 3.

SPEAKING AND WRITING

1 Aim: to practise speaking.

- Ask the students to go round and find people who like swimming, basketball, gymnastics and football. Make sure they ask and answer the questions using *Do you like ...?* and *Yes, I do.* or *No, I don't.* Ask them to write down the names.

2 Aim: to practise speaking.

- Ask the students to think about which sport they like. If they don't like any sports, ask them to think of another hobby or pastime. They can ask you what the English word is.
- Ask the students to go round asking and saying what sports, hobby or pastime they like and to find another student who likes the same thing.

3 Aim: to practise writing.

- Ask the students to write a poster about their favourite sports. Ask them to look for some magazine photos showing their favourite teams, and other favourite sports.
- It would be suitable to set this activity for homework.

4 Tick (✔) the sports Jack, Gwen and Alison like. Put a cross (✘) by the sports they don't like.

	Jack	Gwen	Alison
football			
tennis			
volleyball			
table tennis			
skiing			
running			
basketball			
gymnastics			
swimming			

GRAMMAR

Yes/no questions	Short answers
Do you like swimming?	*Yes, I do.*
Do you like table tennis?	*No, I don't. (= do not)*
Do you live in Berlin?	*Yes, I do. No, I don't.*
	Yes, we do. No, we don't.
Do they work in London?	*Yes, they do. No, they don't.*

1 Tick (✔) the correct answer.

1 Do you like tennis?
a Yes, I do. b Yes, I like.

2 Do you like volleyball?
a No, I no like. b No, I don't.

3 Are you married?
a No, I am not. b No, I don't.

4 Are they from London?
a Yes, they are. b Yes, they do.

5 Do they work in Paris?
a Yes, they do. b Yes, they work.

6 Do you live in Berlin?
a Yes, we do. b No, they don't.

2 Write five questions.

			in a flat?
		live	tennis?
Do	you	work	in a house?
		like	in an office?
			football?

3 Work in pairs. Ask and answer your questions from 2.

4 Answer the questions.

1 Do you like swimming?
2 Do you live in London?
3 Do you have breakfast at five o'clock in the morning?
4 Do you work in an office?
5 Are you married?
6 Are you a doctor?
7 Are you French?
8 Are you nineteen?

5 Work in pairs. Act out the conversations in *Listening and writing activities* 2 and 3.

SPEAKING AND WRITING

1 Find:

Four people who like swimming. Write their names here.

____

____

Four people who like basketball. Write their names here.

____

____

Four people who like gymnastics. Write their names here.

____

____

Four people who like football. Write their names here.

____

____

2 Find someone who likes the same sports as you.

Do you like swimming? Yes, I do.

3 Write a poster about sports.

Say what sports you like.
We like basketball.

Say what your favourite team OR player is.
Our favourite team is ...

Say what the favourite sport in your country is.
People in my country like ...

20 She likes her job

Telling the time (2); present simple: *he, she, it*

VOCABULARY AND SPEAKING

1 Listen and repeat.

a quarter past	a quarter to	half past

What's the time?
A A quarter past one.
B Half past two.
C A quarter to three.

2 Match the sentences in 1 with the correct time.

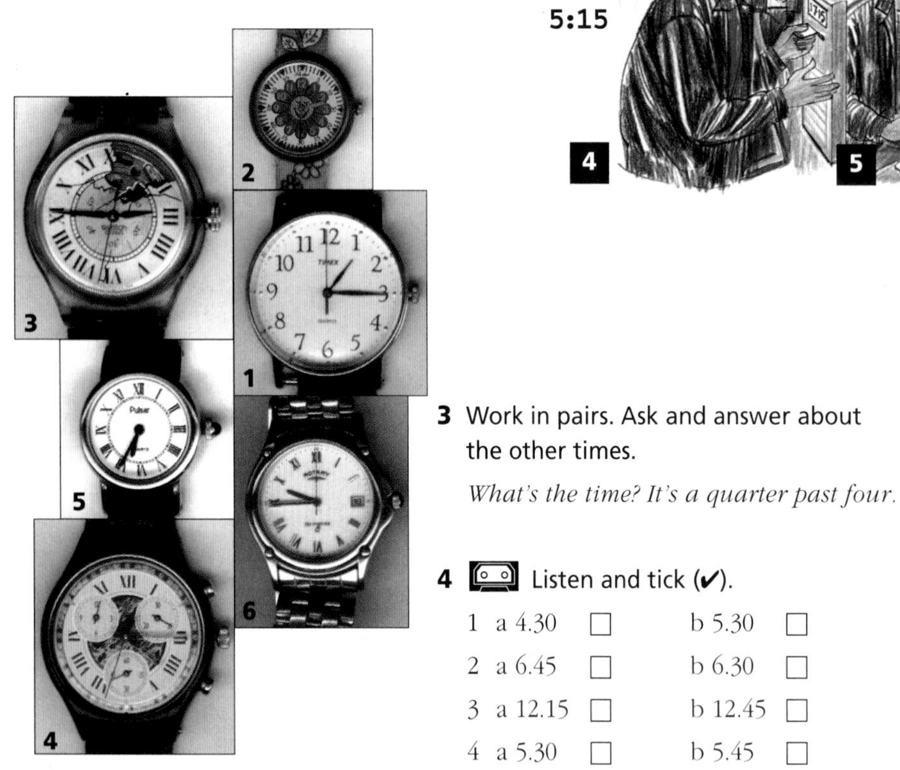

3 Work in pairs. Ask and answer about the other times.

What's the time? It's a quarter past four.

4 Listen and tick (✔).

	a		b	
1	a 4.30	☐	b 5.30	☐
2	a 6.45	☐	b 6.30	☐
3	a 12.15	☐	b 12.45	☐
4	a 5.30	☐	b 5.45	☐
5	a 7.30	☐	b 7.45	☐
6	a 11.15	☐	b 11.30	☐

5 Listen and repeat.

leave arrive go home start
visit finish

6 Match the sentences with the pictures.

a Joe arrives at work at nine o'clock.
b He starts work at a quarter past nine.
c He goes home at a quarter to nine.
d He visits friends at six o'clock on Fridays.
e He finishes work at a quarter past five.
f He leaves home at half past eight.

7 Complete sentences about you.

1 I leave home at ____
2 I arrive at work/school at ___
3 I start work at ___
4 I finish work at ____
5 I go home at ____
6 I visit friends at/on ____

8 Work in pairs. Say your answers to 7.

I leave home at eight o'clock.

20

GENERAL COMMENTS

Present simple: third person

So far, the presentation of the present simple has been restricted to the first and second person singular and plural and the third person plural, all of which have the same form. This lessons introduces the third person singular with the *-s* ending. You may wish to draw the students' attention to the explanation in the *Grammar Review* at the back of the book, where they will see all the forms of the present simple laid out in a chart.

The theme of the lesson continues with the use of the present simple to describe routines and habits.

Telling the time (2)

This is the second of two lessons in which ways of telling the time are presented. Saying *a quarter past one, half past two* and *a quarter to three* is the most common way of expressing 1.15, 2.30 and 2.45, but you may like to tell the students that another common way is to say *one fifteen, two thirty, two forty-five*.

VOCABULARY AND SPEAKING

1 Aim: to present ways of telling the time.

- Ask the students to listen and repeat the expressions. Play the tape.

2 Aim: to present ways of telling the time.

- Ask the students to match the sentences in activity 1 to the correct clock faces.

Answers
A - 1
B - 2
C - 3

3 Aim: to present ways of telling the time.

- Ask the students to work in pairs and to ask and say the time shown in the other clocks.

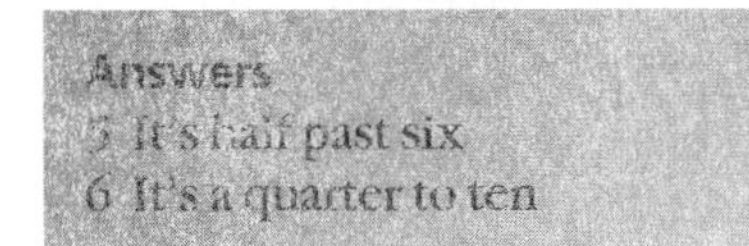

Answers
5 It's half past six
6 It's a quarter to ten

4 Aim: to practise recognising the time.

- As with numbers, your students may have more difficulty recognising the time than telling it. Explain that they will hear one of the two times shown, and that they should tick the time they hear. Play the tape.

Answers
1 b 2 a 3 a 4 b 5 a 6 a

- Check the answers with the whole class. Play the tape again.

- You may want to give further practice in telling and recognising the times. Write some more clocks on the board, and ask the students to tell the time, or say some more times to the whole class and ask them to write them down. Note that the second activity will be more difficult than the first.

5 Aim: to present the pronunciation of the words in the vocabulary box.

- Ask the students to listen and repeat the words.

6 Aim: to focus on the meaning of the words in the vocabulary box.

- Ask the students to match the sentences with the illustrations. This should explain the meaning of the verbs in the box.

- Check the answers with the whole class.

Answers
a - 2 b - 3 c - 6 d - 5 e - 4 f - 1

7 Aim: to practise writing times.

- Ask the students to complete the sentences about themselves with an appropriate time.

- Obviously, *five past/to, ten past/to, twenty past/to* and *twenty-five past/to* have not been presented so encourage your students to answer these questions with full hours, halves and quarters.

8 Aim: to practise speaking.

- Ask the students to work in pairs and to talk about their answers to activity 7.

READING

Aim: to practise using the third person form of the present tense.

- Ask the students to read the passage and to complete the sentences with verbs in the third person singular. Point out that they can simply copy the relevant verb from the passage.

Answers
1 lives 2 works 3 has 4 leaves 5 starts
6 has 7 finishes 8 works 9 goes 10 visit

GRAMMAR

1 Aim: to focus on the form of the third person singular of verbs in the present simple.

- Ask the students to read the information in the grammar box and then to do the exercises.

- Ask the students to look back at the passage and to write the third person for each verb.

Answers
leaves arrives works lives starts visits
goes finishes has

- Draw the students' attention to the fact that sometimes you add an *-es* to form the third person, and that sometimes this ending is pronounced /ɪz/.

2 Aim: to focus on possible mistakes.

- Ask the students to tick the correct sentence.

Answers
1a 2b 3b 4b 5a 6b

LISTENING AND WRITING

1 Aim: to practise listening.

- [cassette] Explain to the students that they are going to hear two people talking about their daily routines. Ask them to listen and tick the information they hear.

	Sarah		Mark	
live	☐ Spain	☑ Italy	☐ Mexico City	☑ Acapulco
work	☐ office	☑ school	☐ school	☑ hospital
have breakfast	☑ 7.30 am	☐ 8 am	☑ 6.30 am	☐ 7.45 am
start work	☑ 3 pm	☐ 2 pm	☐ 6.45 am	☑ 8 am
finish work	☑ 9 pm	☐ 11 pm	☐ 6 pm	☑ 7 pm
go shopping	☑ Saturdays	☑ mornings	☐ Fridays	☑ Saturdays
visit parents/friends	☑ Saturday evenings	☑ Sundays	☐ Saturdays	☑ Sundays

2 Aim: to practise speaking.

- Ask the students to check their answers in pairs.

- [cassette] Check the answers with the whole class. You may like to play the tape a second time as you do so.

3 Aim: to practise writing.

- Ask the students to write a paragraph about Sarah and Mark.

SPEAKING

1 Aim: to practise speaking; to practise using the target structure.

- Ask the students to look at Communication activity 36 on page 99 and to follow the instructions. They should look at the identity card and memorise the information. They should then ask and answer questions about the person and check with one another to see that their answers are correct.

2 Aim: to practise speaking; to practise using the target structure.

- Ask the students to work with other pairs and to check their answers to activity 1.

- You may like to ask the students to write a description of the person for homework.

READING

Read the passage and complete the sentences.

Esther lives in a flat in Boston with her husband and their two sons. She works in a shop from Monday to Saturday. She has breakfast at 6.30 in the morning. She leaves at 7.30, and arrives at work at 8 am. She has lunch at 12.30 in the afternoon, and starts work at 1.30 pm. She finishes work at 6 in the evening and goes home. She works on Saturday, but she likes her job.

Her husband works in a school in Boston. On Saturday afternoon, he goes shopping with their sons and on Sunday they visit Esther's parents. They have a house in Cambridge.

1 Esther ____ in a flat in Boston.
2 She ____ in a shop.
3 She ____ breakfast at 6.30.
4 She ____ at 7.30.
5 She ____ at work at 8 am.
6 She ____ lunch at 12.30 pm.
7 She ____ work at 6 pm.
8 Her husband is a teacher. He ____ in a school in Boston.
9 He ____ shopping with their sons on Saturday afternoon.
10 They ____ Esther's parents on Sunday.

GRAMMAR

Telling the time (2)

What's the time? *It's a quarter past one.*
It's half past two.
It's a quarter to three.

Present simple: ***he, she, it***

*Esther live**s** in a flat in Boston.*
*Her husband work**s** in a school.*
*The train leave**s** at 7.30 am.*
*It arrive**s** at 8 am.*

1 Write the third person.

1 leave arrive work live start visit go finish have
leaves,...

2 Tick (✔) the correct sentence.

1 a She works in a shop. b She work in a shop.
2 a He's live in Boston. b He lives in Boston.
3 a Its leaves at 7.30. b It leaves at 7.30.
4 a He go home at 6 pm. b He goes home at 6 pm.
5 a Her parents live in Cambridge. b Her parents lives in Cambridge.
6 a She have two sons. b She has two sons.

LISTENING AND WRITING

1 Listen and tick (✔).

	Sarah		Mark	
live	☐ Spain	☐ Italy	☐ Mexico City	☐ Acapulco
work	☐ office	☐ school	☐ shop	☐ hospital
have breakfast	☐ 7.30 am	☐ 8 am	☐ 6.30 am	☐ 7.45 am
start work	☐ 3 pm	☐ 2 pm	☐ 6.45 am	☐ 8 am
finish work	☐ 9 pm	☐ 11 pm	☐ 6 pm	☐ 7pm
go shopping	☐ mornings/ Saturdays	☐ mornings/ Sundays	☐ Fridays	☐ Saturdays
visit parents/friends	☐ Saturdays/ Sundays	☐ Sundays/ Mondays	☐ Saturdays	☐ Sundays

2 Work in pairs. Check 1.

3 Write a paragraph about Sarah and Mark.

Sarah lives in Italy.

SPEAKING

1 Work in pairs. Turn to Communication activity 36 on page 99.

2 Work with another pair. Check your information.

Her name is Mary Ward.

Progress check

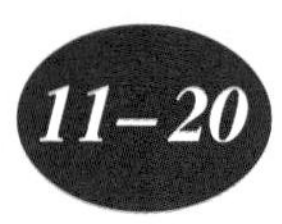

VOCABULARY

1 Tick (✔) the correct answer.

1 A *sweater* is
- a a place ☐
- b a member of the family ☐
- c an item of clothing ☐

2 A *wallet* is
- a a personal possession ☐
- b food ☐
- c a day of the week ☐

3 A *mother* is
- a a drink ☐
- b an eye colour ☐
- c a member of the family ☐

4 *Fair* is
- a a hair colour ☐
- b an item of clothing ☐
- c food ☐

5 *Good looking* is
- a a word to describe character ☐
- b a word to describe appearance ☐
- c a personal possession ☐

6 *Stand up* is
- a an instruction ☐
- b a drink ☐
- c a personal possession ☐

7 A *flat* is
- a a place where people live ☐
- b a day of the week ☐
- c a word to describe character ☐

8 *Thursday* is
- a a day of the week ☐
- b an item of clothing ☐
- c a personal possession ☐

9 *Lunch* is
- a a place where people live ☐
- b food ☐
- c a day of the week ☐

10 *Running* is
- a a day of the week ☐
- b a sport ☐
- c a drink ☐

2 Think of other words for all the categories in 1.

3 Look at the words in Lessons 11 to 20 again. Choose words which are useful to you and write them in your *Wordbank* in the Practice Book.

GRAMMAR

1 Write questions and answers.

1 wallet – £50.00
2 jacket – £39.00
3 jeans – £12.99
4 sweater – £25.50
5 skirt – £20.00
6 shirt – £25.00

1 How much is that wallet?
It's fifty pounds.

Progress check 11–20

You can work through this Progress check in the order shown, or concentrate on areas which may have caused difficulty in Lessons 11 to 20. You can also let the students
… e to or feel the

in Lessons 11

their own, and

10 b

…ulary; to revise
…to 20.
…wers in activity
been presented
…hink of other
…hey should look
…ns 11 - 20 to

…ss.

…cquisition

which are
…hink about
write them in

GRAMMAR

1 Aim: to revise asking and saying how much things cost.

Answers

1 How much is that wallet?	It's fifty pounds.
2 How much is that jacket?	It's thirty-nine pounds.
3 How much are those jeans?	They're twelve pounds ninety-nine.
4 How much is that sweater?	They're twenty-five pounds fifty.
5 How much is that skirt?	It's twenty pounds.
6 How much is that shirt?	They're twenty-five pounds.

2 Aim: to revise saying where things are.

Answers

1 The telephone is on the table.
2 The sweater is under the chair.
3 The magazine is in the coat pocket.
4 The bag is under the table.
5 The keys are in the bag.

3 Aim: to revise *has/have got*.

Answers

The Smiths have got three children. Their son's name is George. He's got fair hair and he's very good looking. Their daughters' names are Judy and Terri. Judy has got dark hair and brown eyes. Terri has got dark hair and green eyes.

4 Aim: to revise imperatives.

Answers

1 b 2 c 3 a 4 d

5 Aim: to revise telling the time.

Answers

1 A quarter past one 2 Half past six
3 A quarter to ten 4 Eleven o'clock

6 Aim: to revise the present simple.

- Ask the students to complete the sentences so they're true for them.

7 Aim: to revise the third person singular.

- Ask the students to work in pairs and to rewrite each other's sentences using the third person singular.

SOUNDS

1 Aim: to focus on /ɑː/, /ʌ/, /ɜː/ and /eə/.

- Ask the students to listen and repeat the words.

- Continue to practise these sounds by asking the students to repeat them in pairs, and then with the whole class.

2 Aim: to focus on stressed syllables in words.

- Ask the students to listen and underline the stressed syllables.

> **Answers**
> sweater jacket glasses father clever wallet

- Ask the students to say the words aloud in pairs, and then with the whole class.

3 Aim: to focus on word stress in sentences.

- Ask the students to predict which words are likely to be stressed.

- Play the tape and ask them to listen and underline the stressed words

> **Answers**
> 1 I've got a brother and two sisters.
> 2 He's got fair hair and blue eyes.
> 3 I live in a house in London.
> 4 It's half past eight.
> 5 I don't like Monday mornings.
> 6 He likes his job.

- Ask them to say the sentences aloud.

LISTENING

1 Aim: to practise listening for text organisation; to listen for enjoyment.

- Remember that the main aim of this activity is to listen for enjoyment to some authentic English. Make sure everyone understands that they won't be able to understand every single word. Say that you'll explain five words and that they must choose these words carefully.

- Point out that the lines are in the wrong order. Ask the students to listen and number them in the order they hear them.

2 Aim: to practise speaking.

- Ask the students to check their answers in pairs.

- Play the song a second time. Go through the correct order of the song, if necessary.

> **Answers**
> Don't worry about a thing
> 'Cause every little thing's gonna be all right
> Singing 'Don't worry about a thing'
> 'Cause every little thing's gonna be all right
> Rise up this morning
> Smiled with the rising sun
> Three little birds beside my doorstep
> Singing sweet songs of melodies pure and true
> Singing 'This is my message to you'

2 Look at the picture and say where the things are.

The telephone is on the table.

3 Complete the passage about the Smiths.

Name	George	Judy	Terri
Family	son	daughter	daughter
Appearance	fair hair,	dark hair,	dark hair,
	good looking	brown eyes	green eyes

The Smiths ____ got three ____. Their ____ name is George. He's got ___ hair. and he's very ____ ____. ____ daughters' ____ are Judy and ____. Judy has ____ hair and ____ eyes. Terri has ____ hair and ____ eyes.

4 Match the instructions with their opposites.

1 Come in. a Close your book.
2 Stand up. b Go out.
3 Open your book. c Sit down.
4 Take your coat off. d Put your coat on.

5 Say what the time is.

6 Complete the sentences so they're true for you.

1 I live in a ____ in ____.
2 I work/go to school in ____.
3 My parents live in ____.
4 We have breakfast at ____.
5 We have dinner at ____.
6 I start school/work at ____.
7 I finish school/work at ____.
8 I like ____.

7 Work in pairs. Look at your partner's answers to 7. Rewrite them like this.

Pierre lives in a flat in Paris. He goes to school in ….

SOUNDS

1 Listen and repeat.

/ɑː/ dark glasses past
/ʌ/ son mother brother
/ɜː/ skirt shirt work Thursday
/eə/ hair fair their

2 Listen and underline the stressed syllable.

sweater jacket glasses father wallet

Now say the words aloud.

3 Listen and underline the stressed words.

1 I've got a brother and two sisters.
2 He's got fair hair and blue eyes.
3 I live in a house in London.
4 It's half past eight.
5 I don't like Monday mornings.
6 He likes his job.

Now say the sentences aloud.

LISTENING

1 You're going to hear *Three Little Birds*, by Bob Marley. The lines are in the wrong order. Listen and number the lines in the order you hear them.

- ☐ Rise up this morning
- ☐ Don't worry about a thing
- ☐ Smiled with the rising sun
- ☐ Singing 'This is my message to you.'
- ☐ 'Cause every little thing's gonna be all right
- ☐ Singing 'Don't worry about a thing
- ☐ Singing sweet songs of melodies pure and true
- ☐ 'Cause every little thing's gonna be all right'
- ☐ Three little birds beside my doorstep

2 Work in pairs and check your answers.

Now listen again and check.

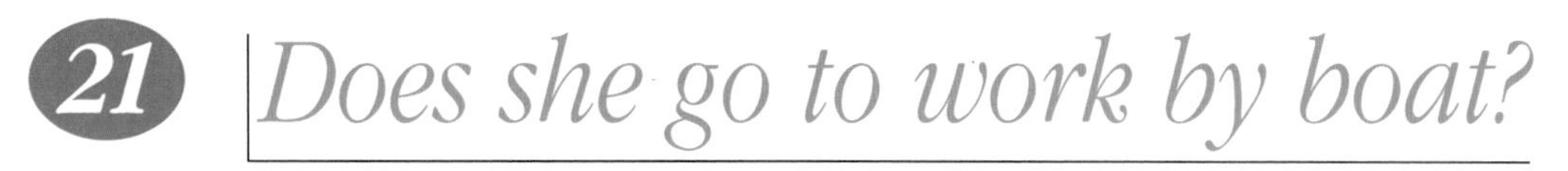

21 Does she go to work by boat?

He/she/it; _Yes/no_ questions and short answers; _by_

VOCABULARY AND SOUNDS

1 Listen and repeat.

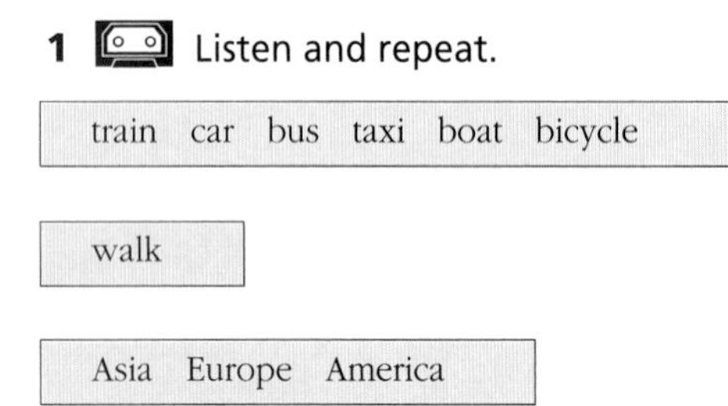

train car bus taxi boat bicycle

walk

Asia Europe America

2 Turn to Communication activity 12 on page 94 and check you know what the words in 1 are.

3 Work in pairs. Say what means of transport you can see in the photo.

4 Listen and repeat.

/eɪ/ train play eight say
/ɑː/ car ask father
/ʌ/ bus number mother
/æ/ taxi bag flat have
/əʊ/ boat go don't
/aɪ/ bicycle time arrive
/ɔː/ walk four quarter

5 Listen and repeat.

car go to work
Do you go to work by car?
bus go to work
Do you go to work by bus?
walk work
Do you walk to work?

READING AND LISTENING

1 Read and complete the chart for Mehmet.

SALLY Good morning! This is Reward Radio. My name's Sally Finch and today on *Going to work ... going home* we're in Turkey on the Galata Bridge in Istanbul. Turkey is in Europe and in Asia. The Galata Bridge is in Europe, but Asia is over there. It's eight o'clock on Monday morning and this is Mehmet. Mehmet, do you live here?

MEHMET No, I don't. I live in Asia.

SALLY Do you work here?

MEHMET Yes, I do.

SALLY So you live on the Asian side but you work in Europe?

MEHMET Yes.

SALLY Do you go to work by car?

MEHMET No. I go to work by boat.

SALLY And are you married?

MEHMET Yes. My wife's name is Belma.

SALLY Does Belma work in Istanbul?

MEHMET Yes, she does.

SALLY And does she go to work by boat?

MEHMET No, she doesn't. She goes to work by car.

SALLY Thank you Mehmet. ... Excuse me!

21

GENERAL COMMENTS

New vocabulary

By now, you should be recommending that the students note down new vocabulary in a notebook. You can suggest that they organise these records according to topics, such as transport, sport, etc. and perhaps a special category, such as words which are personally useful. The vocabulary boxes in *Reward* are organised according to topic or according to new words generated by a specific piece of material. There is space in the Practice Book for the students to note down new words according to topic. You may not wish to discourage translation at this stage, but they should begin to understand that words do not always have direct equivalents in other languages.

VOCABULARY AND SOUNDS

1 Aim: to present the pronunciation of the words in the vocabulary box.

- Ask the students to listen and repeat the words in the vocabulary box as you play the tape.

- Ask the students if there are any words they recognise.

2 Aim: to present the meaning of the words in the vocabulary box.

- Ask the students to match the words and the photos.

3 Aim: to practise speaking; to prepare for listening.

- This activity is designed to help the students think about the topic of the listening material in *Reading and listening*, which is about going to work in Istanbul, which lies in both Europe and Asia. Ask the students to work in pairs and say what means of transport they can see in the photo.

> Answers
> boat/ferry/car/taxi

4 Aim: to practise the pronunciation of /eɪ/, /ɑː/, /ʌ/, /æ/, /əʊ/, /ɑɪ/ and /ɔː/.

- Some or all of these phonemes may already exist in the students' own language(s). If so, you may like to spend less time on this activity.

- Ask the students to listen to the tape and repeat the words.

5 Aim: to focus on stressed words in sentences.

- Ask the students to listen and repeat the sentences as you play the tape.

- Ask three or four students to repeat the sentences.

READING AND LISTENING

1 Aim: to present *yes/no* questions and short answers with the third person singular of the present simple.

- The students have already come across the concept of *yes/no* questions and short answers in Lessons 4, 6 and 19. This lesson presents the third person singular form. Remind them that a short answer uses the same auxiliary (*do/does*) as the question form.

- Ask the students to read the interview and to complete the information about Mehmet and Belma in the chart.

2 Aim: to practise listening.

- Play the rest of the tape and ask the students to try and remember the other means of transport which the speakers mention.

- Ask the students to complete the chart.

Name	goes to work by
Mehmet	boat
Belma	car
Leyla	walks
Mustafa	boat
John	boat
Mary	car

- You will have the opportunity to check the answers in *Grammar* activity 1.

GRAMMAR

1 Aim: to practise using *yes/no* questions and short answers.

- Ask the students to read the information in the grammar box and then to do the exercises.
- Ask a few *yes/no* questions to check the answers to *Reading and listening* activity 2, and elicit a suitable short answer.
- Ask the students to check their answers to *Reading and listening* activity 2 in pairs. They should ask and answer *yes/no* questions.

2 Aim: to practise forming *yes/no* questions.

- Ask the students to complete the sentences with suitable verbs. You may like to write the verbs on the board to prompt them: *work go have live visit* . Tell them that one verb can be used more than once.

Answers

1 Does live	2 Does go	3 Does work
4 Does have	5 Does visit	6 Does go

3 Aim: to practise forming short answers.

- Ask the students to write short answers to the questions in activity 2.

Answers

1 Yes, he does.	2 No, she doesn't.
3 Yes, she does.	4 No, he doesn't.
5 Yes, he does.	6 No, she doesn't.

SPEAKING

1 Aim: to practise speaking; to practise using the target structures.

- Ask the students to work in pairs and to act out the interview in *Reading and listening* activity 1.
- When they're ready ask two or three pairs to act out their interview to the whole class.

2 Aim: to practise speaking.

- Ask the students to act out the interview again, but this time talking about their own journeys to school or work. They should use the interview as a model.

3 Aim: to practise speaking.

- Ask the students to work with new partners, and to follow the instructions. If it's possible, ask them to walk round the class looking for the people and writing their names.

4 Aim: to practise speaking; to practise using the target structures.

- Ask the students to work in pairs, perhaps with their usual partner, and to look at each other's lists of names. They should follow the instructions.
- Explain to the students that they only score a point if they guess correctly first time.
- Find out who has scored the most points.

	goes to work by
Mehmet	
Belma	
Leyla	
Mustafa	
John	
Mary	

2 Listen to the rest of the programme and complete the chart.

GRAMMAR

He/she/it; Yes/no questions

Does Mehmet go to work by boat?	*Yes, he does.*
Does Belma go to work by bus?	*No, she doesn't.*
Does he go to work by car?	*Yes, he does.*
Does she walk to work?	*No, she doesn't.*

By

by car by train by bus by taxi

1 Work in pairs and check your answers to *Reading and listening* activity 1.

Does Mehmet go to work by boat? Yes, he does.

2 Complete.

1 ____ Mehmet ____ in Asia?

2 ____ Belma ____ to work by boat?

3 ____ Leyla ____ in a shop?

4 ____ Mustafa ____ lunch at home?

5 ____ John ____ his parents on Sunday?

6 ____ Mary ____ shopping on Saturday?

3 Answer the questions in 2.

1 Yes 2 No 3 Yes 4 No 5 Yes 6 No

Yes, he does.

SPEAKING

1 Work in pairs and act out the conversation in *Reading and listening* activity 1.

2 Act out the conversation again, but talk about your journey to school/work.

3 Work with other students. Find someone who:

– goes to work/school by car

– goes to work/school by taxi

– goes to work/school by train

– goes to work/school by bicycle

– goes to work/school by bus

– walks to school/work

Now write their names.

4 Work in pairs.

Student A: Look at Student B's list of names. Ask how they go to school/work. You score one point for each *Yes* answer.

Does Piotr go to school by taxi?

Student B: Show your list of names to Student A. Answer the questions.

Yes, he does.

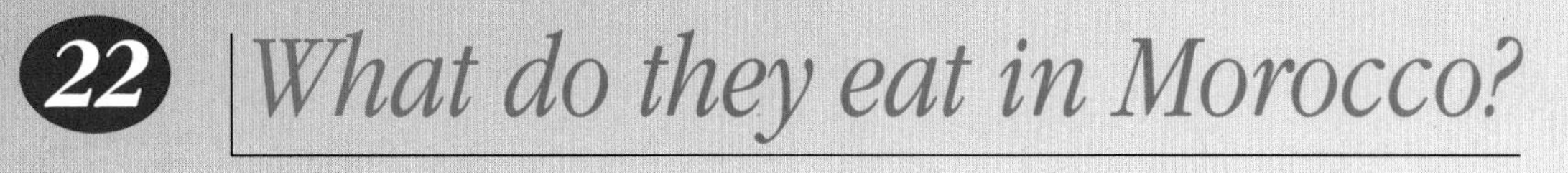

22 *What do they eat in Morocco?*

Present simple: *Wh-* questions

VOCABULARY AND SOUNDS

1 Listen and repeat.

milk yoghurt rice beef
chicken lamb orange lemon
apple wine water juice potato
tomato bread tea coffee beer

2 Work in pairs.

Student A: Turn to Communication activity 13 on page 94.

Student B: Turn to Communication activity 24 on page 96.

3 Ask and say what the food and drink is.

What's this?

Milk. And what's this?

4 Complete.

food drink

Food	*Drink*
orange ...	*water ...*

5 Put the food under these headings.

vegetable meat fruit

Which words don't go under these headings?

READING AND LISTENING

1 Read and match the questions and answers.

Food and drink around the world.

1 What food do you eat in your country?
2 What do you drink?
3 When do you have the main meal of the day?
4 What do you have for breakfast?

A The main meal of the day is lunch. We have lunch at one o'clock in the afternoon. During the week, if you work, the main meal is dinner.
B In Argentina we eat meat, especially beef.
C We have coffee and bread.
D We drink beer and wine with our meals, or water and juice.

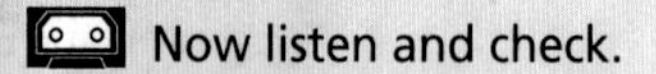

Now listen and check.

22

GENERAL COMMENTS

Wh- questions

Wh- questions are questions formed with words beginning with *wh: who, what, where, when, why*. The term also includes questions beginning with *how*.

Socio-cultural training

Traditional meals in different countries is a popular topic in socio-cultural training. Use this lesson not only to explore the broad cultural traditions of the countries described, but also the personal or family traditions of different students in the class. Remind your students that socio-cultural training includes not only acquiring information about other cultures but also developing socio-cultural self-awareness. The differences in customs and traditions among people of the same culture can often be just as interesting as finding out about other countries.

VOCABULARY AND SOUNDS

1 Aim: to present the pronunciation of the words in the vocabulary box.

- The students may already recognise some of these words. Ask them to listen and repeat them as you play the tape.
- Ask three or four students to say the words aloud. Then play the tape again.

2 Aim: to present the meaning of the words.

- At this stage the students work on their own. In the Communication activities, Student A will find the meaning of some of the words and Student B will find the meaning of the others. This will act as preparation for activity 3.

3 Aim: to present the meaning of the words.

- At this stage, the students work together. Ask them to look at the page and to ask and say what the food and drink is.

4 Aim: to consolidate the vocabulary acquisition process.

- This is a simple categorisation activity which is designed to make the students examine the words again. Ask them to complete the lists with the words they have learned in the previous activity.

Answers

Food: yoghurt rice beef chicken lamb orange lemon apple potato tomato bread

Drink: milk wine water juice tea

5 Aim: to consolidate the vocabulary acquisition process.

- This is a further categorisation activity.
- Ask the students to put the food under the headings and to write down the two words which don't belong to any heading.

Answers

Vegetable: rice potato tomato

Meat: beef chicken lamb

Fruit: orange lemon apple

bread, yoghurt

Note: a tomato is technically a fruit, but it is most often thought of and referred to as a vegetable.

READING AND LISTENING

1 Aim: to listen for main ideas.

- Explain to the students that they are going to hear a person, from Argentina, talking about traditional meals in his country. Ask the students to read the questions and predict what the answers might be.
- Play the tape and ask the students to check their predictions

Answers

1 - B 2 - D 3 - A 4 - C

2 Aim: to check comprehension.

- Ask the students to complete the *Argentina* column of the chart with the letter corresponding to the correct answer.
- The students will hear the rest of the listening passage when they have read the grammar box.

GRAMMAR

1 Aim: to practise speaking; to practise forming *wh-* questions.

- Ask the students to read the information in the grammar box and then to do the exercises.
- At the stage the students are working separately in their groups of three. Ask them to decide who is Student A, B and C and then to follow the instructions.
- Play the tape.

2 Aim: to practise speaking; to practise forming *wh-* questions.

- Ask the students to ask and answer questions about Morocco and India and to complete the chart.

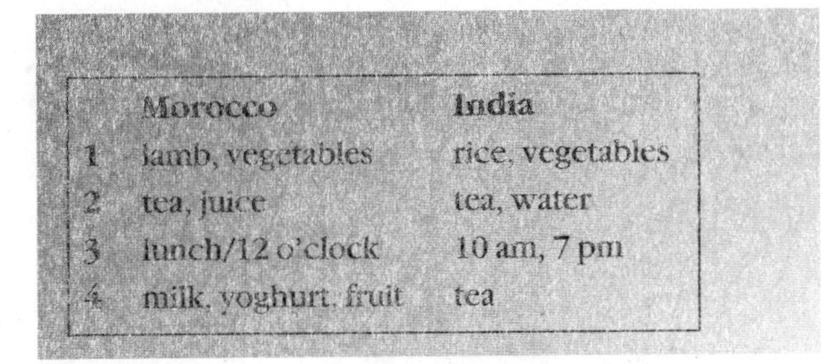

	Morocco	India
1	lamb, vegetables	rice, vegetables
2	tea, juice	tea, water
3	lunch/12 o'clock	10 am, 7 pm
4	milk, yoghurt, fruit	tea

3 Aim: to focus on possible mistakes.

- Ask the students to tick the correct sentences.

> Answers
> 1a 2b 3a 4a

- Ask the students to say why the other questions are wrong. (They all omit the auxiliary.)

4 Aim: to practise writing *wh*- questions.

- Ask the students to write the questions in full.
- Check the answers with the whole class.

> Answers
> 1 What does he have for breakfast?
> 2 When does she have lunch?
> 3 What do you eat?
> 4 What does she drink?
> 5 When do they have the main meal?
> 6 What food do you eat in your country?

SPEAKING AND WRITING

1 Aim: to practise speaking; to prepare for writing.

- Ask the students to talk about food and drink in their country, looking at the questions in *Listening* activity 1.
- You may like to conduct some group feedback at this point. Explore the differences between families and individuals.

2 Aim: to practise writing.

- Ask the students to write a short paragraph answering the questions they discussed in activity 1.
- You may like to leave this to be done for homework.

3 Aim: to practise speaking; to practise using the target structures.

- Ask the students to go round the class asking and answering questions about their eating habits. Ask them to complete the chart.

4 Aim: to practise speaking.

- Ask the students to work in small groups and to talk about the answers to the questions.
- Talk about eating habits with the whole class. What is traditional food and drink at the different meals? Are the country's eating habits changing?

2 Complete the *Argentina* column with the letter corresponding to the correct answer.

Question	Argentina	Morocco	India
1	*B*		
2			
3			
4			

GRAMMAR

Wh- questions
What food do you eat in your country?
When do you have the main meal of the day?

1 Work in groups of three.
Student A: Turn to Communication activity 14 on page 94.
Student B: Turn to Communication activity 25 on page 97.
Student C: Turn to Communication activity 29 on page 97.

2 Work together and complete the Morocco and India columns of the chart with the correct information.

3 Tick (✔) the correct sentence.

1 a When do you drink tea?
  b When you drink tea?
2 a What's he have for breakfast?
  b What does he have for breakfast?
3 a When does she eat?
  b When's she eat?
4 a What do you have for breakfast?
  b What you have for breakfast?

4 Write.

1 what/he/have for breakfast?
2 when/she/have lunch?
3 what/you/eat?
4 what/she/drink?
5 when/they/have the main meal?
6 what food/eat in your country?

What does he have for breakfast?

SPEAKING AND WRITING

1 Work in pairs. Talk about food and drink in your country. Ask and answer the questions in *Listening* activity 1.

2 Write a short paragraph describing food and drink in your country.

In Italy, we eat pasta and pizza.

3 Complete.

Find someone who:	Name
drinks tea in the morning	______
likes beer	______
doesn't like meat	______
has a sandwich for lunch	______
eats pasta	______
doesn't drink tea	______
likes French fries	______
eats burgers for breakfast!	______

What do you drink in the morning? Tea.

4 Work in groups. Ask and say.

What does Marco drink in the morning?
He drinks tea.

23 I don't like lying on the beach

Like + _-ing_; present simple: negatives

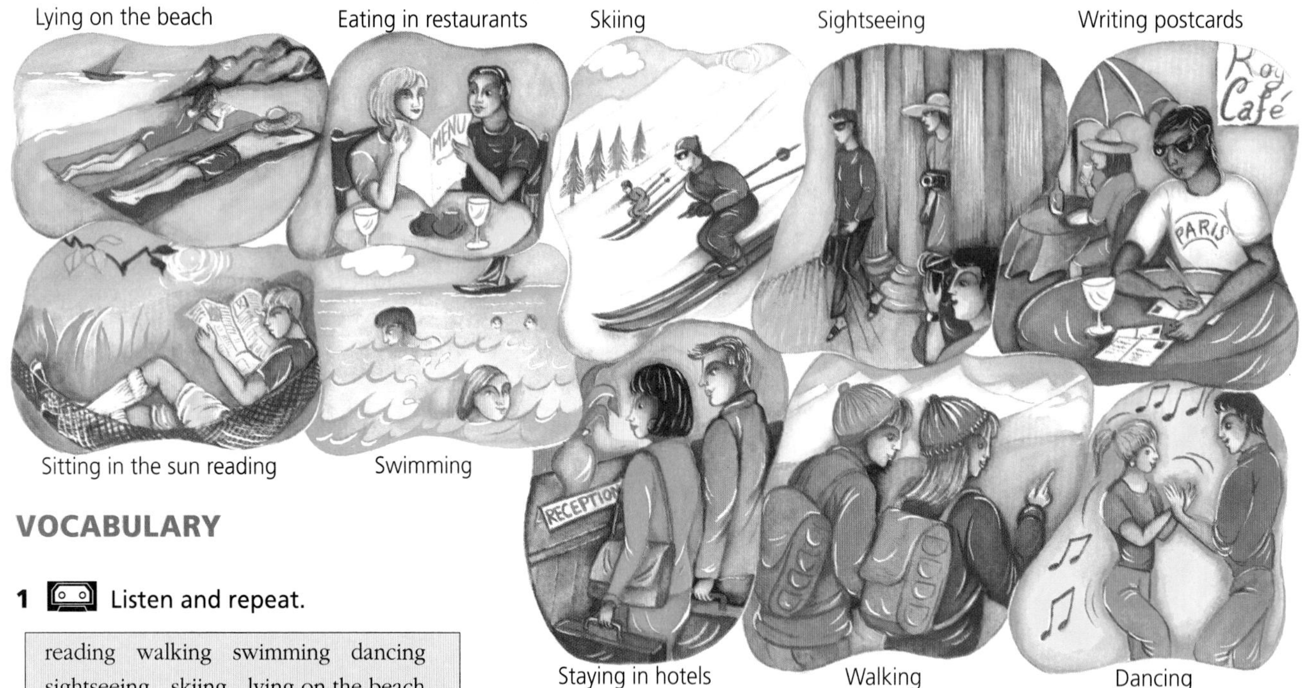

VOCABULARY

1 Listen and repeat.

reading walking swimming dancing sightseeing skiing lying on the beach eating in restaurants staying in hotels writing postcards sitting in the sun

2 Work in pairs. Look at the pictures. Point and say.

3 Write the words in two columns: *I like* and *I don't like*.

I like: reading, swimming...

I don't like: walking...

READING AND LISTENING

1 Read the passages and say who the people in the photo are.

Going on Holiday

Where do you like going on holiday?
What do you like doing on holiday?
What don't you like doing on holiday?
We talk to people about going on holiday.

'I like walking and sightseeing. I don't like lying on the beach. My girlfriend likes sightseeing, but she doesn't like walking.' *Mick.*

'I don't like going on holiday with my family, so I usually go away with my friends, to Spain or to Turkey. We have a great time.' *Dave*

'We don't like staying in hotels. We have friends in the Rocky Mountains in the USA so we go skiing with them.' *Carrie*

'I don't like writing postcards but my parents like to get them, so I write a card to them, and a card to friends.' *Colin*

'I go to Europe during my college holidays. I don't like staying in America. I like travelling by train. I also like walking and sightseeing.' *Brad*

'We go to the sea. I don't like swimming but I like sitting in the sun and reading.' *Patrizia*

23

GENERAL COMMENTS

-ing form verbs

The vocabulary in this lesson consists of *-ing* form verbs, which often follow certain verbs such as *like*. Although they are formed from verbs, usually by adding *-ing* to the infinitive form, they act as nouns.

VOCABULARY

1 Aim: to present the pronunciation of the words in the vocabulary box.

- Ask the students to listen and repeat the words as you play the tape.

- Ask the students if they recognise any words. Some have already been presented in earlier lessons.

2 Aim: to present the pronunciation of the words in the vocabulary box.

- Ask the students to look at the pictures, point to them and say the words.

3 Aim: to consolidate the vocabulary acquisition process.

- Ask the students to categorise the activities according to whether they like or don't like them. They don't need to use the target language yet.

- Ask the students to tell the whole class which column they have put the words in.

READING AND LISTENING

1 Aim: to practise reading for main ideas.

- Ask the students to read the quotations and to match them with the photos of the people who said them.

Answers
1 – Carrie 2 – Patrizia

2 Aim: to check comprehension; to prepare for practice of the target structures.

- Ask the students to read the statements and to say if they are true.

Answers
1 false 2 false 3 false 4 true 5 true 6 false

- Check the answers with the whole class. Are there any comments which the students identify with?

3 Aim: to practise reading for main ideas.

- Explain to the students that they are going to here two people talking about what they like doing on holiday. Check that everyone still remembers the meaning of the words in the chart; remind them that these words and expressions were presented in *Vocabulary* activity 1.

- Ask the students to listen and tick the things the speakers like doing and to put a cross by the things they don't like doing.

	Gary	Margaret
reading		✓
walking	✓	
swimming	✗	✓
dancing		✓
sightseeing	✓	✗
skiing	✗	
lying on the beach	✗	✓
eating in restaurants	✓	
staying in hotels	✓	
writing postcards	✗	✗
sitting in the sun		

4 Aim: to check comprehension; to practise speaking; to provide an opportunity for a second listening.

- Ask the students to check their answers in pairs.

- Play the tape a second time.

GRAMMAR

1 Aim: to practise using *like* + *-ing* and the present simple: negatives.

- Ask the students to read the information in the grammar box and then to do the exercises.

- Ask the students to check their answers to *Vocabulary* activity 3 and to say what they like or don't like doing on holiday.

2 Aim: to practise using *like* + *-ing*.

- Ask the students to look at *Reading and listening* activity 2 and correct the false statements.

Answers
1 Mick doesn't like lying on the beach.
2 Dave doesn't like going on holiday with his family.
3 Carrie and her husband don't like staying in hotels.
6 Patrizia doesn't like swimming.

3 Aim: to focus on some possible mistakes.

- Ask the students to choose the correct sentences.

Answers
1 I don't like swimming.
2 He doesn't like staying in hotels.
3 We don't like sightseeing.
4 They don't like reading.
5 She doesn't like dancing.
6 You don't like walking.

SPEAKING AND WRITING

1 Aim: to practise using the target structures; to provide a model for writing.

- Ask the students to work in pairs and ask and answer the questions in *Reading and listening* activity 1.

2 Aim: to practise writing.

- Ask the students to use the information they collected in activity 1 for a paragraph about their partner's holiday likes and dislikes.

- When they're ready, ask three or four students to read their paragraphs to the whole class.

- You may like to ask the students to do this activity for homework.

2 Say if these statements are true or false.

1 Mick likes lying on the beach.
2 Dave likes going on holiday with his family.
3 Carrie and her husband like staying in hotels.
4 Colin doesn't like writing postcards.
5 Brad likes going to Europe.
6 Patrizia likes swimming.

3 Listen to Gary and Margaret talking about what they like and don't like doing on holiday. Put a tick (✔) by the things they like doing and a cross (✗) by the things they don't like doing.

	Gary	Margaret
reading		
walking		
swimming		
dancing		
sightseeing		
skiing		
lying on the beach		
eating in restaurants		
staying in hotels		
writing postcards		
sitting in the sun		

4 Work in pairs and check your answers.

Gary likes sightseeing but Margaret doesn't.

Now listen again and check.

GRAMMAR

Like + *-ing*

I like swimming.
Patrizia likes sitting in the sun.
Mick likes walking and sightseeing.

Present simple: negatives

I don't like lying on the beach.
She doesn't like walking.
We don't like staying in hotels.

1 Work in pairs. Check your answers to *Vocabulary* activity 3.

I like swimming but I don't like sightseeing.

2 Correct the false statements in *Reading and listening* activity 2.

Mick doesn't like lying on the beach.

3 *Doesn't* or *don't?* Choose the correct sentences.

1 I doesn't/don't like swimming.
2 He doesn't/don't like staying in hotels.
3 We doesn't/don't like sightseeing.
4 They doesn't/don't like reading.
5 She doesn't/don't like dancing.
6 You doesn't/don't like walking.

SPEAKING AND WRITING

1 Work in pairs. Ask and answer the questions in *Reading and listening* activity 1.

2 Write a paragraph about your partner's holiday likes and dislikes. Read it to the class.

Marco likes going on holiday to Europe. He likes …

24 There's a telephone in the hall

There is/are; any

VOCABULARY AND SOUNDS

1 Listen and repeat.

kitchen bathroom bedroom living room garden dining room hall

downstairs upstairs front back

small large

2 Read and label the rooms.

The *kitchen, living room* and *dining room* are downstairs.

The *dining room* is at the front.

There is a door from the hall to the *kitchen*.

The *living room* has a window. You see the garden.

There are two *bedrooms upstairs*.

The *bathroom* is upstairs, at the back.

3 Work in pairs. Ask and answer.

What rooms do you have in your home?

4 Listen and repeat.

cooker cupboard armchair sofa bed shower

5 Work in pairs. Look at the picture. Point and say these words.

6 Work in pairs. Say what's in each room.

kitchen – cooker, table ...

Now listen and check.

24

GENERAL COMMENTS

There is/are* and *any

The position of *there is/are* in the sequence of lessons is designed to break up the run of lessons on the present simple with a relatively simple structure. *Any* can be more complex, especially when the students are asked to consider whether it can be replaced with *some*. Its use with plural negatives and questions does not encroach on the more complex area. Explain that this simplified rule is useful at the moment, but will require further examination later in the course. Students will return to *any* in *Reward* Elementary.

VOCABULARY AND SOUNDS

1 Aim: to present the pronunciation of the words in the vocabulary box.

- Explain that the words in the first box are rooms of the house, the words in the second box are locations in the house, and the words in the last box are adjectives of size. Don't translate the words yet. The students nevertheless need to understand the meaning of *downstairs, upstairs, front and back.*

- Ask the students to listen and repeat the words as you play the tape.

2 Aim: to present the meaning of the words in the vocabulary box.

- This is a problem-solving activity through which they will learn the meaning of the words for rooms. Ask the students to read the sentences and to label the rooms.

- Check the answers with the whole class.

Answers
a - kitchen b - bathroom c - bedroom
d - living room e - dining room

3 Aim: to practise using the new vocabulary.

- Write on the board *We have*... Ask two or three students to say what rooms they have in their homes. Tell them the rooms in your own home.

- Ask the students to work in pairs and say what rooms they have.

4 Aim: to present the words in the vocabulary box.

- Ask the students to listen and say the words in the box.

5 Aim: to focus on the words in the vocabulary box.

- Ask the students to look at the picture, point to and say the items of furniture.

6 Aim: to practise using the new vocabulary.

- Ask the students to work in pairs and say what's in each room.

- Ask the students to listen and check.

READING AND LISTENING

1 Aim: to practise reading and listening for specific information.

- Ask the students to listen to the tape and read through the passage and find the answers to the questions.

Answers
Three rooms downstairs and eight rooms upstairs.

2 Aim: to practise reading and interpreting information.

- Explain that the three descriptions are of people, one of whom lives in the house which has been described.

- Ask the students to listen to the tape and read the descriptions and to decide who lives in the house.

Answer
Angie Ashton

3 Aim: to practise speaking; to check activity 2.

- Ask the students to work in pairs and to check their answers to activity 2.

- Play the tape again and ask the students to listen and check.

GRAMMAR

1 Aim: to focus on possible mistakes.

- Ask the students to read the information in the grammar box and then to do the exercises.
- Ask the students to tick the correct sentence.
- Correct this activity with the whole class. Try to focus on why one of the sentences in each pair is wrong.

Answers
1a 2a 3b 4b 5a 6b

2 Aim: to practise using the target structures.

- Ask the students to write sentences describing what they can see in the picture.

3 Aim: to practise using the target structures.

- Ask the students to work in pairs and ask and answer questions about what they can see in the house in the picture.

SPEAKING AND WRITING

1 Aim: to practise speaking.

- Ask the students to work in pairs and to decide who is Student A and who is Student B. Explain that Student A will ask about Student B's living room, and Student B will ask about Student A's kitchen. Both students should complete the chart. Ask them to follow the instructions.

2 Aim: to practise writing.

- Ask the students to write a description of a room in their own home.
- You may like to ask students to do this activity for homework.

READING AND LISTENING

1 Listen and read. Say how many rooms there are.

'Hello and welcome to *Through the keyhole*, the game where I describe a house and you decide who lives here. Today I'm in a very large and beautiful house in the country. Downstairs there's a living room, a dining room with a window onto a large garden, and a kitchen. In the dining room there's a table and chairs for four people. Upstairs there are five bedrooms and three bathrooms. In the kitchen there's a cooker, a table, and five chairs. There's lots of food – fruit, vegetables but no meat. In the bedroom at the back, there's a large bed, and a television. There aren't any chairs. There's a cupboard with jeans, jackets, skirts and shoes. There's also a tennis racquet. At the moment, we're downstairs in the living room, there's a radio and there are some books, but there isn't a television. There are three sofas and four armchairs, so he or she likes having friends here. There's a table here with lots of photos of the man or woman who lives here, with his or her family.'

2 Listen to descriptions of three people. Who lives in the house?

George Mandelson ☐ Angie Ashton ☐ Frances Peters ☐

3 Work in pairs. Check your answer to 2.

GRAMMAR

> **There is/are**
> *There's a garden. There are five bedrooms.*
> *Are there any chairs in the dining room?*
> *Yes, there are. No, there aren't. (= there are not)*
> *Is there a shower?*
> *Yes, there is. No, there isn't. (= there is not)*
> **Any**
> *Plural negative* — *There aren't any cupboards in the bathroom.*
> *Plural questions* — *Are there any chairs in the kitchen?*

1 Tick (✔) the correct sentence.

1 a Is there a garden?
  b Are there a garden?

2 a There are two chairs.
  b There is two chairs.

3 a There isn't any plants.
  b There aren't any plants.

4 Is there a shower?
  a Yes, there are.
  b No, there isn't.

5 Are there any cupboards?
  a Yes, there are.
  b No, there isn't.

6 Is there a television?
  a Yes, there's.
  b No, there isn't.

2 Look at the picture and write sentences.

1 In the living room, there's ...
2 In the kitchen, there's a table ...
3 In the bedroom, ...
4 In the bathroom, ...

3 Work in pairs. Ask and answer questions about the house in the picture.

Are there any chairs in the dining room?
Yes, there are.

SPEAKING AND WRITING

1 Work in pairs.

Student A: Turn to Communication activity 28 on page 97.

Student B: Turn to Communication activity 35 on page 99.

2 Write a description of a room in your house.

In my bedroom there are some cupboards . . .

25 I usually have a party

Present simple: adverbs of frequency

VOCABULARY AND SOUNDS

1 Put the months in the right order.

April August December February January July June March May November October September

2 Listen and check 1. As you listen, repeat the words.

3 Match.

first second third fourth fifth sixth seventh eight ninth tenth eleventh twelfth

9th 7th 3rd 6th 10th 12th 1st
5th 2nd 8th 11th 4th

4 Say these numbers.

13th 14th.. 15th 16th 17th 18th 19th 20th
21st 22nd 23rd 24th 25th 26th 27th
28th 29th 30th 31st

Now listen and repeat.

5 Listen and repeat.

the first of January — the fourth of April
the second of February — the fifth of May
the third of March — the sixth of June

6 Say these dates.

7th July 8th August 9th September 10th October
11th November 12th December

Now listen and check.

7 Complete.

1 My birthday is on ___.
2 My friend's birthday is on ___.
3 My mother's birthday is on ___.
4 My father's birthday is on ___.

READING AND SPEAKING

Read and find answers to the questions.

1 What do you usually do on your birthday?
2 Who do you usually spend your birthday with?
3 Do you usually get presents and birthday cards?
4 Which birthdays are always very special?

'We don't often do very much. I usually invite my friends to a bar for a drink after work. We have a cup of coffee or a drink, and then we go home.' Pablo, Spain

'Children always have a party at home. Their friends bring presents and we play games and then we have something to eat and drink. Then everyone always sings Happy Birthday.' Alexis, England

'I don't often do anything special. I sometimes go to the theatre with my wife or for a meal in a restaurant.' Dave, USA

'For us, every twelfth year of life is special, and there's usually a party. The sixtieth birthday is always very special. We usually give presents of fruit, flowers and cakes.' Kanda, Thailand

25

GENERAL COMMENTS

Adverbs of frequency

All aspects of the present simple have now been presented. The grammar focus of this lesson creates the opportunity for further word recycling the present simple tense. You may need to refer to the *Grammar review* to help the students learn where adverbs of frequency go in the sentence.

Socio-cultural training

This lesson focuses on birthday traditions in different countries. As usual, this information is presented not simply to provide an interesting view of different cultures, but to stimulate a reflection on the students' own culture(s) and traditions.

VOCABULARY AND SOUNDS

1 Aim: to present the words in the vocabulary box.

- Ask the students to put the months in the right order.

2 Aim: to present the words in the vocabulary box.

- Write the months on the board. Play the tape and ask the students to repeat the words.

- Point to various months and ask students to say them aloud, individually and in chorus.

3 Aim: to present the words in the vocabulary box.

- Ask the students to match the words in the box with the numbers.

- Play the tape and ask the students to repeat the numbers.

4 Aim: to present ordinal numbers 13th to 31st.

- To put all the ordinal number in a box would give the impression of vocabulary overload. But there is enough information in activity 3 to allow the students to guess how the remaining ordinal numbers are pronounced. Ask the students to work in pairs and to decide how they are pronounced.

- Ask three or four students to say the numbers aloud.

- Ask the students to listen to the tape and repeat the numbers.

5 Aim: to present ways of saying the date.

- Ask the students to listen and repeat the dates as you play the tape.

6 Aim: to present ways of saying the date.

- The students have enough information in activity 5 to guess how the dates in this activity are pronounced.

- Play the tape and ask the students to check.

7 Aim: to practise writing dates.

- Ask the students to complete the sentences with the dates of people's birthdays.

- Check that the students can say the dates in their answers accurately.

READING AND SPEAKING

1 Aim: to practise reading for main ideas; to practise reading for specific information.

- The questions focus on the three main pieces of information in the quotations. However, the process of extracting these main ideas involves some careful reading for specific information.

- The answers are clear in the reading material, so go through the questions and ask the students to read out the relevant parts of the quotations.

You may want to expand on the reading activity in the following ways:

- Ask the students to go round the class asking and answering questions about their birthdays.

- Ask the students to work in groups of three or four and to discuss their answers to the questions in 1.

- Open the discussion to the whole class. Invite different students to talk about the ways they spend their birthdays.

- You may like to ask the students to write about the different ways they spend their birthdays for homework.

GRAMMAR

1 Aim: to focus on the position of the adverb of frequency.

- Ask the students to read the information in the grammar box and then to do the exercises.

- Ask the students to look at the position of the adverbs of frequency in the grammar box.

Answers
Between the noun/pronoun and the verb

- You may need to explain to the students that this is not an invariable rule.

2 Aim: to focus on the position of the adverb of frequency.

- Ask the students to write the sentences with the adverbs in the right position.

Answers
1 He often goes out with friends.
2 They never have a party.
3 She usually sees her parents.
4 Do you often go out to a restaurant?
5 I sometimes have a drink with some friends.
6 I usually get some cards and presents.

- Ask three or four students to tell the whole class what they do on their birthdays.

LISTENING AND SPEAKING

1 Aim: to prepare for listening.

- The words shown are essential for understanding the listening material, but the vocabulary load for this lesson is already quite high, so they should be presented as receptive rather than productive items. If necessary, translate these words.

- Ask the students to look at the chart and tick the statements which are true for them or correct them with a suitable adverb of frequency.

2 Aim: to practise listening.

- Explain to the students that they're going to listen to three people talking about what they do on their birthday. Ask the students to listen to the tape and to tick the statements which are true for the speakers.

	You	Karen	Pete	Molly	Your partner
I always get presents and birthday cards.	✔	✔	✔		
I usually go out with friends.			✔		
I often go to a restaurant.				✔	
I sometimes invite friends home.			✔		
I always have a meal with my family.					
I usually have a party.					
I never do anything special.					

3 Aim: to practise using adverbs of frequency.

- Ask the students to work in pairs and check their answers to activity 3.

4 Aim: to practise using adverbs of frequency.

- Ask the students to work in pairs and to complete the *Your partner* column in activity 2.

5 Aim: to practise speaking.

- Ask the students to go round the class asking and answering questions to find the information.

GRAMMAR

Present simple: adverbs of frequency

*I **always** have a party.* 100%
*I **usually** go out with friends.*
*I **often** go to a restaurant.*
*I **sometimes** invite friends home.*
*I **never** do anything special.* 0%

1 Answer the question.

Where do you put the adverb of frequency?

2 Decide where the adverbs in brackets go.

1 He goes out with friends. (often)
2 They have a party. (never)
3 She sees her parents. (usually)
4 Do you go out to a restaurant? (often)
5 I have a drink with some friends. (sometimes)
6 I get some cards and presents. (usually)

LISTENING AND SPEAKING

1 Look at the statements in the chart below. Tick (✔) the statements which are true for you or correct them with a suitable adverb of frequency.

2 Listen to Karen, Peter and Molly and tick the statements which are true for them.

3 Work in pairs and check your answers to 2.

Karen always has a party.

4 Work in pairs and complete the *Your partner* column.

What do you do on your birthday?
I usually go out with friends.

5 Find people with a birthday:
in the same month.
on the same day.
What do they do?

	You	Karen	Pete	Molly	Your partner
I always get presents and birthday cards.					
I usually go out with friends.					
I often go to a restaurant.					
I sometimes invite friends home.					
I always have a meal with my family.					
I usually have a party.					
I never do anything special.					

26 I can cook

can for ability

PARENTS NEED HELP!
Do you like children? Do you like to travel? Can you speak English? Can you play the guitar? Have you got six weeks in July and August?
We need someone to go on holiday with us to the USA and help us with our three children.
Write to Mr and Mrs Burroughs, 11, Belsize Park, London.

FLAT SHARE
Three students need a fourth who can sing, do the shopping, ride a bicycle and cook to share a flat in Finchley. £250 per month. Write to 4, Kings Close, Bromley

INTERNATIONAL SUMMER SCHOOL ASSISTANT needed.
Can you swim, play the piano, speak any languages, play tennis and football? You can? Do you need a holiday job?
Great! Ring Dave on 27566.

SECRETARY needed.
We need someone to use a computer and understand French for three mornings/week. Some weekend work. Ring 099875

VOCABULARY AND SOUNDS

1 Listen and repeat.

dance swim draw cook sing drive type

2 Turn to Communication activity 30 on page 97.

3 Match the words in the two boxes.

play ride use speak understand

piano bicycle football computer guitar French English Italian tennis

play the piano

Now look at the adverts and check your answers.

4 Look at the cartoon and check you understand these words.

need help

5 Listen and repeat.

/æ/	Can you swim?	Yes, I can.
	Can you type?	No, I can't.
/æ/	Can you use a computer?	No, I can't.
/ə/	I can swim.	I can play the piano.
	I can't use a computer.	

26

GENERAL COMMENTS

Modal verbs

Can is the only modal verb presented in *Reward* Starter. In this lesson, its use for expressing ability is presented. In Lesson 27 its use for making polite requests *Can I have a sandwich?* is presented implicitly under the functional heading of talking about food and drink. The students may possibly add an *-s* to the third person singular, so draw their attention to the fact that its form is the same for all persons early in the lesson.

Expressing ability

Some cultures find it difficult to express ability because it suggests a lack of suitable modesty even when the statement is one of factual information. If you think your students come from such a culture, you may want to avoid the activities in the lesson, (for example in *Listening and speaking*) which personalise the function.

VOCABULARY AND SOUNDS

1 Aim: to present the pronunciation of the words in the vocabulary box.

- Ask the students to repeat the words as you play the tape.

2 Aim: to present the meaning of the words in the vocabulary box in activity 1.

- Ask the students to turn to Communication activity 30 on page 97 and to match the verbs with the drawings which illustrate their meaning.
- Check the answers with the whole class.
- Explain that the verbs in the box in activity 1 can be used intransitively, i.e. they don't need a noun to follow them.

3 Aim: to present the words in the vocabulary boxes.

- This is a collocation activity. The verbs in the first box are often transitive, i.e. they can be followed by a noun. The students may recognise some of the words, so encourage them to say what the words mean before you give an explanation,
- Ask the students to read the three advertisements to check their answers. They can do this in pairs and then you can check with the whole class.

Possible answers
play the piano, the guitar, football, tennis
ride a bicycle
use a computer
speak/understand French, English, Italian

- Explain that *play the piano, play the guitar* is a set expression using the definite article. The other verb and noun combinations use the indefinite article or no article.

4 Aim: to present the words in the vocabulary box.

- Ask the students to look at the cartoon which is designed to explain the meaning of the two words. Translate them if necessary.

5 Aim: to practise the pronunciation of the target language.

- Ask the students to listen and repeat the sentences as you play the tape.
- Make sure they understand that *can* in a whole sentence is pronounced /ə/, whereas it's pronounced /æ/ when it's used in a short answer.

READING AND LISTENING

1 Aim: to practise reading for main ideas.

- Ask the students to read the adverts in *Do you need help?* and to make notes on what each person needs.
- Check the answers with the whole class. Ask the students to make sentences with '*They need...*'

2 Aim: to prepare for listening; to practise reading and interpreting information.

- Ask the students to read the one-sided conversation and to guess which advert it goes with.

Answer
International Summer school assistant

3 Aim: to prepare for listening.

- Ask the students to work in pairs and predict what Frank's replies are. There may be one or two replies which they can't guess accurately, but this will make the listening passage more informative.
- Play the tape. Ask the students to look at the notes they made in activity 1. As they listen, they should put *F* by the things he can do. The answers will be checked in *Grammar* activity 2.

GRAMMAR

1 Aim: to practise using *can*.

- Ask the students to read the information in the grammar box and then to do the exercises.
- Ask the students to act out the interview in *Reading and listening* activity 2 in pairs.
- Ask two or three pairs of students to act out the interview for the whole class.

2 Aim: to practise using *can*.

- Do this activity with the whole class.

> **Answers**
> He can swim, play the guitar, speak French and German, play tennis and football.
> He can't play the piano and speak Italian.

3 Aim: to practise speaking; to practise using *can*.

- Act out the interview with one or two students but ask them to give true answers.
- Ask the students to act out the interview in pairs.

4 Aim: to practise speaking; to practise using *can*.

- Ask the students to work in pairs and to say what they *can* and *can't* do, using the other adverts as prompts.

5 Aim: to practise speaking; to practise using *can*.

- Ask the students to work in new pairs and to tell each other what their old partner *can* and *can't* do.

LISTENING AND SPEAKING

1 Aim: to practise listening for main ideas.

- Understanding the main ideas of these two interviews will allow the students to decide which candidate should get the job.
- Ask the students to listen to the tape and write what each person can do.

> **Answers**
> **Janie:** swim, play the piano, speak a little Spanish, play tennis
> **Lois:** play the piano, guitar, violin, the trumpet; swim; speak French, Italian, Russian, Spanish; play tennis and football

2 Aim: to practise speaking.

- Ask the students to decide who gets the job.

> **Probable answer**
> Lois

3 Aim: to prepare for the role play in 4.

- Ask the students to work in groups of four and to decide who is the interviewer and who are the interviewees.
- Ask the students to follow the instructions. At this stage they should be working alone. Student A should write questions to ask Students B, C and D, who should think about what they can do for the job.

4 Aim: to practise speaking.

- Ask the students to act out their job interviews in groups.
- Ask one or two groups to act out their role plays to the whole class.

READING AND LISTENING

1 Read the adverts in *Do you need help?* Make notes on what each person needs to do.

2 Read the interview. Which advert is it for?

INTERVIEWER	So, are you a student?
FRANK	____
INTERVIEWER	And you need a holiday job?
FRANK	____.
INTERVIEWER	Can you swim?
FRANK	____.
INTERVIEWER	And music? Can you play the piano?
FRANK	____. But I can play the guitar.
INTERVIEWER	OK, and can you speak any languages?
FRANK	____. I can speak French and German.
INTERVIEWER	And what about sport? Can you play tennis and football?
FRANK	____.
INTERVIEWER	Good.

3 Work in pairs and guess what Frank says.

Now look at the notes you made in 1 and listen. Put a tick (✔) by the things he can do.

GRAMMAR

Can	
Can you swim?	*Yes, I can.*
Can you play the piano?	*No, I can't.*
Can he swim?	*Yes, he can.*
Can he play the piano?	*No, he can't.*
I can swim. He can dance.	*She can cook.*
I can't cook. He can't drive.	*She can't play the piano.*

1 Work in pairs. Act out the interview in *Reading and listening* activity 2.

2 Say what Frank can and can't do.

He can swim, but he can't play the piano.

3 Work in pairs. Act out the interview again. Give true answers. Change round when you're ready.

4 Work in pairs. Look at the other adverts. Which things can you do?

I can speak English, but I can't play the guitar.

5 Work in new pairs. Tell each other what your old partner can and can't do.

Fabrice can speak English, but he can't play the guitar.

LISTENING AND SPEAKING

1 Listen to two more interviews, with Janie and Lois, for the job. Write what each person can do.

Janie - swim, play the piano

2 Work in pairs. Who gets the job?

3 Work in groups of four. Choose one of the adverts.

Student A: You need help. Write questions you want to ask Students B, C and D.

Students B, C and D: You need a job. Working alone, think about what you can do for the job.

4 Act out job interviews in your groups.

27 Can I have a sandwich, please?

Talking about food and drink

VOCABULARY AND SOUNDS

1 Listen and repeat.

coffee orange milk water bread cake apple pie cheese tomato lettuce

2 Work in pairs. Look at the picture. Point and say.

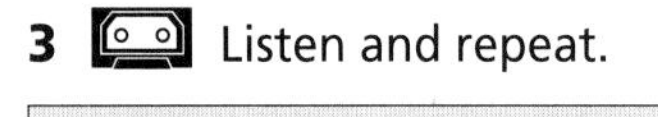

3 Listen and repeat.

cup glass bottle piece

4 Listen and repeat.

/ə/ a cup of coffee
a cup of tea

a glass of wine
a glass of milk

a bottle of wine
a bottle of water

a piece of cake
a piece of cheese
a piece of pie

Now point and say.

LISTENING

Halley Court Café Menu

Sandwiches £2.50
Cheese
Cheese and tomato
Chicken and lettuce
Beef
Halley Court Special

Pizzas £3.00
Cheese and tomato

Drinks 75p
Cola
Fanta
Milk
Mineral water
Coffee
Tea

Baked potatoes £2.00
filled with
Cheese
Chilli
Tuna and Mayonnaise

Pasta £3.00
Spaghetti

Desserts £1.00
Chocolate cake
Apple pie
Yoghurt (50p)

27

GENERAL COMMENTS

Personalising vocabulary

The items of vocabulary in this lesson are all frequently used words in certain cultures, but not in others. Although you will find it useful to introduce these words in order to do the rest of the activities, you may want to spend time on food words which are more useful to the students. Adapting the items of vocabulary so that they respond more to the students' personal requirements will contribute towards the vocabulary acquisition process.

VOCABULARY AND SOUNDS

1 Aim: to present the words in the vocabulary box.

- Ask the students to listen and repeat the words.

2 Aim: to practise the words in the vocabulary box.

- Ask the students to work in pairs. Ask them to point to and say the words in the picture.

- Say the words aloud and ask the students to repeat them.

3 Aim: to present the words in the vocabulary box.

- Play the tape and ask the students to repeat the words.

- Say the words aloud and ask the students to repeat them.

4 Aim: to practise the pronunciation of the expressions.

- Ask the students to listen and repeat the expressions as you play the tape.

- Check the pronunciation of five or six students. Check that everyone says /ə/ for *of.*

- Ask the students to point to the pictures and say the expressions.

LISTENING

1 Aim: to prepare for listening; to practise reading for specific information.

- Ask the students to read the conversation and to say where it takes place.

- Ask the students to decide where the sentences go in the conversation.

Answers
1e 2f 3b 4d 5a 6c

2 Aim: to practise listening for specific information.

- Ask the students to work in pairs and check their answers.

- Play the tape and ask the students to listen and check.

FUNCTIONS

1 Aim: to focus on the meaning and the use of the expressions in the functions box.

- Ask the students to read the information in the functions box and then to do the exercises.

- Ask the students to decide if it is the waiter or the customer who uses the expressions.

Answers

Waiter:	Anything to drink?
	Anything to eat?
	Anything else?
	Here you are.
	Enjoy your meal.
Customer:	What's a Halley Court Special?
	Can I have a sandwich?
	Thank you.
	How much is it?
	Can I have a cup of coffee?

- Draw the students' attention to the fact that the waiter uses *Enjoy your meal!* but there isn't really a suitable statement for people to say to each other when they start eating.

2 Aim: to practise talking about food and drink.

- Ask the students to act out the conversations in pairs.

LISTENING AND SPEAKING

1 Aim: to revise vocabulary; to prepare for listening.

● Ask the students to list all the words for food and drink they learned in this lesson and in Lesson 22. They will use this as their checklist for the listening in activity 2.

2 Aim: to practise listening for specific information.

● [cassette] Ask the students to listen to two people talking about food and drink and to tick the things in the checklist in activity 1 which the speakers like and to put a cross by the things the speakers don't like.

Answers

Selina

Likes: salad, lettuce, tomatoes, vegetables, pizza, pasta, cheese, potatoes, mineral water, Cola, tea, chocolate cake

Doesn't like: coffee

Finn

Likes: chicken, tomatoes, lettuce, potatoes, baked potatoes with tuna and mayonnaise, tea, chocolate cake

Doesn't like: beef

3 Aim: to check comprehension; to practise interpreting information.

● Ask the students to work in pairs and to decide what Finn and Selina chose from the menu in *Listening* activity 1.

● [cassette] Play the tape and ask the students to listen and check.

4 Aim: to practise speaking.

● Ask the students to work in pairs and to use the expressions in the functions box to act out conversations.

● Ask two or three pairs to act out their conversations for the whole class.

5 Aim: to practise using the vocabulary presented in this lesson and in Lesson 22; to prepare for speaking.

● Ask the students to write a favourite/typical restaurant menu.

6 Aim: to practise speaking.

● Ask the students to work in groups of four or five and use the menus they wrote in activity 5 to act out conversations between a waiter and customers.

1 Decide where these sentences go.

WAITER Can I help you?
JANE (1) ____
WAITER It's a sandwich with chicken, lettuce, tomato and mayonnaise.
JANE (2) ____
WAITER It's £2.50.
JANE (3) ____
WAITER Certainly. And anything to drink?
JANE (4) ____
WAITER OK, a Halley Court Special and a cup of coffee. Anything else?
JANE (5) ____
WAITER Thank you, . . . OK, a Halley Court Special, a cup of coffee and a piece of chocolate cake. Here you are.
JANE (6) ____
WAITER Enjoy your meal.

a A piece of chocolate cake, please.
b OK, can I have a Halley Court Special, please?
c Thank you very much.
d A cup of coffee, please.
e Yes, what's a Halley Court Special?
f How much is it?

2 Work in pairs and check your answers to 1.
Now listen and check.

FUNCTIONS

Talking about food and drink

What's a Halley Court Special?	*How much is it?*
Can I have a sandwich?	*Can I have a cup of coffee?*
Anything to drink?	*Anything to eat?*
Anything else?	*Enjoy your meal.*
Here you are.	
Thank you.	

1 Look at the expressions in the functions box. Who says them, *waiter* or *customer*?

Waiter *Anything to drink?*
Customer *What's a Halley Court Special?*

2 Work in pairs. Act out the conversation in *Listening* activity 1.

LISTENING AND SPEAKING

1 Make a list of food and drink words from this lesson and from Lesson 22.

2 Listen to Finn and Selina talking about food and drink. Use the list from 1 and tick (✔) the things they like and cross (✗) the things they don't like. Add any items they like or don't like.

3 Work in pairs. Guess what they choose from the menu in *Listening* activity 1.
Now listen and check.

4 Work in pairs. Act out conversations in the café. Use the menu in *Listening* activity 1. Ask and say.

Can I help you?
Yes, can I have a baked potato?

5 Write a typical restaurant menu for your country.

Pasta ...
Pizza ...

6 Work in groups of four or five.

Student A: You're a waiter. Act out a conversation with Students B, C and D. Use the menu you wrote in 5.

Students B, C and D: Look at Student A's menu. Act out a conversation in a restaurant.

Can I help you?
Yes. I'd like some pasta, please.

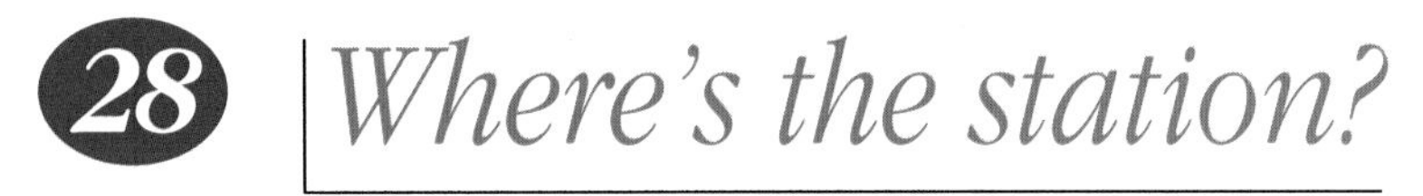

28 Where's the station?

Asking for and giving directions

VOCABULARY AND SOUNDS

1 Listen and repeat.

bank pub baker cinema chemist
market station restaurant library
bookshop car park post office

2 Use some of the words in 1 and complete the map.

3 Work in pairs.

Student A: Turn to Communication activity 31 on page 98.

Student B: Turn to Communication activity 41 on page 101.

Now complete the rest of the map.

4 Match the words and expressions with the signs.

turn left go straight ahead turn right

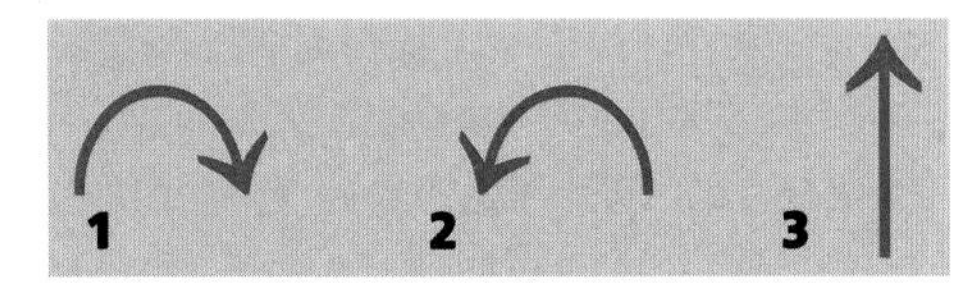

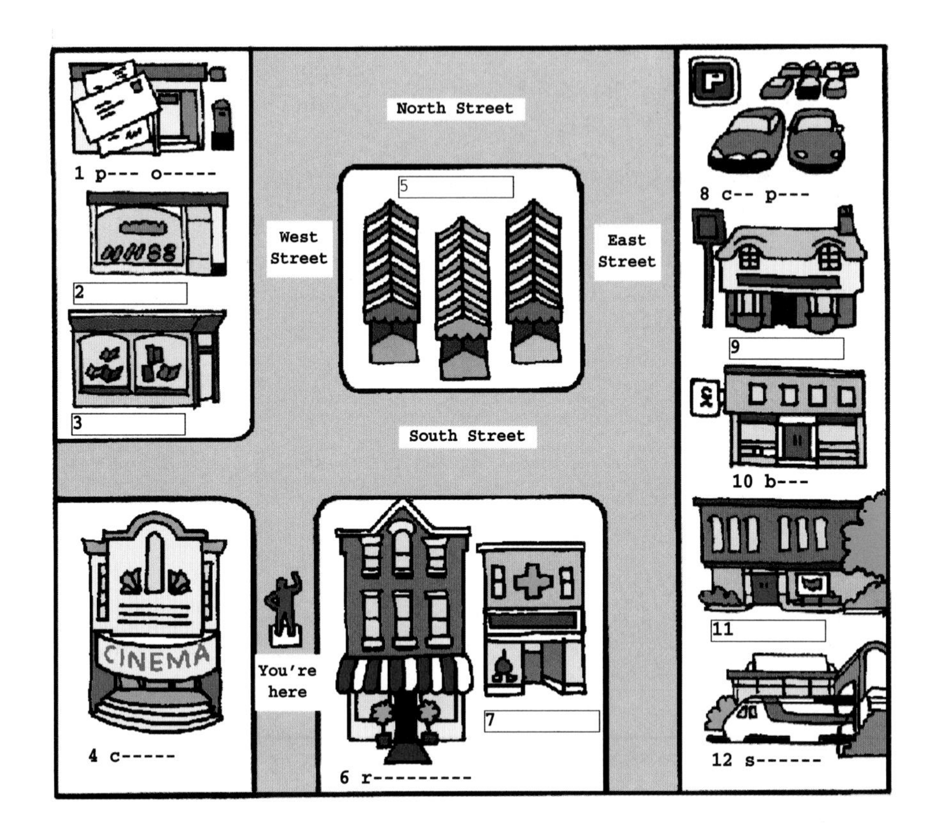

LISTENING

1 Match the question and answers.

1 Where's the station?
2 Where's the bookshop?
3 Where's the market?
4 Where's the chemist?

a It's in North Street.
b It's in West Street.
c It's in South Street.
d It's in East Street.

Now listen and check

2 You're at the point marked YOU'RE HERE. Match the questions and answers.

1 Where's North Street?	a Turn right.
2 Where's West Street?	b Go along West Street. Turn right into North Street.
3 Where's South Street?	c Turn right into South Street. Turn left into East Street
4 Where's East Street?	d Go straight ahead.

Now listen and check.

3 Listen to four people and follow their routes. Say where they want to go.

First person - post office

4 Work in pairs and check your answers.

28

GENERAL COMMENTS

Politeness conventions

The students will have learnt the words *please* and *thank you* and may have realised that in English words to demonstrate polite behaviour are used frequently. Even instructions and imperatives are given in a certain intonation in order to make them sound more polite. Giving directions is one of the few functions in which the effect is not toned down, since the purpose is to make oneself as clear as possible.

VOCABULARY AND SOUNDS

1 Aim: to present the pronunciation of the words in the vocabulary box.

- Ask the students to listen and repeat the words as you play the tape.
- Check the pronunciation of several individual students.

2 Aim: to present the meaning of some of the words in the vocabulary box.

- The students should be able to complete the missing letters of words in the map by looking for words in the vocabulary box.

3 Aim: to present the meaning of the other words in the vocabulary box.

- Ask the students to work in pairs and to decide who is Student A and who is Student B. They should look at the names of the other places in the Communication activities and complete the map.

Answers

1 post office	7 chemist
2 baker	8 car park
3 bookshop	9 pub
4 cinema	10 bank
5 market	11 library
6 restaurant	12 station

4 Aim: to present the meaning of the words in the vocabulary box.

- Ask the students to match the words and expressions with the directions. Make sure everyone understands *left* and *right*. Hold up your hands in turn and ask the students to say *left* or *right*.

Answer

1 - turn right 2 - turn left 3 - go straight ahead

LISTENING

1 Aim: to present the language of asking for and giving directions.

- Ask the students to use the map to match the questions and the answers
- Check the answers with the whole group.

Answers

1 - d 2 - b 3 - a 4 - c

- Play the tape and ask the students to listen and check.

2 Aim: to practise the language of asking for and giving directions.

- Make it clear to the students where they are on the map.
- Ask the students to match the questions and answers.

Answers

1 - b 2 - d 3 - a 4 - c

- Play the tape and ask the student to listen and check their answers.

3 Aim: to practise listening for specific information.

- Ask the students to listen to four conversations and follow the routes they hear. Where does each speaker want to go? Play the tape.

Answers

Speaker 1: post office
Speaker 2: bank
Speaker 3: cinema
Speaker 4: car park

4 Aim: to check comprehension.

- Ask the students to check the answers to activity 3 in pairs.
- Check the answers with the whole class.

FUNCTIONS

1 Aim: to focus on asking for and giving directions.

- Ask the students to read the information in the functions box and then to do the exercises.

- Ask the students to complete the conversation with expressions from the functions box.

> **Answers**
> Where's the post office?
> It's in West Street.
> Where's West Street?
> Go along South Street and turn right. It's on the left.

2 Aim: to practise asking for and giving directions.

- Ask the students to use the map to write sentences to say where the places are.

> **Answers**
> Sherlock Holmes pub: It's in Northumberland St.
> Charing Cross station: It's in the Strand.
> Odeon cinema: It's in Leicester Square.
> Covent Garden market: It's in Bedford Street.
> Foyles bookshop: It's in Charing Cross Road.

3 Aim: to practise giving directions.

- Ask the students to work in pairs and write directions to the places in activity 2.

LISTENING AND READING

1 Aim: to practise listening for specific information.

- Check everyone understands what a walking tour is. Ask the students to listen and to decide at which position the tour starts.

> **Answer**
> Trafalgar Square

- Ask the students to listen again and, as they listen, point to the places on the map that are mentioned in the walking tour.

2 Aim: to practise reading for specific information.

- This activity involves some careful reading. Ask the students to read the guided tour and to follow the route.

WRITING

- Ask the students to write a walking tour of their city, showing some interesting things to see.

- You may like to ask the students to do this activity for homework.

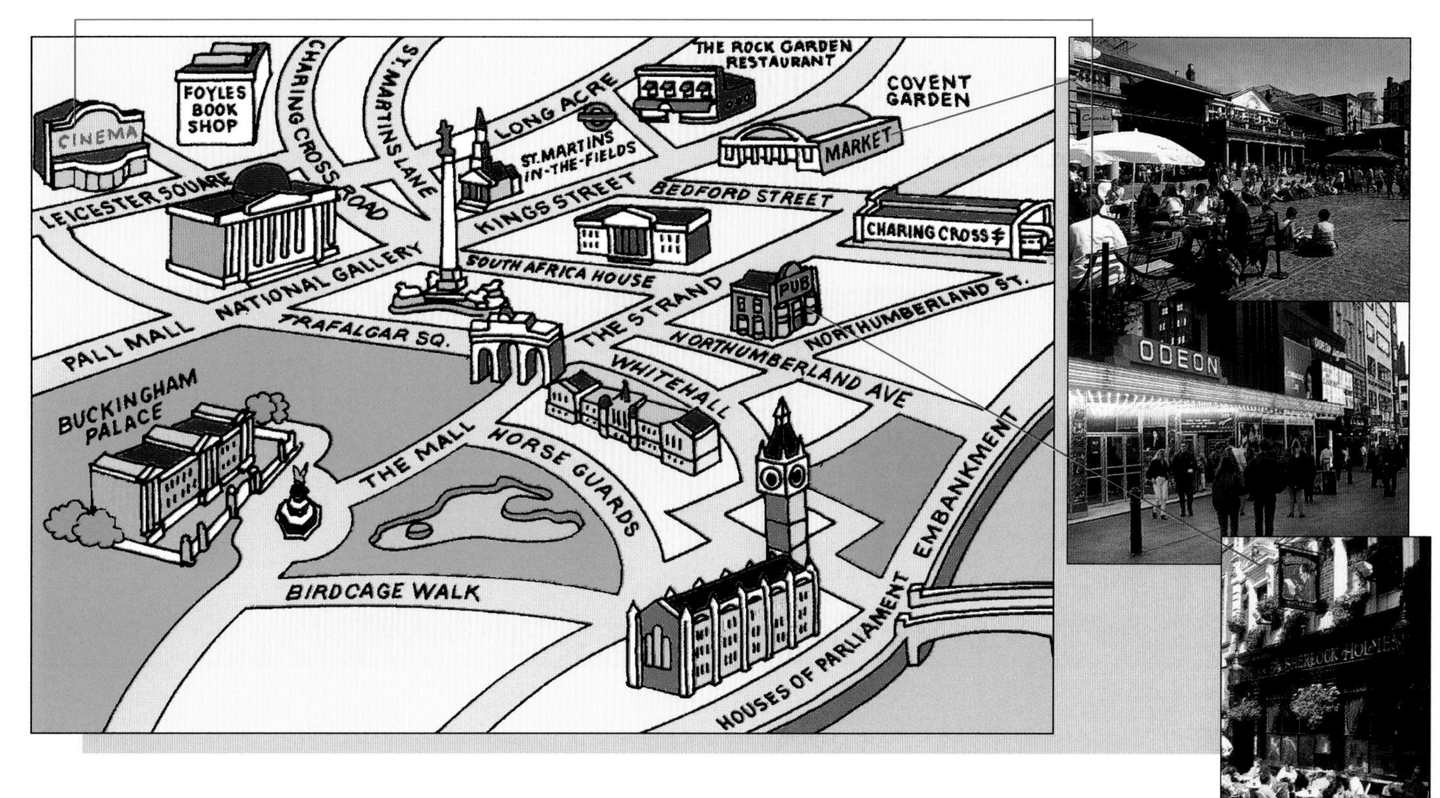

FUNCTIONS

Asking for and giving directions

Where's the station?	*It's in East Street.*
Where's West Street?	*Go along South Street.*
	Turn left. Turn right.
	It's on the left. It's on the right.
	It's straight ahead.

1 Complete.

Where's the post office?

_____ in West Street.

_____ West Street?

Go ____South Street and _____ right. It's on the ____.

2 Look at the map on this page. Write sentences and say where these places are.

Sherlock Holmes pub   Charing Cross Station
Odeon cinema   Covent Garden market
Foyles bookshop

3 Work in pairs. Decide where you are on the map. Now write directions to the places in 2.

Where's Charing Cross Station?

Go along Pall Mall. Turn right into Trafalgar Square. Turn left into the Strand. Go straight ahead and it's on the right.

LISTENING AND READING

1 You're tourists on a walking tour of London. Listen and point to where you are. Now point to these places:
– Buckingham Palace – The Houses of Parliament.

2 Read *Walking tour of Covent Garden and Trafalgar Square* and point.

Walking tour of Covent Garden and Trafalgar Square

Start your tour at Trafalgar Square. Go along Northumberland Avenue and turn left into Northumberland Street, where the Sherlock Holmes pub is. Turn left into the Strand and go past Charing Cross Station. Go along the Strand and turn left into Bedford Street. The old Covent Garden Market is on the right.

WRITING

Write a walking tour of your city/town.

Start your tour at the station. ...

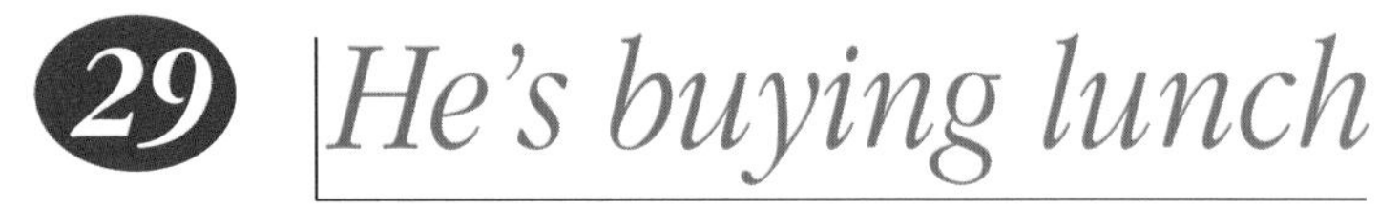

29 *He's buying lunch*

Present continuous (1)

VOCABULARY AND READING

1 Match the sentences with the photos.

buy sit run drive stand

a He's buying lunch.
b They're sitting in a theatre.
c They're running.
d They're standing in a queue.
e They're driving to work.

2 Match the clocks to the photos.

3 Say where you think the people in the photos are.

A In London at the moment, people are stopping work and leaving their offices. They're standing in queues for buses, running for trains or walking to pubs or cafés and having something to eat.

B In New York at the moment, people are having something to eat and drink, such as a sandwich and coffee. They're seeing friends and having lunch or shopping.

C In Moscow at the moment, some people are having dinner in restaurants, going to the theatre or having a coffee in bars. Many families are at home. They're watching television, reading the newspaper or playing games.

D In Hong Kong at the moment, most people are lying in bed asleep, but some people are standing in queues outside clubs, or are inside and drinking or dancing.

E In Los Angeles at the moment, people are getting up, washing, getting dressed and having breakfast or driving to work.

29

GENERAL COMMENTS

Present continuous

This is the first of three lessons on the present continuous (or progressive) tense. Before you start work on this tense, you must make sure that everyone understands the uses of the present simple: to talk about states, customs, habits and routines. The present continuous can, confusingly, be used to talk about both something happening at the present time, and something going to happen in the future, although usually the context makes the meaning clear. This lesson focuses on the present use. The tense can cause difficulty to students whose mother tongue has no progressive aspect.

VOCABULARY AND READING

1 Aim: to present the pronunciation and meaning of the words in the vocabulary box.

- Read the words and the sentences aloud several times and ask five or six students to read them aloud.

- Ask the students to match the sentences and the photos.

Answers
1-a 2-d 3-e 4-c 5-b

2 Aim: to prepare for reading; to check comprehension.

- Ask the students to check their answers to activity 1 and to discuss which time of day it is in the photos. Ask them to match the clocks to the photos.

3 Aim: to practise reading for specific information; to present the present continuous.

- This activity focuses on the different time zones around the world. Ask the students to read the paragraphs and match them with the photos.

Answers
A-4 B-1 C-5 D-2 E-3

GRAMMAR

1 Aim: to focus on the form of the present participle.

- Ask the students to read the information in the grammar box and then to do the exercises.

- Ask the students to complete the missing information.

Answer
You form the present continuous with the verb *be* and the present participle.
You use *am* with *I*. You use *are* with *we, you* and *they*. You use *is* with *he, she* and *it*.

2 Aim: to focus on the form of the present participle.

- Ask the students to look at the passages in *Vocabulary and reading* activity 3 for the present participle form of the verb.

Answers
dancing drinking getting dressed driving getting up having lying playing reading running seeing shopping stopping walking washing watching

3 Aim: to focus on the form of the present participle.

Answers
Verbs ending in *-e*: - dance, drive, have
Verbs ending in 2 vowels: lie
Verbs ending in *n, p, t*: run, shop, stop, get

4 Aim: to practice using the present continuous.

- This activity is designed to reinforce the use of the tense. Ask the students to write true sentences using other verbs, saying what the people are doing at the moment.

SOUNDS

1 Aim: to focus on the pronunciation of the present participle.

- Explain that the ending of the present continuous is pronounced /ŋ/. Some students may have difficulty with this sound. Spend some time practising saying present participles. Say an infinitive and ask students to say the present continuous.

- Play the tape and ask the students to listen and tick the words they hear.

Answers
1-a 2-b 3-b 4-a 5-b 6-b 7-a 8-b

2 Aim: to practise the pronunciation of the present participle.

- Ask the students to listen to the tape and repeat the words in 1.

SPEAKING

1 Aim: to practise using the present continuous; to practise speaking.

- The present continuous is often use to describe something the listener cannot actually see. Ask the students to say what people are doing. Ask them to look at Communication activity 32 in pairs and follow the instructions.

2 Aim: to practise using the present continuous; to practise speaking.

- Ask the students to use the present continuous to say what people are doing at the moment in their country and around the world.

GRAMMAR

> Present continuous (1)
> **Present participle form**
> *play – playing drink – drinking*
> *stand – standing run – running*
> *shop – shopping lie – lying sit – sitting*
>
> | | |
> |---|---|
> | *I'm playing tennis.* | *(= I am)* |
> | *You're standing in a queue.* | *(= you are)* |
> | *We're driving to work.* | *(= we are)* |
> | *They're sitting in a bar.* | *(= they are)* |
> | *He's buying a newspaper.* | *(= he is)* |
> | *She's running.* | *(= she is)* |
> | *It's stopping.* | *(= it is)* |

1 Complete the sentences.

You form the present continuous with the verb ____ and the present participle. You use ____ with *I*. You use ____ with *we, you* and *they*. You use ____ with *he, she* and *it*.

2 Look at the passages in *Vocabulary and reading* activity 3 and write the *-ing* form of the following verbs.

> dance drink get dressed drive get up
> have lie play read run see shop
> stop walk wash watch

3 Look at the verbs in 2. Put them in groups.

Verbs ending in *-e*: *dance*

Verbs ending in two vowels: *lie*

Verbs ending in *n, p, t*: *run*

Now write the present participle with these verbs.

4 Say what people are doing at the moment.

1 My father/mother ____.
2 My sister/brother ____.
3 My friend ____.
4 My teacher ____.
5 I ____.
6 We ____.

1 My mother is going to work .

SOUNDS

1 Listen and tick (✔) the correct words.

1	a stand in	b standing	5 a play in	b playing
2	a read in	b reading	6 a run in	b running
3	a shop in	b shopping in	7 a lie in	b lying
4	a sit in	b sitting	8 a write in	b writing

2 Listen and repeat the words in 1.

SPEAKING

1 Work in pairs. Turn to Communication activity 32 on page 98.

2 Work in pairs. Say

– what the time is at the moment
It's 3 pm.

– what people are doing at the moment in your country
In my country, people are ...

– what people are doing in London, New York, Moscow, Hong Kong and Los Angeles at the moment.
In London, people are ....

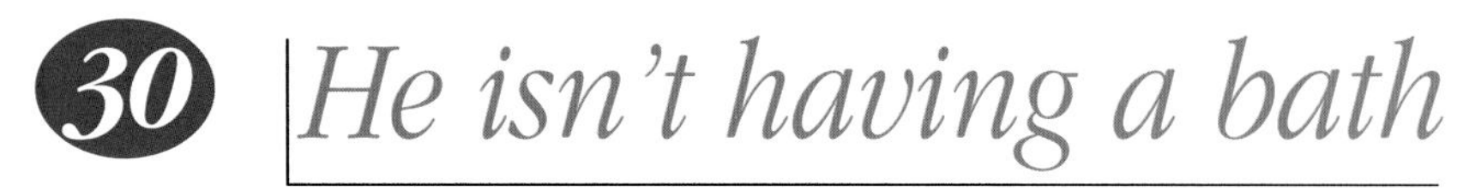

30 He isn't having a bath

Present continuous (2): negatives; questions

LISTENING AND VOCABULARY

1 Match the *wh-* questions with the correct picture.

a What's he doing?
b What's she doing?
c What are they doing?

Now work in pairs and check your answers.

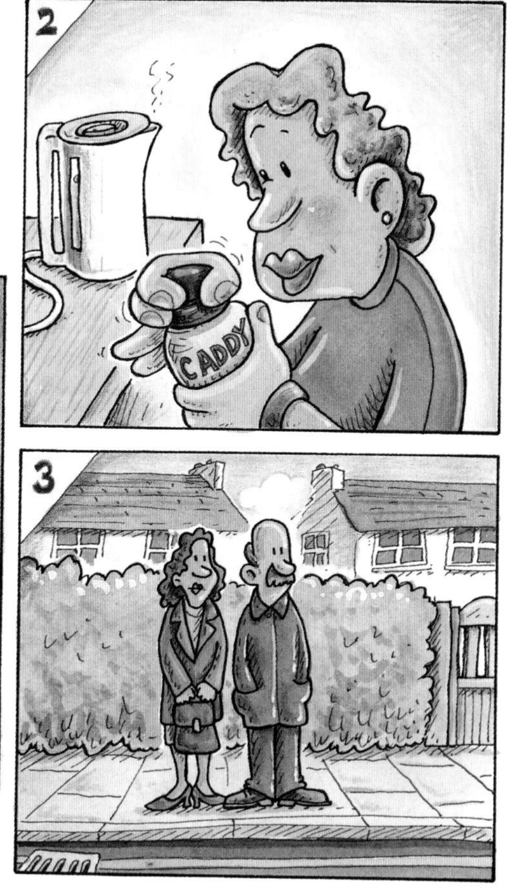

2 Match the *yes/no* questions with the correct picture.

d Is she talking to her daughter?
e Is she making tea?
f Is he listening to the radio?
g Is he having a bath?
h Are they waiting for a bus?
i Are they having dinner?

3 Listen and check your answers to 1 and 2.

Picture 1 What's he doing?
Is he listening to the radio?

4 Match.

talk wait listen

for to

5 Match.

make have

coffee tea lunch dinner
a bath shower

6 Listen and tick (✔) the right sentences.

1 a He's listening to the radio.	☐	b He's listening to the CD.	☐
2 a She's making tea.	☐	b She's making coffee.	☐
3 a They're waiting for a bus.	☐	b They're waiting for a taxi.	☐
4 a He's having a bath.	☐	b He's having a shower.	☐
5 a She's talking to her son.	☐	b She's talking to her daughter.	☐
6 a They're having dinner.	☐	b They're having lunch.	☐

30

GENERAL COMMENTS

Vocabulary revision

The vocabulary load in this lesson is quite low. You may want to use this opportunity to revise some of the vocabulary boxes in previous lessons. Ask the students to look back at the boxes, to choose ten or twelve verbs and to write the present continuous.

LISTENING AND VOCABULARY

1 Aim: to present *wh-* questions in the present continuous.

● Ask the students to look at the pictures and match the questions with the pictures.

> **Answers**
> a - 1/4 b - 2/5 c - 3/6

● Check the answers in pairs and then with the whole class.

2 Aim: to present the present continuous in *yes/no* questions.

● Ask the students to match the questions with the pictures.

> **Answers**
> d - 5 e - 2 f - 1 g - 4 h - 3 i - 6

3 Aim: to check comprehension.

● Ask the students to listen and check their answers.

4 Aim: to present the words in the vocabulary box.

● The students will have already come across verbs which require prepositions to follow them. This activity ensures that the suitable preposition will be learnt and recorded in their vocabulary records.

● Ask the students to match the words in the box with the prepositions.

> **Answers**
> talk to wait for listen to

● There are other possibilities for preposition combinations with these verbs, but these are the most common.

5 Aim: to present the words in the vocabulary box.

● *Make* and *have* are among the most common words which have a variety of collocations. Do this activity with the whole class.

● You may need to check the difference between *make lunch* and *have lunch*, etc.

> **Answers**
> make dinner tea lunch coffee
> have dinner tea lunch a shower coffee

● Ask the students to suggest other possible collocations and then correct them.

6 Aim: to check comprehension, to listen for specific information.

● Ask the students to listen and tick the correct answers to the questions.

> **Answers**
> 1 - b 2 - b 3 - b 4 - b 5 - a 6 - b

GRAMMAR

1 Aim: to practise using negatives.

● Ask the students to read the information in the grammar box and then to do the exercises.

● Ask the students to write the answers to *Listening and vocabulary* activity 2.

2 Aim: to practise using negatives.

● Explain that the sentences are all wrong. Ask the students to correct them using a negative and an affirmative sentence.

3 Aim: to focus on the form of questions.

● Ask the students to form questions.

> **Answers**
> 1 Are you speaking English?
> 2 Is your teacher reading?
> 3 Are your friends listening to the teacher?
> 4 Is your brother going to work/school?
> 5 Is your mother/wife/husband waiting outside?
> 6 Are you writing questions?

4 Aim: to practise using the present continuous.

● Ask the students to write answers to the questions using a negative and an affirmative sentence.

SPEAKING AND WRITING

1 Aim: to practise forming questions.

● Ask the students to work in pairs and to follow the instructions. Explain that in Communication activity 33 they will see two similar pictures. They should describe the differences they can find.

2 Aim: to practise writing.

● Ask the students to write down as many differences between the two pictures as they can in 1 minute.

● When they've finished, ask the students to count up the differences. Who has the most written down? Check the answers with the class.

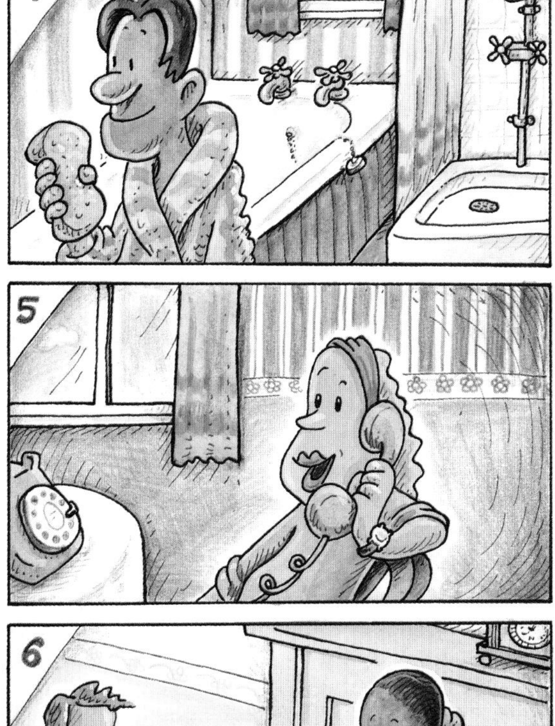

GRAMMAR

Present continuous (2): negatives

I'm not having	*(= am not)*
he isn't having	*(= is not)*
she isn't having	
you aren't having	*(≠ are not)*
we aren't having	
they aren't having	

Questions

Are you having?	*Yes, I am.* *No, I'm not.*
Are they having?	*Yes, they are.* *No, they aren't.*
Is he/she having?	*Yes, he/she is.* *No, he/she isn't.*
What are you doing?	*What are they doing?*
What is he doing?	*What is she doing?*

1 Write answers to the questions in *Listening and vocabulary*, activity 2.

Is he listening to the radio?

No, he isn't. He's listening to a CD.

2 Tick (✔) or correct the sentences.

At the moment, ...
1 ... my teacher is dancing.
2 ... my friends are playing badminton.
3 ... my teacher is wearing a yellow hat.
4 ... I'm reading the newspaper.
5 ... I'm lying on the beach.
6 ... we're having breakfast.

My teacher isn't dancing. She's working.

3 Write questions.

1 you are speaking English
2 your teacher is reading
3 your friends are listening to the teacher
4 your brother is going to work/school
5 your mother/wife/husband is waiting outside
6 you are writing questions

Are you speaking English?

4 Answer the questions you wrote in 3.

SPEAKING AND WRITING

1 Work in pairs. Turn to Communication activity 33 on page 98.

2 Write down as many differences between the pictures as you can in 1 minute.

Progress check 

VOCABULARY

1 Look at the words below. They are all nouns.

a car   the bicycle   a chicken   a bathroom
the bedroom   a piano   the cinema   a restaurant

Look at these words. They are all verbs.

draw   sing   use   speak   buy   have

Now look at these words. They are all adjectives.

blue   large   small   red   this

These words are all pronouns.

I   you   he   she   it   we   they

These words are all prepositions.

in   at   on   under   from   to   by

These words are all adverbs.

always   often   sometimes

Work in pairs and say what *part of speech* (noun, verb or adjective) these words are.

noun   verb   adjective   pronoun   preposition

white   at   kitchen   we   black   sofa   take   to
understand   they   read   from

2 Here are the titles of Lessons 21 – 30. Say what part of speech the underlined words are.

Does she go to work by boat?
I can cook.

What do they eat in Morocco?
Can I have a sandwich, please?

I don't like lying on the beach.
Where's the station?

There's a telephone in the hall.
He's buying lunch.

I usually have a party.
He isn't having a bath.

3 Some verbs and nouns often go together.

go to work   have breakfast   play the piano
speak English   make coffee   get up

Which verbs go with these nouns?

dressed   the guitar   to school   French   tea   dinner

4 Look at the words in Lessons 21 to 30 again. Choose words which are useful to you and write them in your *Wordbank* in the Practice Book.

GRAMMAR

1 Match the questions and answers.

1 Does he like football?	a Yes, she does.
2 Do you like Cola?	b No, I don't.
3 Are you married?	c Yes, he is.
4 Is he French?	d Yes, he does.
5 Does she walk to school?	e No, they don't.
6 Do they go by train?	f No, I'm not.

2 Write questions.

1 what/you/eat/at dinner?
2 what/he/like doing on holiday?
3 when/they/have breakfast?
4 where/she/have her meals at home?
5 how/you/get to work?
6 when/you go to school?

What do you eat at dinner?

3 Complete with *don't* or *doesn't.*

1 I ____ like swimming.
2 He ____ like staying in hotels.
3 She ____ write postcards.
4 We ____ go on holiday.
5 You ____ like skiing.
6 They ____ like meat.

Progress check 21–30

GENERAL COMMENTS

You can work through this Progress check in the order shown, or concentrate on areas which may have caused difficulty in Lessons 21 to 30. You can also let the students choose the activities they would like or feel the need to do.

VOCABULARY

1 Aim: to focus on parts of speech.

- Ask the students to look at the words listed under the different parts of speech. Then ask them to work in pairs and decide what part of speech the remaining words belong to.

- Ask the students to decide what part of speech the words are.

Answers
white – adjective at – preposition kitchen – noun
we – pronoun black – adjective sofa – noun
take – verb to – preposition understand – verb
they – pronoun read – verb from – preposition

- Point out that some words can be more than one part of speech.

2 Aim: to focus on parts of speech.

- Ask the students to say what part of speech the underlined words are.

Answers
she – pronoun boat – noun
cook – verb
they – pronoun eat – verb in – preposition
can – (modal) verb sandwich – noun
like – verb on – preposition beach – noun
station – noun
telephone – noun hall – noun
he – pronoun buying – present participle/-ing form
lunch – noun
usually – adverb have – verb
he – pronoun having – present participle/-ing form

3 Aim: to focus on words which go together.

- Remind the students that in Lesson 30, there was an activity which focused on words which go together.

Answer
get dressed play the guitar go to school
speak/learn/read/write French have/make tea
have/make dinner

4 Aim: to help the students organise their vocabulary learning.

- Encourage the students to write the new words they have learnt in their *Wordbanks*.

GRAMMAR

1 Aim: to revise *yes/no* questions and short answers in the present simple.

Answers
1d 2b 3f 4c 5a 6e

2 Aim: to revise the formation of questions.

Answers
1 What do you eat at dinner?
2 What does he like doing on holiday?
3 When do they have breakfast?
4 Where does she have her meals at home?
5 How do you get to work?
6 When do you go to school?

3 Aim: to revise the use of *don't* and *doesn't*.

Answers
1 don't 2 doesn't 3 doesn't
4 don't 5 don't 6 don't

4 Aim: to revise the position of adverbs.

Answers
1 I often go swimming at the weekend.
2 We sometimes go to the cinema on Sundays.
3 They always go to a restaurant with friends.
4 He never goes out on Sunday.
5 She usually invites her friends to her flat.
6 You always have a shower in the morning.

5 Aim: to revise *can*.

Answers
1 He can swim.
2 He can't drive.
3 He can use a computer.
4 He can play the piano.
5 He can't cook.
6 He can't speak French.

6 Aim: to revise the present continuous.

Answers
1 They aren't singing. They're dancing.
2 She isn't playing the guitar. She's playing the piano.
3 He isn't running. He's swimming.
4 They aren't playing football. They're playing tennis.
5 He isn't eating. He's drinking.
6 She isn't washing. She's cooking.

SOUNDS

1 Aim: to focus on /ɑɪ/, /ɪ/, /uː/, /iː/ and /ʊ/.

- Ask the students to listen and repeat the words as you play the tape.

2 Aim: to focus on stressed syllables in words.

- Ask the students to listen to the tape and underline the stressed syllables. Then ask them to say the words aloud.

Answers
bicycle vegetable telephone restaurant library
America December September computer

3 Aim: to focus on stressed syllables in words.

- Ask the students to predict which syllables are stressed.
- Play the tape and ask the students to check. They should repeat the words.

Answers
Asia February November sightseeing eleventh

4 Aim: to focus on contrastive stress.

- Explain that when you correct a statement, you stress the information which is wrong and the information which is right.
- Play the tape and ask the students to listen and repeat.

5 Aim: to focus on contrastive stress.

- Ask the students to underline the stressed words in the last three sentences of *Grammar* activity 6. Play the tape and ask the students to check the stress and to repeat the sentences.

Answers
They aren't playing football. They're playing tennis.
He isn't eating. He's drinking.
She isn't washing. She's cooking.

LISTENING

1 Aim: to practise listening for specific information; to listen for pleasure.

- Ask the students to listen to the song and to underline any words which are different.

Answers
Daniel is travelling tonight on a train
I can see the red tail lights heading for Spain,
Oh, and I can't see Daniel waving goodbye
God, it looks like Daniel, must be the clouds in my ears.
They say Spain's pretty, though I've never been,
Well, Daniel says its the next place he's ever seen,
Oh and he should know who's been there enough,
Lord, I miss Daniel, oh I miss him so much.
Oh Daniel my father,
You are older than him
Do you still feel the train
Of the scars that won't heal?
Your eyes have died, but you see more than I,
Daniel, you're a car in the place of the sky.

2 Aim: to check comprehension; to practise speaking.

- Your students may find this activity quite hard. Give them plenty of support and help them with any words which they don't understand. This may be a rare occasion when you need to explain every word.
- Ask the students to check their answers in pairs, then check as a class. Play the tape again.

4 Put the adverbs in the right position.

1 I go swimming at the weekend. (often)
2 We go to the cinema on Sundays. (sometimes)
3 They go to a restaurant with friends. (always)
4 He goes out on Sunday. (never)
5 She invites her friends to her flat. (usually)
6 You have a shower in the morning. (always)

5 Write sentences saying what Pete can do.

1 Can he swim? ✓
2 Can he drive? ✗
3 Can he use a computer? ✓
4 Can he play the piano? ✓
5 Can he cook? ✗
6 Can he speak French? ✗

6 Correct these sentences and say what people are doing at the moment.

1 They're singing. (dance)
2 She's playing the guitar. (play the piano)
3 He's running. (swim)
4 They're playing football. (play tennis)
5 He's eating. (drink)
6 She's washing. (cook)

They aren't singing. They're dancing.

SOUNDS

1 Listen and repeat.

/aɪ/ wine knife ninth drive rice
/ɪ/ drink swim sing sit
/uː/ spoon room
/iː/ eat read speak leave
/ʊ/ book cook look football

2 Listen and underline the stressed syllables.

bicycle vegetable telephone restaurant library
America December September computer

Now say the words aloud.

3 Underline the stressed syllables.

Asia February November sightseeing eleventh

Now listen and check. As you listen, say the words aloud.

4 Listen to and repeat the first three sentences of *Grammar* activity 6.

1 They aren't singing. They're dancing.
2 She isn't playing the guitar. She's playing the piano.
3 He isn't running. He's swimming.

5 Underline the stressed words in the last three sentences of *Grammar* activity 6.

Now listen and check. As you listen, say the sentences aloud.

LISTENING

1 You're going to hear *Daniel,* by Elton John. The words below are not the exact words of the song. Listen and underline anything which is different.

Daniel is travelling tonight on a train
I can see the red tail lights heading for Spain,
Oh, and I can't see Daniel waving goodbye
God, it looks like Daniel, must be the clouds in my ears.
They say Spain's pretty, though I've never been,
Well, Daniel says it's the next place that he's ever seen,
Oh and he should know who's been there enough,
Lord, I miss Daniel, oh I miss him so much.
Oh, Daniel my father,
You are older than him
Do you still feel the train
Of the scars that won't heal?
Your eyes have died, you see more than I,
Daniel, you're a car in the place of the sky.

2 Work in pairs and check your answers. Can you correct the words you underlined?

Now listen again and check.

31 We're going to Australia

Present continuous (3): future plans

VOCABULARY

1 Listen and repeat.

beach sea city outback mountains

2 Work in pairs. Point and say.

3 Check these words in the dictionary.

meet spend wear camp get pack

cases tickets plane hat

103 Creswell Avenue
Sydney
New South Wales

Dear Mum and Dad,

Thanks for your letter. It's great that you're coming! Here's what we're doing. You're arriving on Sunday 29 December and Bruce is meeting you at the airport. You're staying with us in Sydney for a week and then, on Sunday, we're driving to Port Stephens (it's about three hours away).

We're spending a week in a hotel on the beach there (you can go swimming, sailing or just lie in the sun!).

After this we're going to Cobar, a town in the outback. We're camping for a week here. It's always very hot, so bring a hat to wear! Then it's back to England for you.

Looking forward to seeing you soon.

Lots of love,

Fran

xxx

PS Bruce sends his best wishes too.

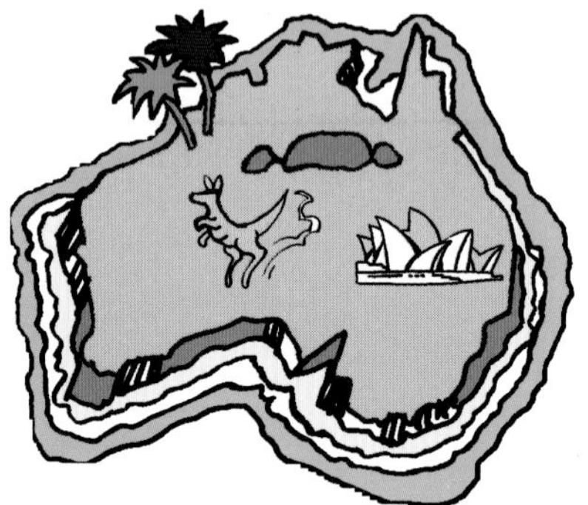

READING AND LISTENING

1 Read the letter and write short answers to the questions.

1 Where are Fran's parents going?
2 Who is meeting them at the airport?
3 Where are they staying in Sydney?
4 Where are they going after Sydney?
5 Where are they staying?
6 Where are they going then?
7 Are they staying in a hotel?

31

GENERAL COMMENTS

Present continuous

This is the third lesson on the present continuous, and it focuses on the future use of the tense. Students may find it difficult to understand why the tense can be used for both the present and the future. Stress that the tense is used to talk about a definite arrangement in the future, rather than a decision taken at the moment of speaking, when *will* is used.

You may find it appropriate to tell the students that there are some verbs which are not normally used in the continuous form: *hear, know, like, love, understand, want*.

VOCABULARY

1 Aim: to present the words in the vocabulary box.

● Ask the students to listen and repeat the words in the vocabulary box.

2 Aim: to focus on the words in the vocabulary box.

● Ask the students to work in pairs and point to the photos and say what they see.

3 Aim: to focus on words which go together; to present the words in the vocabulary box.

● Remind the students that there are many verb and noun combinations in English. When two words often go together, this is called a collocation.

● Ask the students to match the verbs and the nouns. They may check these in a dictionary.

Possible answers
meet - plane
wear - hat
get - plane
pack - cases

READING AND LISTENING

1 Aim: to practise reading for main ideas.

● Ask the students to read the letter and write short answers to the questions.

Answers
1 - Australia 2 - Bruce 3 - at Fran's and Bruce's
4 - Port Stephens 5 - hotel 6 - Cobar
7 - no (camping)

2 Aim: to practise reading for specific information.

● Ask the students to read the letter again and to fill in the missing words in the conversation.

Answers
1 going 2 staying 3 going 4 spending
5 going 6 camping

● Ask the students to check their answers in pairs and then listen and check.

GRAMMAR

1 Aim: to encourage the students to compare English with their own language.

● Ask the students to read the information in the grammar box and then to do the exercises.

● Ask the students if they can use a present tense in their own language to talk about the future.

2 Aim: to revise the uses of the present continuous.

● Ask the students to think about the uses of the present continuous which they have come across in Lessons 29, 30 and 31.

Answers
You can use the present continuous:
- to talk about definite arrangements in the future ✓
- to talk about something happening at the moment ✓
- to talk about habits and routines ✗

3 Aim: to practise using the present continuous for future arrangements.

● Ask the student to write full answers to the short answers they wrote in *Reading and listening* activity 1.

Answers
1 They're going to Australia.
2 Bruce is meeting them at the airport.
3 They're staying with Bruce and Fran.
4 They're going to Port Stephens.
5 They're staying in a hotel.
6 They're going to Cobar.
7 They aren't staying in a hotel. They're camping.

4 Aim: to practise using the present continuous for future arrangements.

● Ask the students to read the diary and to say what Fran's parents are doing.

Answers
1 They're getting the plane tickets.
2 They're going to the doctor.
3 They're getting visas from Australia House.
4 They're packing (their) cases.
5 They're staying the night at a friend's house.
6 They're getting the plane.

5 Aim: to practise using the present continuous for future arrangements.

● Ask the students to complete the diary with things they are doing next week.

● In pairs, ask the students to ask and say what they are doing next week.

LISTENING AND SPEAKING

1 Aim: to practise listening for specific information.

● Explain to the students that the telephone call they will hear contains some important changes to the plans. Ask them to listen and underline the plans which are different.

2 Aim: to practise listening; to practise using the present continuous for future plans.

● Ask the students to work in pairs and say what the new plans are.

Answers

Bruce isn't meeting them at the airport. Fran's meeting them.
They aren't staying with Fran and Bruce. They're staying in a hotel.
They aren't spending a week in Port Stephens. They're spending 10 days.
They aren't camping for a week in the outback (Cobar). They camping for 3 days.

● Play the tape again and ask the students to listen and check.

3 Aim: to practise speaking.

● Ask the students to work in pairs and to plan a visit to somewhere special. It can be anywhere in the world.

4 Aim: to practise speaking.

● Ask several pairs to tell the whole class what they're doing and where they're going.

● You may like to ask the students to write about their plans for homework.

2 Complete the conversation between Fran's parents, Don and Sue, and a friend, Tony.

TONY What are your plans for the holiday? Where are you going?

DON We're ____ to Australia.

TONY Australia!

SUE Yes, for three weeks. We're ____ with Fran in Sydney. We're spending a week there.

DON And then we're ____ to Port Stephens, about three hours away, and we're ____ a week on the beach.

TONY Wonderful!

SUE Then we're ____ to a town called Cobar in the outback. We're ____ there.

TONY Well, have a great time!

DON Thanks. What are you doing?

TONY Oh, I'm staying at home.

Now listen and check.

GRAMMAR

Present continuous (3): future plans

*I'**m** stay**ing** at home.*
*You'**re** arriv**ing** on Sunday 29 December.*
*He'**s** meet**ing** you at the airport.*
*We'**re** go**ing** to Cobar.*
*They'**re** spend**ing** a week in Sydney.*

1 Answer the question.

Can you use a present tense to talk about the future in your language?

2 Tick (✔) the true statements.

You can use the present continuous:

- to talk about definite arrangements in the future ☐
- to talk about something happening at the moment ☐
- to talk about habits and routines ☐

3 Write full answers to the questions in *Reading and listening* activity 1.

They're going to Australia.

4 Look at the diary. Say what Fran's parents are doing next week.

5 Complete the diary with things you're doing next week.
Now work in pairs. Ask and say what you're doing next week.

What are you doing on Monday?

I'm going to my English lesson.

LISTENING AND SPEAKING

1 Listen to a phone call from Fran. Underline any plan in the letter which is different from what you hear.

2 Work in pairs and say what the new plans are.

Bruce isn't meeting them at the airport. Fran's meeting them at the airport.

Now listen again and check.

3 Work in pairs. Plan a trip to somewhere special. Say:

– where you're going
– what you're doing

4 Tell the rest of the class what your plans are.

We're flying to London. We're staying ...

December

MONDAY
Get plane tickets

TUESDAY
Go to doctor

WEDNESDAY
Get visas from Australia House

THURSDAY
Pack cases

FRIDAY
Stay the night at friend's house

SATURDAY
Get the plane

SUNDAY

32 Let's go to the cinema

Making suggestions; accepting and refusing; talking about the cinema and theatre

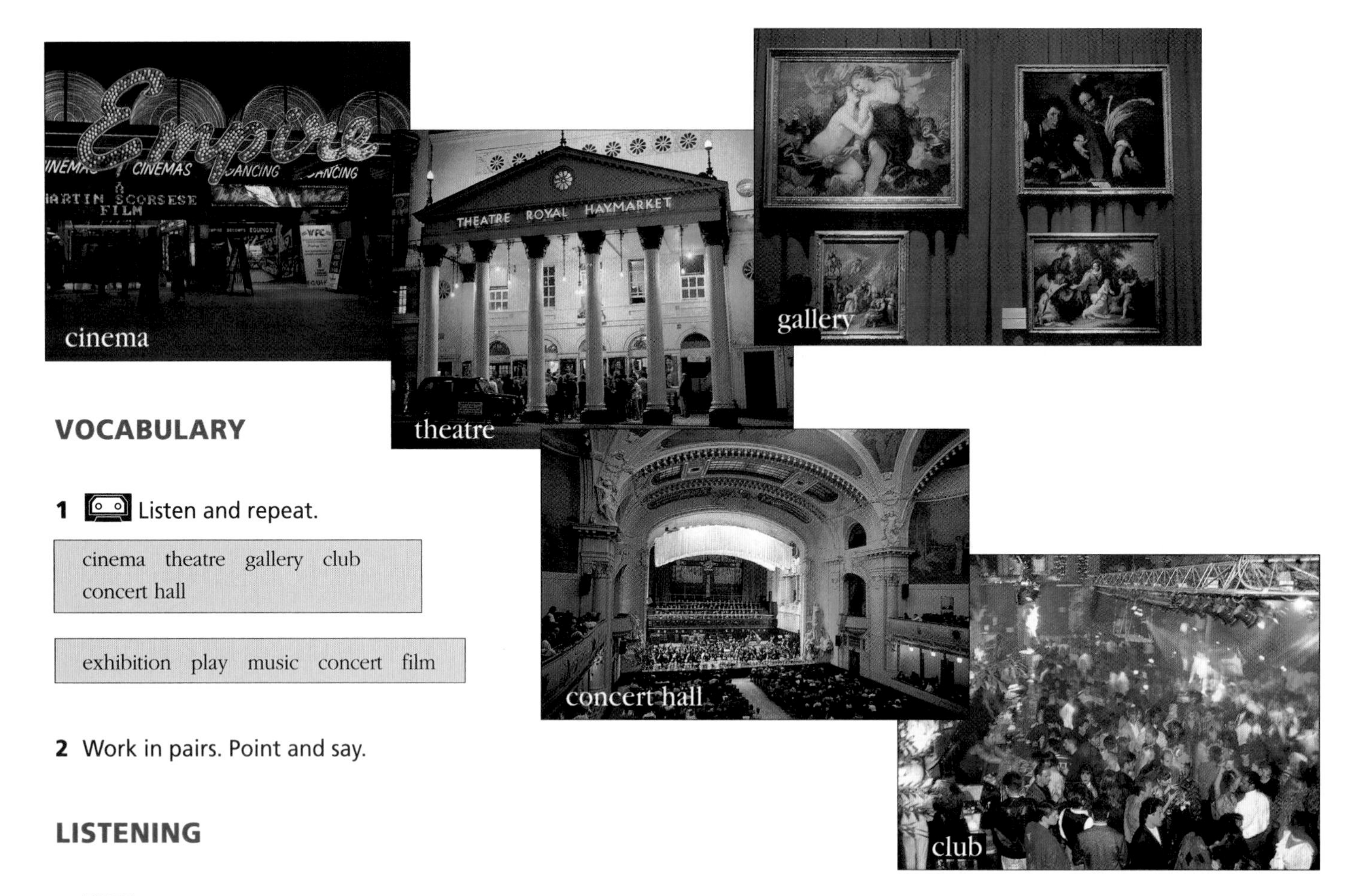

VOCABULARY

1 Listen and repeat.

cinema theatre gallery club concert hall

exhibition play music concert film

2 Work in pairs. Point and say.

LISTENING

1 Listen and read.

A
STEVE Let's go to a club this evening.
ANNA I'm sorry but I don't like clubs.
STEVE OK. Well, let's go to the cinema.
ANNA I'm sorry but I don't like films.
STEVE How about going to the theatre, then?
ANNA I'm sorry but I'm busy this evening. I'm going out with Jack.
STEVE Oh!

B
TOM Let's go to the cinema.
ALISON Yes, OK. What's on?
TOM The new James Bond film.
ALISON Where's it on?
TOM At the Odeon.

2 Complete.

JACK Let's go to the cinema.
ANNA (1) ____
JACK How about going to the theatre, then?
ANNA (2) ____
JACK An Agatha Christie play.
ANNA (3) ____
JACK At the Theatre Royal.
ANNA (4) ____

a Where's it on?
b Yes, OK. What's on?
c Great!
d I'm sorry but I don't like films.

Now listen and check your answer.

32

GENERAL COMMENTS

Making suggestions

The function of *making suggestions* implies a sense of future, so this lesson continues the series of lessons on expressing future time. You may like to explain that in English, when someone refuses an invitation, it is very common to give some kind of explanation. In other cultures, a simple no is perfectly acceptable. You may also like to point out that an apology is very common when someone refuses an invitation.

VOCABULARY

1 Aim: to present the words in the vocabulary box.

- Ask the students to listen and repeat the words.

2 Aim: to present the meaning of the words in the vocabulary box.

- Ask the students to point to the photos and say the words.
- Ask the students to match the places and the events that take place there.

> **Answers**
> cinema – film theatre – play gallery – exhibition
> club – music concert hall – concert

LISTENING

1 Aim: to present the language for making suggestions.

- Ask the students to listen and read the conversations. Ask the students to say in which conversation someone accepts an invitation and in which one someone refuses a conversation.

> **Answers**
> A – refuses
> B – accepts

2 Aim: to practise listening for specific information.

- Ask the students to decide where the sentences go in the conversation.

> **Answers**
> 1d 2b 3a 4c

- Play the tape and ask the students to check their answers.

SOUNDS

1 Aim: to practise stress and intonation patterns.

- Ask the students to listen and read the sentences as you play the tape.
- Ask the students to say the sentences aloud as a whole class, and individually.

2 Aim: to practise stress and intonation patterns.

- Ask the students to listen and repeat the sentences as you play the tape.

3 Aim: to practise stress and intonation patterns.

- Ask the students to predict which words the speaker is likely to stress and to underline them.
- Play the tape and ask the students to check their answers and repeat the sentences.

FUNCTIONS

1 Aim: to focus on the language of making, accepting and refusing invitations.

- Ask the students to read the information in the functions box and then to do the exercises.
- Ask the students to complete the conversations with words from the functions box.

> **Answers**
> 1 A Let's go to the cinema.
> B I'm sorry but I'm busy.
> A How about going tomorrow night?
> B Yes, OK.
>
> 2 A Let's go to the theatre.
> B Yes, OK.

2 Aim: to focus on word order.

- Ask the students to put the words in the correct order to form sentences.

> **Answers**
> 1 I'm sorry but I don't like films.
> 2 I'm sorry but I'm busy this evening.
> 3 Let's go to an exhibition.
> 4 How about going to a concert?

3 Aim: to practise using the language of making, accepting and refusing suggestions.

- Ask the students to act out the conversations in *Listening* activities 1 and 2.

4 Aim: to practise using the language of making, accepting and refusing suggestions.

- Ask students to look at the posters from *Vocabulary* activity 1, and using the information in pairs, to act out similar conversations to *Functions* activity 1.

SPEAKING

1 Aim: to practise speaking.

- Ask the students to work in pairs and to make notes on two or three things that are on in their town at the moment.

2 Aim: to practise speaking.

- Ask the students to work in larger groups and to talk about the things that are on in their town. Try to get an agreement on what to do from as many people as possible in the group.

SOUNDS

1 Listen and read.

Let's go to the cinema.

How about going to the theatre?

Let's go to an exhibition.

How about going to a concert?

Now say the sentences aloud.

2 Listen and repeat.

I'm sorry but I don't like clubs.

I'm sorry but I'm busy this evening.

I'm sorry but I don't like Picasso.

3 Underline the stressed words.

I'm sorry but I don't like music.

I'm sorry but I'm busy tomorrow evening.

I'm sorry but I don't like Spielberg.

Now listen and repeat 3.

FUNCTIONS

Making suggestions

Let's go *to the cinema.*

How about going *to the theatre?*

Accepting	Refusing
Yes, OK.	***I'm sorry but*** *I don't like films.*
	I'm sorry but *I'm busy.*

Talking about the cinema and theatre

What's on?	*The new James Bond film./The new Agatha Christie play.*
Where's it on?	*At the Odeon/Theatre Royal.*

1 Complete.

1 A ____ go to the cinema.
 B I'm ____ but I'm busy.
 A ____ about going tomorrow night?
 B Yes, ____.

2 A ____ go to the theatre.
 B Yes, ____.

2 Put the words in the correct order to form sentences.

1 I'm don't films but I like sorry
2 sorry I'm evening but busy this I'm
3 go exhibition to an let's
4 to concert how going about a?

3 Work in pairs and act out the conversations in *Listening* activities 1 and 2.

4 Look at the posters in *Vocabulary* activity 1. Work in pairs and act out conversations.

SPEAKING

1 Work in pairs. Write down things which are on in your town at the moment. Choose two or three things you want to see.

2 Work in groups. Make suggestions about things to see, and accept or refuse the suggestions. Try to get as many people as possible to go and see something with you.

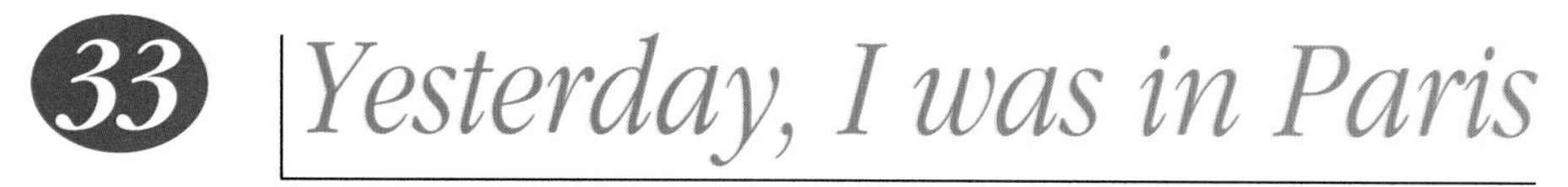

33 Yesterday, I was in Paris

Past simple (1) *be: was/were*

VOCABULARY

1 Translate the words.

tired happy cold bored
unhappy warm hot awful fine

Now listen and repeat.

2 Complete the sentences so they are true for you.

1 At eleven o'clock in the evening, I'm ____.
2 In April, it's ____.
3 In January, it's ____.
4 When I listen to music, I'm ____.
5 In August, it's ____.
6 On Friday evening, I'm ____.
7 On Monday morning, I'm ____.
8 If I don't have a holiday, I'm ____.

3 Work in pairs. Check your answers to 2.

LISTENING AND READING

1 Listen and read.

JENKINS Today, I'm in the office, but yesterday I was in Paris. In Paris with the woman of my dreams! Today I'm in England, but yesterday I was in France. In France, in Paris, at the Hotel des Amores. Today I'm bored and unhappy. Yesterday we were happy. Yesterday it was warm and everything was fine. Today it's cold and everything is awful. Oh Paris! Oh Marie Claire!

BOSS Jenkins!

JENKINS Oh no!

33

GENERAL COMMENTS

Past simple

This is the first of seven lessons on the past simple. As with the other tenses, the past simple is deconstructed into its component parts, and no lesson will cover more than one or two aspects. This lesson presents the past simple of the verb *be*. Lesson 34 presents *yes/no* questions and short answers with *was/were*. Lesson 35 presents *had*, Lesson 36 presents the past simple of regular verbs, Lesson 37 presents negatives using the auxiliary *didn't* + infinitive, Lesson 38 is on *yes/no* questions and short answers, and Lesson 39 on irregular verbs and *wh-* questions. This slow but careful progression is designed not to overload the students.

VOCABULARY

1 Aim: to present the words in the vocabulary box.

- Ask the students to match some of the words with the drawings. Ask the students to translate the words.
- Play the tape and ask the students to listen and repeat.

2 Aim: to practise using the words in the vocabulary box.

- Ask the students to use the words in the box to make true sentences.

3 Aim: to practise using the words in the vocabulary box.

- Ask the students to work in pairs and to compare their answers to the questions.

LISTENING AND READING

1 Aim: to present the past simple of *be*.

- Ask the students to listen and follow the conversation as you play it.

2 Aim: to check comprehension; to practise using *was/were*.

- Ask the students to read the passage again and to complete the sentences.

Answers

1 ... he was in Paris.
2 ... he was in France.
3 ... they were happy.
4 ... it was warm.
5 ... everything was fine.

SOUNDS

1 Aim: to focus on the pronunciation of *was/were*.

- Ask the students to listen and notice how *was* and *were* are pronounced when used in an unstressed word in a sentence. Play the tape.

- Ask the students to say the sentences aloud. Make sure they say /wəz/ and /wɜː/.

2 Aim: to focus on the pronunciation of *was/were*.

- Ask the students to say the sentences aloud. Make sure they say /wəz/ and /wɜː/.

- Play the tape and ask them to listen and check.

GRAMMAR

1 Aim: to focus on the use of was and were.

- Ask the students to read the information in the grammar box and then to do the exercises.

- Ask the students to say when you use *was* and *were*

Answer
Was is for *I, he* and *she*
were is for *you, we* and *they*

2 Aim: to practise using *was* and *were*.

- Ask the students to complete the sentences using either *was* or *were*.

Answers
1 was 2 were 3 were 4 were 5 was 6 was

3 Aim: to practise using *was* and *were*.

- Ask the students to complete the sentences with true information.

4 Aim: to practise using the *was* and *were*.

- Ask the students to work in pairs and to compare their answers to 3.

- Check several students' answers with the whole class.

SPEAKING AND WRITING

1 Aim: to practise speaking.

- Ask the students to work in pairs and decide who is Student A and who is Student B.

- Ask the students to follow the instructions in Communication activity 34 on page 99.

2 Aim: to practise writing.

- Ask the students to complete the missing information for the description of the photo.

Answers
There **were** four people and a dog in the photo. There **was** a man, a woman and two children. They **were** outside. They **weren't** on the beach, but they **were** in the country. They **weren't** Asian. They **were** probably American. The woman **was** probably the children's mother. She **was** quite pretty. The man **was** probably the children's father. He **was** quite good-looking. The children **were** probably brother and sister, but they **weren't** twins. The dog **was** brown and white. It **wasn't** a cold day. It **was** probably summer. It **wasn't** night, so it **was** probably midday. Their lunch **was** on the grass in front of them. There **were** sandwiches and cakes to eat. There **wasn't** any hot food. It **wasn't** a modern photo. It **was** probably from 1960.

2 Work in pairs and complete the sentences.

Today he's in the office, but yesterday he ____ .

Today he's in England, but yesterday he ____ .

Today he's bored and unhappy, but yesterday they ____ .

Today it's cold, but yesterday it ____ .

Today everything is awful, but yesterday everything ____ .

SOUNDS

1 [cassette] Listen to the pronunciation of *was* and *were*.

1 I was tired.
2 I was cold.
3 We were happy.
4 We were bored.

Now say the sentences aloud.

2 Say these sentences aloud.

1 He was hot.
2 She was cold.
3 They were tired.
4 They were happy.
5 It was awful.

[cassette] Now listen and check.

GRAMMAR

Past simple (1): *be*
I was
You were
He/she/it was
We were
They were

1 When do we use *was* and when do we use *were*?

2 Complete the sentences.

1 Yesterday I ____ in New York.
2 In February they ____ in Spain.
3 You ____ at work yesterday.
4 Last year we ____ in Australia.
5 He ____ at home at ten o'clock.
6 She ____ in Italy last year.

3 Complete the sentences for you.

The last time I was...
tired was ____.
unhappy was ____.
cold was ____.
bored was ____.
The last time we were...
at school/work was ____.
on holiday was ____.

4 Work in pairs. Say your answers to 3.

SPEAKING AND WRITING

1 Work in pairs. Turn to Communication activity 34 on page 99.

2 Complete the text.

There ___ four people and a dog in the photo. There ___ a man, a woman and two children. They ___ outside. They ___ on the beach, but they ___ in the country. They ___ Asian. They ___ probably American. The woman ___ probably the children's mother. She ___ quite pretty. The man ___ probably the children's father. He ___ quite good-looking. The children ___ probably brother and sister, but they ___ twins. The dog ___ brown and white. It ___ a cold day. It ___ probably summer. It ___ night, so it ___ probably midday. Their lunch ___ on the grass in front of them. There ___ sandwiches and cakes to eat. There ___ any hot food. It ___ a modern photo. It ___ probably from 1960.

34 Was she in the kitchen?

Past simple (2): *yes/no* questions and short answers

VOCABULARY

1 Complete these sentences with *food* and *drink*.

hungry thirsty

When you're hungry, you need some ____.

When you're thirsty, you need a ____.

2 Here are some new words in the story in this lesson. Check you understand them.

professor colonel detective sergeant lady Miss Mrs butler murder knife murderer scream dead cook alone

What kind of story do you think it is?

READING AND LISTENING

1 Match the drawings and the paragraphs.

A It was eight o'clock in the evening at Ripley Grange, the home of Lady Scarlet. There were six people at the table in the dining room: Colonel White, Miss Green, Professor Peacock, Mrs Mustard, Doctor Plum, and Lady Scarlet.

B It was cold in the dining room. They were hungry because the food wasn't very good. There was a cold potato, a piece of cold meat and a piece of cold lettuce.

C They were thirsty, but there wasn't any wine, only a glass of water.

D Probe, Lady Scarlet's butler and cook was at the door of the dining room. He was tall with black hair but he wasn't very good-looking. He wasn't a very good butler, and he was an awful cook.

Now listen and check.

2 Look at these sentences from the next part of the story. Put them in the correct order.

☐ Then, there was a scream. It was Lady Scarlet. Was she in the kitchen? Yes, she was.

☐ Was there something on the table? Yes, there was – there was a knife on the table. It was red. Was it murder? Who was the murderer?

☐ It was ten o'clock in the evening at Ripley Grange. It was quiet ... very quiet. Was there anyone in the dining room? No, there wasn't.

☐ Was she alone in the kitchen? No, she wasn't. Probe was also in the kitchen. He was dead.

Now listen and check.

34

Theme of the lesson

The theme of the lesson is an old-fashioned murder mystery in a parody of an Agatha Christie story or the game *Cluedo*. The story and the characters are deliberately humorous. It's set in an old-style English country house.

VOCABULARY

1 Aim: to present the words in the vocabulary box.

- The vocabulary load in this lesson is light, so you may want to add a few extra adjectives to describe physical requirements, feelings, mood etc.

- Ask the students to complete the sentences with the words *food* and *drink*.

2 Aim: to pre-teach some important vocabulary.

- The words in this activity are not essential for the students to learn at this level, but are nevertheless important for the story. You can either translate the words or ask the students to use dictionaries to check them.

- Ask the students to predict what kind of story they think it is.

READING AND LISTENING

1 Aim: to practise reading for main ideas.

- Ask the students to read the first part of the story and to match the drawings with the paragraphs.

Answers
1 - D 2 - C 3 - A 4 - B

2 Aim: to prepare for listening.

- Ask the students to predict the order in which the next paragraphs should come. They should do this in pairs.

Answers
2 Then, there was a scream. It was Lady Scarlet. Was she in the kitchen? Yes, she was.
4 Was there something on the table? Yes, there was - there was a knife on the table. It was red. Was it murder? Who was the murderer?
1 It was ten o'clock in the evening at Ripley Grange. It was quiet ... very quiet. Was there anyone in the dining room? No, there wasn't.
3 Was she alone in the kitchen? No, she wasn't. Probe was also in the kitchen. He was dead.

- Play the tape and ask the students to listen and check.

GRAMMAR

Aim: to focus on word order.

- Ask the students to read the information in the grammar box and then to do the exercises.

- Ask the students to put the words in the right order to make sentences.

> **Answers**
> 1 Was Colonel White in the kitchen?
> 2 Was Mrs Mustard in the dining room?
> 3 Was Miss Green in the bedroom?
> 4 Was Dr Plum in the living room?
> 5 Was Professor Peacock in the garden?
> 6 Was Lady Scarlet in the kitchen?

LISTENING AND SPEAKING

1 Aim: to practise listening for main ideas.

- Check everyone understands that Detective Prune and Sergeant Peach are policemen.

- [tape] Ask the students to listen to the interviews and to complete the chart by ticking the rooms the characters were in from 8 pm to 10 pm.

	Colonel White	Miss Green	Professor Peacock	Mrs Mustard	Doctor Plum	Lady Scarlet
kitchen					✓	✓
bathroom						
bedroom						✓
dining room	✓	✓	✓	✓	✓	✓
living room	✓		✓		✓	
garden		✓		✓		

2 Aim: to practise using *yes/no* questions and short answers.

- Ask the students to work in pairs and check their answers to activity 1 by asking and answering questions about the characters.

- You can do this activity orally with the whole class.

3 Aim: to check comprehension.

- Ask the students to complete the sentences.

> **Answers**
> Colonel White – living room
> Miss Green – garden
> Professor Peacock – living room
> Mrs Mustard – garden
> Doctor Plum – living room (and kitchen)
> Lady Scarlet – bedroom

4 Aim: to practise speaking.

- Ask the students to decide who the murderer was. Ask them to work in pairs and then to work with other pairs. Can anyone think of a motive for the murder?

5 Aim: to practise listening for main ideas.

- [tape] Play the tape and ask the students to find out who the murderer was.

> **Answers**
> Lady Scarlet was the murderer. Only she was alone, and she was tired of the cold house and the bad food.

GRAMMAR

Past simple (2): *yes/no* questions and short answers

Was I in the kitchen?	*Yes, you were.*
	No, you weren't.
Were you in the kitchen?	*Yes, I was.*
	No, I wasn't.
Was he/she in the kitchen?	*Yes, he/she was.*
	No, he/she wasn't.
Were we in the kitchen?	*Yes, we were.*
	No, we weren't.
Were they in the kitchen?	*Yes, they were.*
	No, they weren't.

Put the words in order and write questions.

1 was Colonel White the kitchen in?
2 Mrs Mustard was in the dining room?
3 Miss Green in the bedroom was?
4 was Doctor Plum the living room in?
5 Professor Peacock in the garden was?
6 Lady Scarlet was in the kitchen?

LISTENING AND SPEAKING

1 Detective Prune and Sergeant Peach come to Ripley Grange next morning. Listen to their interviews and find out where people were at 8 pm and 10 pm. Put a tick (✔) in the chart below.

2 Work in pairs and check your answers.

Was Colonel White in the kitchen at ten o'clock?

No, he wasn't. He was in the living room.

3 Complete the sentences. Say where people were at 10 pm

Colonel White was in the ____.
Miss Green was in the ____.
Professor Peacock was in the ____.
Mrs Mustard was in the ____.
Doctor Plum was in the ____.
Lady Scarlet was in the ____.

4 Work in pairs. Who was the murderer?

5 Listen and find out who was the murderer, and why.

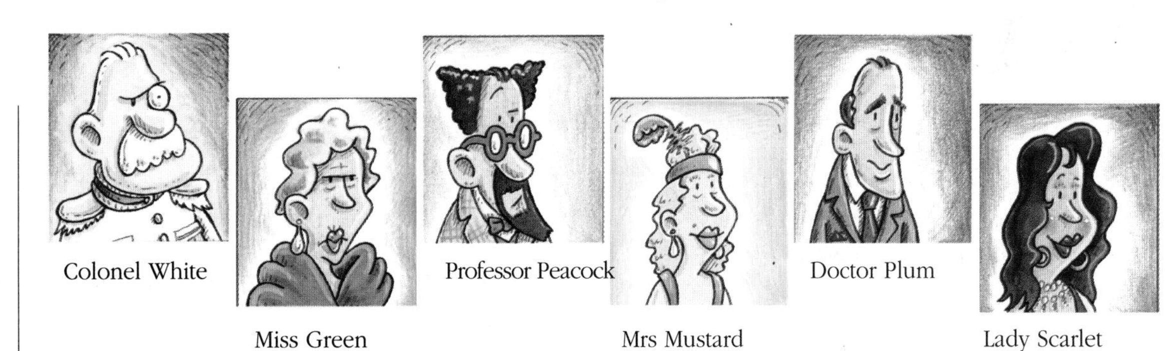

	Colonel White	Miss Green	Professor Peacock	Mrs Mustard	Doctor Plum	Lady Scarlet
kitchen						
bathroom						
bedroom						
dining room						
living room						
garden						

35 *They didn't have any computers*

Past simple (3): *had*

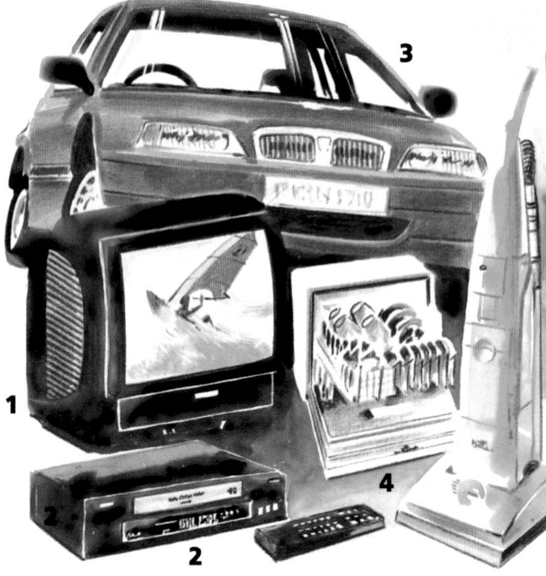

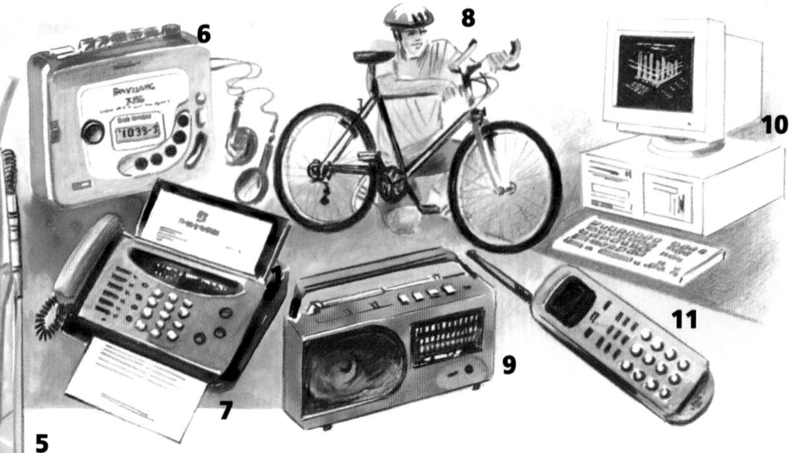

VOCABULARY AND SOUNDS

1 Match the words with the pictures.

television video recorder telephone radio computer personal stereo car bicycle fax machine dishwasher vacuum cleaner

2 Tick (✔) the things you or your family have at home.

3 Listen and underline the stressed syllables in the words in 1.

television

Now listen and repeat.

4 Work in pairs. Ask and say which things in 1 you have at home.

We've got a television and a video recorder.

5 Circle the things your grandparents had.

READING AND LISTENING

1 Mary is 80. Read about her and her family. Tick (✔) the things they had and put a cross (✗) by the things they didn't have when she was a child.

MARY Well, when I was a child, we had a telephone in the hall, but we didn't have a television. No one had television. And, of course, we didn't have a video recorder.

INTERVIEWER What about a radio?

MARY Yes, we had a radio. The radio programmes were very good.

INTERVIEWER And computers, did you have computers or personal stereos?

MARY Oh, no, we didn't have computers or personal stereos. And I was fifty before I had my own radio.

INTERVIEWER Did you have a car?

MARY Yes, some families had a car, but we didn't. We had bicycles, all six of us.

INTERVIEWER And no fax machine, of course. Or vacuum cleaner or dishwasher?

MARY No, we didn't have a fax machine. But we had a kind of vacuum cleaner. And we didn't have a dishwasher.

35

GENERAL COMMENTS

Defining culture

One's culture is not simply defined by geography, nationality or ethnic background. Other factors play a role in defining one's culture: gender, socio-economic background, education and age. Exploring any of these factors in the classroom will allow cross-cultural training to take place as much as discovering the customs, traditions, attitudes and beliefs of people from different countries. In this lesson, the differences in living standards between now and when people were younger are explored.

VOCABULARY AND SOUNDS

1 Aim: to present the meaning of the words in the vocabulary box.

- Ask the students to match the words with the pictures.

Answers
television - 1
video recorder - 2
telephone - 11
radio - 9
computer - 10
personal stereo - 6
car - 3
bicycle - 8
fax machine - 7
dishwasher - 4
vacuum cleaner - 5

2 Aim: to practise using the words in the vocabulary box.

- Ask the students to tick the things they have at home.

3 Aim: to present the pronunciation of the words in the vocabulary box.

- Ask the students to listen and underline the stressed syllable in the words in 1.

Answers
television video recorder telephone radio
computer personal stereo car bicycle
fax machine dishwasher vacuum cleaner

4 Aim: to practise using the words in the vocabulary box.

- Ask the students to work in pairs and ask and answer which things they have at home. Is there anyone who has all of the items? Is there anyone who has none of them?

5 Aim: to prepare for listening; to practise using the words in the vocabulary box.

- Ask the students to circle the items their grandparents had.

READING AND LISTENING

1 Aim: to practise reading for specific information; to prepare for listening; to present the past simple *had* and *didn't have*.

- Ask the students to read the conversation and tick the things Mary had, or put a cross by the things she didn't have.

Answer
telephone ✓
television ✗
video recorder ✗
radio ✓
computer ✗
personal stereo ✗
car ✗
bicycle ✓
fax machine ✗
vacuum cleaner ✓
dishwasher ✗

2 Aim: to check comprehension.

- Ask the students to work in pairs and to check their answers.

3 Aim: to practise listening for specific information.

- Explain that the recorded version of the conversation has some extra words. Ask the students to listen and mark the conversation in activity 1 when they hear anything extra. Play the tape.

4 Aim: to check comprehension; to practise speaking.

- Ask the students to check their answers to 3 in pairs.
- Play the tape a second time.
- If you wish, you can refer students to page 115 of their Student's Books to check their answers against the tapescript.

GRAMMAR

1 Aim: to practise using the past simple *had* and *didn't have.*

● Ask the students to read the information in the grammar box and then to do the exercises.

● Ask the students to do this activity in writing. You may want to teach the link words *and, but* and *or*.

Answers
They had a telephone but they didn't have a television or a video recorder.
They had a radio but they didn't have computers or personal stereos.
They didn't have a car but they all had bicycles.
They didn't have a fax machine or a dishwasher, but they had a kind of vacuum cleaner.

2 Aim: to practise using the past simple *had* and *didn't have.*

● Ask the students to write sentences saying what their grandparents had or didn't have.

3 Aim: to focus on the difference between *was, were* and *had.*

● Ask the students to complete the sentences with *was, were* or *had*.

Answers
1 was 2 had 3 had 4 was/were 5 had 6 was/had

SPEAKING AND LISTENING

1 Aim: to practise speaking.

● Ask the students to work in pairs and say what the mistakes are. There are many anachronisms in the drawing and they should make sentences using *They didn't have* ....

2 Aim: to practise speaking.

● Ask the students to work in pairs and to check their answers to activity 1.

● Ask the students to tell the whole class their answers.

3 Aim: to prepare for listening.

● Make sure everyone understands what these words mean.

4 Aim: to present the pronunciation of the dates shown.

● Play the tape and ask the students to repeat the dates.

5 Aim: to practise speaking.

● Ask the students to work in pairs. Each student in turn should make a sentence using *Did they have ...?* and a date of their choice. The other student should give short answers *Yes, they did. No, they didn't.*

6 Aim: to practise listening for specific information.

● Play the tape and ask the students to listen and see how many correct answers the speaker gets and how many correct answers they got in activity 5.

Answers
The speaker gets 9 correct

7 Aim: to practise speaking.

● Finish the lesson with a discussion about things the students *had* or *didn't have* when they were children. Ask the students to work in groups of three or four.

● You might like to ask the students to make a poster with magazine pictures showing what they didn't have when they were younger.

telephone		
television		
video recorder		
radio		
computer		
personal stereo		
car		
bicycle		
fax machine		
vacuum cleaner		
dishwasher		

2 Work in pairs and check your answers.

3 Listen to Mary and put a \ if you hear any extra words or phrases.

4 Work in pairs and check your answers. Try to remember the extra words or phrases.

Now listen again and check.

GRAMMAR

Past simple (3): ***had***

I		*I*	
you		*you*	
he		*he*	
she	*had*	*she*	***didn't*** *have (= did not have)*
it		*it*	
we		*we*	
they		*they*	

We ***had*** *a telephone in the hall, but we* ***didn't have*** *a television.*

1 Write sentences saying what Mary's family had or didn't have.

They had a telephone, but they didn't have a television.

2 Write sentences saying what your grandparents had or didn't have.

My grandparents had a television, but they didn't have a personal stereo.

3 Complete with *was, were* or *had.*

1 It ____ a great film.
2 You ____ breakfast at seven o'clock.
3 They ____ dinner at eight o'clock.
4 The play ____ awful. We ____ bored.
5 We ____ a holiday in August.
6 He ____ thirsty so he ____ a drink.

SPEAKING AND LISTENING

1 Work in pairs. Turn to Communication activity 38 on page 100.

2 Work in pairs and check your answers to 1.

They didn't have telephones.

3 Here are some more discoveries and inventions which are now everyday items.

aeroplanes trains cameras newspapers steam engines

4 Listen and repeat these dates.

1950 1850 1750 1650 1550

5 Work in pairs. You're going to play *When in the World ...?* Ask and say:

Did they have trains in 1850? Yes, they did.

Did they have trains in 1550? No, they didn't.

6 Listen to two people playing *When in the World ...?* and check your answers. Score one point for each correct answer.

7 Work in groups of three or four. Talk about things you had or didn't have when you were a child.

36 We listened to the radio

Past simple (4): regular verbs

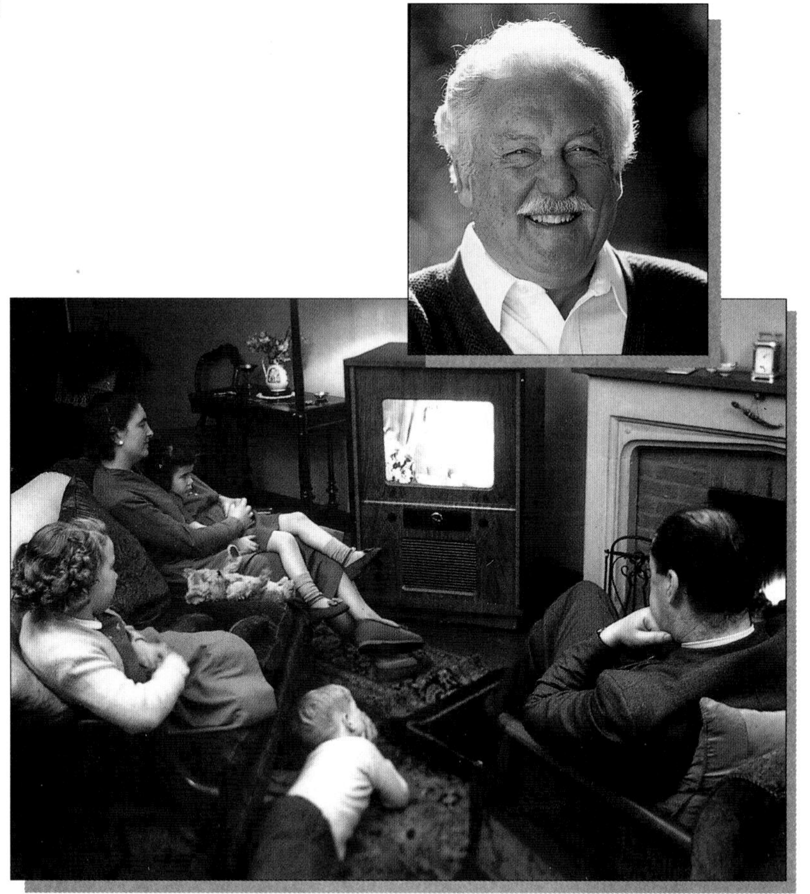

VOCABULARY

1 Write these words in the correct column.

last month	this year	this month	today
this week	last week	last year	yesterday

In the past	In the present
last year	*this year*

2 Read.

This year is 1997. Last year was 1996.

3 Complete.

1 This year is ____. Last year was ___.
2 This month is ____. Last month was ____.
3 Today is ____. Yesterday was ____.

READING AND LISTENING

1 Read about Brian's childhood. Match the headings and the paragraphs. There is one extra heading.

Holiday Sunday Work Sport
Entertainment at home

A 'We had a television set and we watched it in the evening. We listened to the radio or played records. There weren't any computers or computer games, but sometimes my brother played the piano and my sister and I danced to the music. In the summer,we played games in the garden until eight o'clock.'

B 'When I lived in London with my parents, I played tennis a lot, but I don't play it now. I wanted to play football, but I was terrible. On Sunday mornings,I watched the local football team in the park. I started running when I was at university in 1973.'

C 'On Sunday my mother cooked Sunday lunch and we had Sunday lunch together. Then in the afternoon, we had a walk in the country or I visited my friends. In summer we watched the village cricket match. We stayed at home on Sunday evenings.'

D 'My father worked five days a week. He started at 9 am and finished at 5 pm. He worked in a bank in London. We lived in South London, so every day he travelled over two hours by train to the city centre to get to work and back.'

36

GENERAL COMMENTS

Theme of the lesson

The theme of the lesson is childhood. It doesn't matter if your students are quite young, as most people, however old they are, have some childhood memories. The lesson also includes some expressions of past time. These will also appear in Lesson 38.

VOCABULARY

1 Aim: to present the expressions of time in the vocabulary box.

- Say the expressions of time aloud and ask the students to repeat them.
- Make sure everyone understands the expressions of time. Ask the students to put the expressions in two columns

Answers

in the past:	last month last week last year yesterday
in the present:	this year this month today this week

2 Aim: to present the meaning of the expressions.

- Simply ask the students to look at the sentence to help them remember what the time expressions mean. Check everyone remembers *day, week, month* and *year*. Tell them that *this* goes with present time, and *last* goes with past time.

3 Aim: to check the meaning of the expressions in the vocabulary box.

- Ask the students to complete these sentences to check they have understood the meaning of the expressions of time.

READING AND LISTENING

1 Aim: to practise reading for main ideas; to present the past simple form of some regular verbs.

- The headings constitute an extremely reduced summary of the paragraph. Ask the students to read the paragraphs and to match them with the headings

Answers
A Entertainment at home **B** Sport
C Sunday **D** Work

2 Aim: to practise using the past simple form of regular verbs.

- Explain that some of the sentences about Brian's childhood are wrong. Ask the students to rewrite them so they are right.

Answers
1 His brother played the piano.
2 He started running at university.
3 He visited his friends on Sunday afternoon.
4 His father worked in a bank.
5 They lived in (South) London.
6 They watched television in the evening.
7 He had Sunday lunch with his family.
8 His father travelled to work by train.

GRAMMAR

1 Aim: to focus on the form of the past simple regular verbs.

- Ask the students to read the information in the grammar box and then to do the exercises.
- Ask the students to look at the verbs in this lesson and to try and complete the rule.

Answer
You form the past simple of most regular verbs by adding *-ed*.

2 Aim: to focus on the form of the past simple regular verbs.

- Ask the students to do this on their own and then check their answers with the whole class.

Answer
1 listened played wanted started cooked visited watched stayed worked
2 danced lived
3 travelled

- Point out that the three categories refer to
  1 = verbs to which you add *-ed*
  2 = verbs to which you add *-d*
  3 = verbs which double the last consonant and to which you add *-ed*.

SOUNDS

1 Aim: to focus on the pronunciation of the endings of regular verbs in the past simple.

- Ask the students to listen and repeat the verbs as you play the tape.

2 Aim: to focus on the pronunciation of the endings of regular verbs in the past simple.

- Ask the students to put these verbs in the columns according to their pronunciation in the past simple.

Answers
/d/ lived arrived opened listened changed
/t/ liked cooked stopped danced helped
/ɪd/ started hated

- Play the tape and ask the students to check their answers.

LISTENING AND WRITING

1 Aim: to practise listening for specific information.

- Explain that the sentences with letters are summaries of what the speakers say. Ask the students to listen and put the letter corresponding to what the speakers say in the chart.

	Ben	Judy
Entertainment at home	h	j
Sport	d	c
Sunday	e	i
Holiday	a	b
Work	f	g

2 Aim: to practise speaking.

- Ask the students to check their answers in pairs.
- Play the tape and ask them to listen again.

3 Aim: to practise writing; to practise using regular verbs in the past simple.

- Ask the students to write sentences about themselves five or ten years ago using some of the verbs in the list.
- You may like to ask the students to do this for homework.

4 Aim: to practise speaking.

- Ask the students to find out what their partners said and tell the rest of the class.

2 Correct the sentences.

1 His sister played the piano.
2 He started running at school.
3 He visited his friends on Sunday evening.
4 His father worked in a shop.
5 They lived in the country.
6 They watched television in the morning.
7 He had Sunday lunch with his friends.
8 His father walked to work.

GRAMMAR

Past simple (4): regular verbs
/d/ **played stayed**
He played tennis. *They stayed at home.*
/t/ **worked watched**
My father worked in London. *He watched the cricket.*
/ɪd/ **wanted visited**
He wanted to play football. *He visited her friends.*

1 Complete the sentence.

You form the past simple of most regular verbs by adding ____.

2 Look for the past simple form of these verbs in *Reading and listening* activity 1, and write them down.

1 listen play want start cook visit watch stay work
2 dance live
3 travel

SOUNDS

1 Listen and repeat.

/d/ played stayed
/t/ worked finished
/ɪd/ wanted visited

2 Write these words in the correct column.

liked lived arrived cooked stopped danced started opened hated listened helped changed

/d/ /ɪd/ /t/

Now listen and check your answers.

LISTENING AND WRITING

1 Listen to two more people, Ben and Judy, talking about when they were children. Put the letter corresponding to what they say in the correct column of the chart.

	Ben	Judy
Entertainment at home		
Sport		
Sunday		
Holiday		
Work		

a 'We stayed in a small hotel in Devon.'
b 'We travelled around France.'
c 'I played tennis in my school team.'
d 'I played football with friends.'
e 'We often had friends for lunch.'
f 'My father was an engineer and he travelled a lot.'
g 'My father and my mother were doctors.'
h 'We played cards.'
i 'My mother cooked lunch.'
j 'I played the piano.'

2 Work in pairs and check your answers.

Now listen again.

3 Write five sentences about yourself ten years ago. Use some of these verbs.

live start play cook visit stay work finish watch listen dance

4 Work in pairs. Show your sentences to each other. Tell the rest of the class what your partner wrote.

37 Picasso didn't live in Spain

Past simple (5): negatives

1

VOCABULARY AND READING

1 Check the verbs you don't know in a dictionary.

be born start study live work paint finish die

2 Write the past simple of the verbs in 1.

3 Complete the sentences with the verbs in the past simple.

1 I ____ work at 9 am yesterday morning.
2 She ____ medicine at university.
3 We ____ in Paris for ten years.
4 Picasso ____ Guernica.
5 He ____ in a bank last year.
6 She ____ work at five yesterday afternoon.
7 Shakespeare ____ in 1564 and ____ in 1616.

4 Match these words with the photos.

sculpture painting

5 Work in pairs. You're going to read about Pablo Picasso. Do you know:

– who he was?
– when and where he was born?
– where he lived?
– what he did?
– where and when he died?

6 Read and check your answers to 5.

7 Tick (✔) the true statements.

1 Picasso was Spanish.
2 He was born in 1881.
3 He started to paint when he was fifteen.
4 He lived in Barcelona in 1904.
5 He worked in Madrid from 1904.
6 He finished Guernica in 1938.
7 He returned to Spain to live.
8 He died in 1972.

PICASSO, Pablo (1881 – 1973)

Pablo Picasso was a great Spanish artist. He made over 20,000 sculptures and paintings in his life. He was born in Malaga in 1881, and started to paint when he was ten. When he was fifteen, he studied at the Barcelona School of Fine Arts. From 1904 he lived and worked in Paris. Guernica was his most famous painting. He painted it in 1937 and finished it in two months. He didn't want the painting to be in Spain so it was in a gallery in New York for many years. You can see it now in the Prado Museum, in Madrid. For most of his life he didn't live in Spain. He lived in France and died there in 1973.

37

GENERAL COMMENTS

Picasso

You may like to tell your students more about the Spanish painter Picasso. He was also famous for his Cubist paintings and his paintings from his Blue and Rose periods. He left Spain after the Spanish Civil War and was determined not to live there again until the death of Franco, the Spanish Head of State. For this reason, his most famous painting, Guernica, was kept in New York. But in recent years, it has been returned to Spain and now can be seen in the Prado Museum in Madrid.

VOCABULARY AND READING

1 Aim: to present the words in the vocabulary box.

- The words are essential for the students to understand the passage, so ask them to look the words up in a dictionary or simply translate them for the students.

2 Aim: to check the past simple form of the verbs in the vocabulary box.

- Remind the students of the rules formulated in Lesson 36 concerning the past simple endings (Lesson 36, *Grammar* activity 2)

> **Answers**
> was born started studied lived worked painted finished died

3 Aim: to practise using the verbs in the vocabulary box.

- Do this activity orally with the whole class. Ask the students to complete the sentences with the verbs in the past simple.

> **Answers**
> 1 started 2 studied 3 lived 4 painted
> 5 worked 6 finished 7 was born/died

4 Aim: to present the words in the box.

- These two nouns are also important for the passage. Ask the students to match the words in the vocabulary box to the photos. Translate them if necessary.

5 Aim: to prepare for reading.

- You may need to give your students a lot of background information to Picasso if they are unsure who he was. First of all, ask the questions and find out how much they know.
- Then use the information at the top of this page to give the students further background knowledge about the painter.

6 Aim: to practise reading for specific information.

- Ask the students to read the passage and find the answers to the questions in activity 5.
- Ask the students to work in pairs and to check their answers.

> **Answers**
> 1 He was a great Spanish artist.
> 2 He was born in Malaga in 1881.
> 3 He lived in Paris.
> 4 He worked in Paris and painted Guernica.
> 5 He died in France in 1973.

7 Aim: to prepare for the presentation of the negative of past simple verbs; to practise reading for specific information.

- Ask the students to read the passage again and to tick the true statements.

> **Answers**
> 1 true 2 true 3 false 4 false
> 5 false 6 false 7 false 8 false

GRAMMAR

1 Aim: to focus on the form of negatives.

- Ask the students to read the information in the grammar box and then to do the exercises.
- Ask the students to look at the examples of negatives in the grammar box and in the passage, and then to complete the rule.

> **Answer**
> To form the past negative you write *didn't* before the infinitive of the verb.

2 Aim: to practise forming the negative of past simple verbs.

- Ask the students to write full sentences correcting the sentences in *Vocabulary and reading* activity 7.

> **Answers**
> 3 He didn't start to paint when he was fifteen. He started to paint when he was ten.
> 4 He didn't live in Barcelona in 1904. He lived in Paris.
> 5 He didn't work in Madrid from 1904. He worked in Paris.
> 6 He didn't finish Guernica in 1938. He finished it in 1937.
> 7 He didn't return to Spain to live. He stayed in France.
> 8 He didn't die in 1972. He died in 1973.

3 Aim: to practise forming the negative of past simple verbs.

- Ask the students to write sentences.
- Ask five or six students to read their sentences to the whole class.

SOUNDS

1 Aim: to focus on contrastive stress.

● Remind the students that when you correct information which is wrong, you stress both the wrong information and the correct information.

● Play the tape and ask the students to repeat the sentences.

2 Aim: to focus on contrastive stress.

● Ask the students to underline the wrong information and the correct information in the last three sentences in *Grammar* activity 2.

● Play the tape and ask the students to check if they have underlined the stressed words. Ask the students to repeat the sentences.

SPEAKING AND WRITING

1 Aim: to practise speaking; to prepare for writing.

● Ask the students to work in pairs and choose someone famous from their country, and about whom they know a lot. Ask them to make notes as suggested.

● You may like to give this activity for homework.

2 Aim: to practise speaking.

● Ask the students to work in groups. One student describes the famous person they made notes on in 1 without saying the name and the other students have to guess who it is. They should take it in turns to give their descriptions.

3 Aim: to practise writing.

● Ask the students to write a paragraph about the famous person.

● You may like to correct the paragraphs when they have finished.

4 Aim: to practise writing.

● Continue the writing practice by asking the students to write two true statements and one false statement about themselves.

● Encourage them to be as imaginative as they like about the false information!

5 Aim: to practise speaking.

● Ask the students to read their partner's sentences and to guess which is the false one.

● Place the information on the wall for everyone to see. Which is the most unlikely piece of false information?

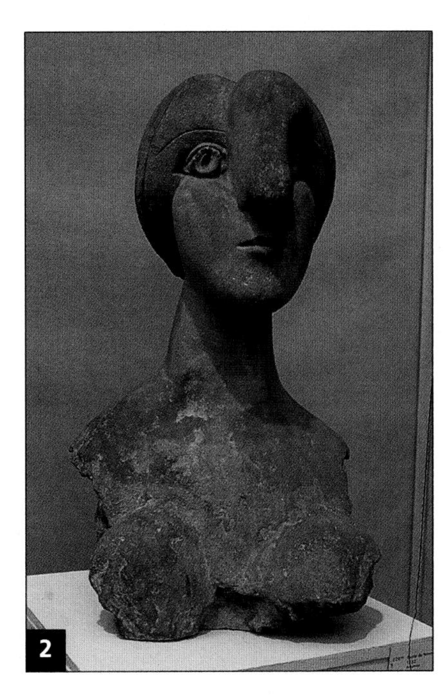
2

GRAMMAR

Past simple (5): negatives

I		
you		
he		
she	*didn't live*	*(= did not)*
it		
we		
they		

*He **didn't** want the painting to be in Spain.*
*He **didn't** live in Spain.*

1 Complete.

To form the past negative you write ____ before the infinitive of the verb.

2 Correct the false statements in *Vocabulary and reading* activity 7.

3 He didn't start to paint when he was fifteen. He started to paint when he was ten.

3 Write things you did and didn't do:

– yesterday – last week
– last month – last year

Yesterday I played football.
I didn't listen to the radio.

SOUNDS

1 Listen and repeat.

He didn't start to paint when he was fifteen. He started to paint when he was ten.

He didn't work in Madrid from 1904. He worked in Paris.

He didn't finish Guernica in 1938. He finished it in 1937.

2 Underline the stressed words in your other answers to *Grammar* activity 2.

Now listen and check. As you listen say the sentences aloud.

SPEAKING AND WRITING

1 Work in pairs. Think about the life of a famous person, and make notes on:

– when he or she was born – where he or she lived
– what he or she did – where and when he or she died

Atatürk, Kemal – born in 1881

2 Work in groups of three or four. Describe the famous person you made notes on in 1. Don't say his or her name. The others should guess who he/she is.

3 Write a paragraph about the famous person.

Kemal Atatürk was born in 1881.

4 Write two true sentences about your life, and one false sentence.

I was born in Italy.
I lived in Milan and Florence.
I painted the Last Supper.

5 Work in pairs. Show your partner your sentences. Can he or she guess which is the false one?

You didn't paint the Last Supper!

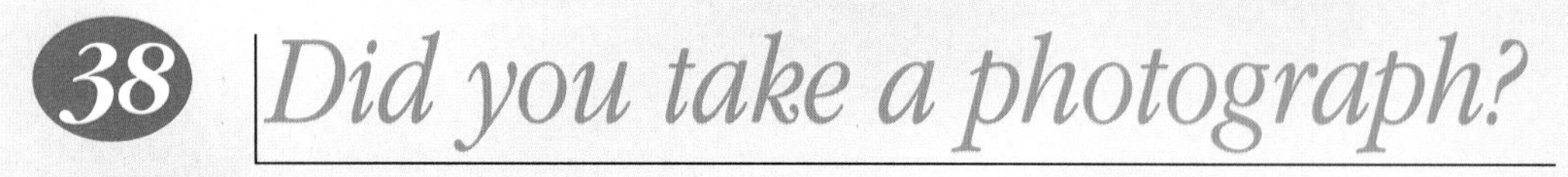

38 Did you take a photograph?

Past simple (6): *yes/no* questions and short answers

VOCABULARY

You are going to read three stories in this lesson. Check these words in the dictionary.

weather foggy dark bark village disappear dog cat climb

READING AND LISTENING

1 Read the conversation and decide where these sentences go.

a No, we didn't. c No, we didn't.
b Yes, he did. d No, he didn't.

STEVE When we started, the weather was fine. We walked about fifteen kilometres. About four hours later, we started to come home. Suddenly, the weather changed. It was very foggy. We were still in the mountains.

PHILIP Did you stay there?

STEVE (1) ____ . We walked for an hour but it was very cold and dark. We decided to stop walking and wait.

PHILIP Did you wait for a long time?

STEVE Well, no, we didn't. You see, after about two or three minutes, something happened. A dog, a big black dog suddenly appeared out of the fog. He had red eyes. Then he barked at us.

PHILIP Did he want to help you?

STEVE (2) ____ . So we walked for two hours behind the dog. Then we arrived back at the village.

PHILIP Did the dog stay with you?

STEVE (3) ____ . When we arrived at the village, he disappeared into the mountains.

PHILIP Did you take a photograph?

STEVE (4) ____ .

2 Work in pairs and check your answers.

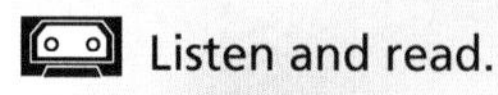

Now listen and check.

SOUNDS

Listen and read.

1 Did you stay there?
2 Did he want to help you?
3 Did the dog stay with you?
4 Did you take a photograph?

Now listen and repeat the sentences.

38

GENERAL COMMENTS

Stories

This lesson contains three stories about animals. Some of the most effective teaching material available can be found in stories, which can create genuine motivation among the students. It's important to remember that a story must not be too long. If it is, it should be cut into manageable parts, up to 150 words at this level. There also needs to be tasks which don't simply test the students' comprehension but which help them get to the heart of the story, such as the plot, the characters, the imagery. The whole of the film and novel industries are based on our love of stories, and this pleasure needs to be catered for in the language classroom.

VOCABULARY

Aim: to present the words in the vocabulary box.

- Make sure the students understand the meaning of these words. Ask them to look them up in a dictionary or translate them.

READING AND LISTENING

1 Aim: to practise reading and understanding text organisation; to prepare for listening; to present *yes/no* questions and short answers.

- Explain to the students that they are going to read a story about a mysterious incident in the mountains. Ask them to decide where the sentences go in the conversation.

Answers
1c 2b 3d 4a

2 Aim: to practise listening .

- [cassette] Ask the students to listen and check their answers to activity 1 as you play the tape.

SOUNDS

1 Aim: to present and practise the pronunciation of *yes/no* questions.

- [cassette] Ask the students to listen and follow the sentences.
- Ask the students to listen and repeat the sentences.

GRAMMAR

1 Aim: to focus on the form of *yes/no* questions.

- Ask the students to read the information in the grammar box and then to do the exercises.
- Ask the students to look at the examples of *yes/no* questions in the conversation and in the grammar box and to complete the rule about the form of *yes/no* questions.

Answers
You form *yes/no* questions with *did* + subject + infinitive.

2 Aim: to focus on the form of *yes/no* questions.

- Ask the students to match the questions and the answers.

Answers
1e 2d 3a 4c 5b

3 Aim: to practise using short answers.

- Ask the students to complete the sentences.

Answers
1 Yes, I did.
2 No, she didn't.
3 Yes, they did.
4 Did he say hello? No, he didn't.
5 Did I answer the question? Yes, you did.
6 Did I take your keys? No, you didn't.

4 Aim: to focus on word order in *yes/no* questions.

- Ask the students to put the words in the correct order and make questions

Answers
1 Did you go to the cinema last night?
2 Did you watch television yesterday?
3 Did you see your friends last weekend?
4 Did you go swimming last week?
5 Did you go to school last week?
6 Did you bring your books today?

5 Aim: to practise using short answers.

- Ask the students to work in pairs and ask and answer the questions in activity 4.

READING AND WRITING

1 Aim: to practise reading for specific information; to practise using *yes/no* questions and short answers.

- Ask the students to read the passage and find the answers to the questions.

Answers
1 Yes, she did.
2 No, it didn't.
3 No, she didn't.
4 Yes, she did.
5 No, she didn't.
6 Yes, it did.

2 Aim: to practise predicting.

- Explain to the students that they are going to read a story about a faithful dog, but they are going to answer questions about it before they read it. In fact, the questions are simply a way of stimulating motivation to read.

- Ask the students to guess the answers to the questions. Go through the questions with the whole class.

3 Aim: to practise writing.

- Ask the students to write as much of the story as they can without having read it. You'll be surprised by how much they can predict accurately.

4 Aim: to practise reading for specific information.

- In activity 3, the students have effectively created their own reading comprehension check for this activity. Ask them to read the story in Communication activity 37 and to correct the versions they wrote in activity 3.

- You may like to ask the students to do this for homework.

GRAMMAR

Past simple (6): *yes/no* questions and short answers

	I		*Yes, you did.*	*No, you didn't.*
	you		*Yes, I did.*	*No, I didn't.*
	he		*Yes, he did.*	*No, he didn't.*
Did	*she*	*take a photo?*	*Yes, she did.*	*No, she didn't.*
	we		*Yes, we did.*	*No, we didn't.*
	they		*Yes, they did.*	*No, they didn't.*

Did you take a photo? No, we didn't.

1 Complete this sentence.

You form *yes/no* questions with ____ + subject (*I, you, he* etc.) + ____.

2 Match questions and answers.

1 Did you follow the dog? a Yes, you did.
2 Did she get lost? b Yes, he did.
3 Did I say hello? c No, they didn't.
4 Did they get lost? d No, she didn't.
5 Did he want to follow him? e Yes, I did.

3 Complete the questions and answers.

1 Did you sleep well? Yes, ____.
2 Did she call you? No, ____ .
3 Did they come by train? Yes, ____.
4 ____ he say hello? No, ____.
5 ____ I answer the question? Yes, ____.
6 ____ I take your keys? No, ____.

4 Write the questions.

1 you go cinema last did to night the?
2 did watch you yesterday television?
3 you did see friends your last weekend?
4 week you swimming did last go ?
5 school last you go to did week?
6 today your you did bring books?

5 Work in pairs. Answer the questions in 4.

1 Did you go to the cinema last night? No, I didn't.

READING AND WRITING

1 Read and answer the questions.

Barbara Paule lived in Pennsylvania with her cat, Muddy Water. On 23 June, 1985, she was in her car with the cat in Dayton, Ohio. The car stopped and the cat climbed out of the window and disappeared. She was very unhappy and went home to Pennsylvania. In June 1988, a cat arrived at the door of her house. She washed it and then saw it was Muddy Water. The cat came home after three years and 800 kilometres.

1 Did Barbara Paule live in Pennsylvania?
2 Did the cat climb out of a window at home?
3 Did Barbara find the cat in Dayton?
4 Did Barbara go home to Pennsylvania?
5 Did she know the cat at the door?
6 Did Muddy Water return home?

2 Read these questions which come from a story about a dog. Try to answer the questions before you read the story.

1 Was Dr Ueno a teacher at a university in Tokyo?
2 Did he walk with his dog, Hachiko, to the station every day?
3 Did Hachiko then walk home?
4 Did he return in the evening to meet Dr Ueno?
5 Did Dr Ueno arrive one day?
6 Did Hachiko wait for him?
7 Did Hachiko return to the station and wait for his friend every day?
8 Did he do this for nine years?

3 Now try to write as much of the story as you can, using your answers to the questions in 1.

Dr Ueno was a teacher at a university in Tokyo.

4 Turn to Communication activity 37 on page 99 and read the story. Correct the version you wrote in 3.

39 We went to New York!

Past simple (7): questions; irregular verbs

VOCABULARY AND SOUNDS

1 Listen and repeat.

bill tickets receipts brochure

2 Work in pairs. Point and say.

3 Write the present tense of these verbs.

drank spent got left flew saw
took ate sat went bought thought

drink ...

Now work in pairs and check your answers.

4 Work in pairs. Check the meaning of the verb in the dictionary.

5 Listen and repeat the verbs in 3.

Brochure
Visit the Statue of Liberty

JOE ALLEN
RESTAURANT BILL

Drinks	$23.00
Food	$40.00
TOTAL	$63.00

Bloomingdale's

RECEIPT

Lady's Jacket	$70.00
TOTAL	$70.00

Bloomingdale's

RECEIPT

Man's Seiko Watch	$150.00
TOTAL	$150.00

FEB 9TH
8.00 PM
$40.00
CIRCLE
E41

MAJESTIC THEATRE
247 W. 44TH ST. BROADWAY
The Phantom of the Opera
Saturday February 9th
8.00 PM

CIRCLE
E40
Saturday February 9th
8.00 PM

Jo's Taxis

Receipt

TO: *Broadway (Majestic Theatre)*	*$30.00*

FLYAWAYS LONDON
WALTON/DAVID MR
LONDON TERM 4 LGW
NEW YORK JFK

LISTENING AND READING

1 Listen and read the letter.

David and I went to New York for the weekend! We flew from London airport and arrived in New York at 12 am on Saturday. We took a taxi from the airport to our hotel near Central Park and then went for lunch at Joe Allen, a famous restaurant on Broadway. The food was great!

In the afternoon, we went shopping in Bloomingdale's (a very famous shop in New York). I bought a lovely red jacket and David got a new watch.

In the evening we went to a theatre on Broadway and saw The Phantom of the Opera. A wonderful day!

2 Write short answers to the questions.

1 Where did David and Kate go for the weekend?
2 When did they arrive?
3 How did they get to the hotel?
4 Where did they go for lunch?
5 What did they do in the afternoon?
6 What did they buy?
7 What did they see in the evening?

39

GENERAL COMMENTS

Past simple

This is the last lesson covering the past simple. It focuses on irregular verbs. It may be a suitable moment to show the list of irregular verbs on page 108. Do emphasise that to a large extent, the forms of irregular verbs have to be learnt as vocabulary items, rather than as grammatical structures.

VOCABULARY AND SOUNDS

1 Aim: to present the pronunciation of the words in the vocabulary box.

- The words in the vocabulary box can be used to talk about travel and sightseeing situations. Ask the students to listen and repeat the words as you play the tape.

- Check the pronunciation of the words individually and as a whole class.

2 Aim: to present the meaning of the words in the vocabulary box.

- Ask the students to look at the photos and match them to the words in the vocabulary box. Ask them to say the words as they point.

3 Aim: to focus on the form of the verbs.

- Explain that these verbs have an irregular past simple. Ask the students to say what verbs they look like.

Answers
drink spend get leave fly see
take eat sit go buy think

- Ask the students to work in pairs and check their answers.

4 Aim: to focus on the meaning of the verbs.

- Ask the students to check the meaning of any verbs they are not sure of in the dictionary.

5 Aim: to present the pronunciation of the past simple of the verbs in activity 3.

- Ask the students to listen and repeat the verbs as you play the tape.

LISTENING AND READING

1 Aim: to practise reading for specific information; to prepare for the presentation of irregular past simple forms; to present *wh*- questions.

- Ask the students to read and listen to the diary entry.

2 Aim: to practise reading for specific information.

- Ask the students to look at the diary entry again and write short answers to the questions.

Answers
1 New York 2 12 am 3 by taxi 4 Joe Allen
5 shopping 6 a red jacket and a watch
7 Phantom of the Opera

3 Aim: to deduce information.

- Ask the students to look at the various documents and write complete answers to the questions.

Answers
1 - 0400 (4 o'clock a.m.)
2 - 8 hours
3 - $70.00
4 - $150.00
5 - by taxi
6 - circle, E40/E41
7 - $40.00 each

4 Aim: to check comprehension.

- Ask the students to work in pairs and check their answers to the questions.

GRAMMAR

1 Aim: to focus on the form of the irregular verbs in the past simple.

- Ask the students to read the information in the grammar box and then to do the exercises.

- Ask the students to write the past tense of these verbs.

Answers
went thought bought saw flew took got

2 Aim: to focus on the form of irregular verbs in the past simple.

- Ask the students to match the infinitive and the irregular past simple form.

Answers
run - ran find - found bring - brought
do - did come - came give - gave
read - read (check the pronunciation)
hear - heard say - said make - made
stand - stood wear - wore

3 Aim: to practise using irregular verbs in the past simple.

- Ask the students to write complete answers to *Reading and listening* activity 2.

WRITING AND SPEAKING

1 Aim: to practise writing; to practise past simple *wh*- questions.

- Ask the students to read the passage and then to write questions for the missing information using the question word prompts.

- Ask the students to work in pairs and check their answers.

Answers
1 When did they leave their hotel?
2 What did they take to the airport?
3 Where did they go by boat?
4 How long did they spend there?
5 What did they buy for lunch?
6 Where did they eat them?
7 How long did they sit in the park?
8 Where did they go in the afternoon?
9 What did they see?
10 What did they take to the airport?
11 When did they get the plane?
12 Where did they fly back to?

2 Aim: to practise speaking.

- Ask the students to follow the instructions to the Communication activities. They should work in pairs to find the answers to the questions they wrote in activity 1.

3 Aim: to practise speaking.

- Ask the students to work in pairs and ask and answer the questions they wrote in 1 to complete the passage.

4 Aim: to practise writing.

- Ask the students to write a short paragraph about a special weekend.

- You may like to ask them to do this for homework.

3 Look at the items in *Vocabulary and sounds*, activity 1. Write complete answers to the questions.

1 When did the plane leave London?
2 How long did the journey take?
3 How much did Kate spend on her jacket?
4 How much did David spend on his watch?
5 How did they get to the theatre?
6 Where did they sit?
7 How much were the tickets?

4 Work in pairs and check your answers to 3.

GRAMMAR

Past simple (7): irregular verbs

fly – flew take – took go – went buy – bought
get – got see – saw drink – drank spend – spent
leave – left eat – ate sit – sat think – thought

Questions

Where did they go for the weekend?
When did they arrive?
What did they do in the afternoon?
How did they get to the hotel?
How long did the journey take?
How much did David spend?

1 Write the past tense of these verbs.

go think buy see fly take get

went

2 Match the present and past of these verbs.

run find bring do come give read hear say make stand wear

did came gave read ran found brought heard said made stood wore

3 Write complete answers to *Listening and reading* activity 2.

They went to New York for the weekend.

WRITING AND SPEAKING

1 Read the next part of the letter and write questions for the missing information.

On Sunday morning we left our hotel at (1) *when* _____ in the morning and took our (2) *what* _____ to the airport. Then we went to (3) *where* _____ by boat. We spent (4) *how long* _____ there and then we returned to Manhattan. We bought some (5) *what* _____ for lunch and ate them in (6) *where* _____. We sat in the park for about (7) *how long* _____. In the afternoon, we went to the (8) *where* _____ and saw a (9) *what* _____. By now it was time to go to the airport for our flight home, so we took (10) *what* _____. We got the plane at (11) *when* _____ and flew back to (12) *where* _____. The end of a wonderful weekend!

Now work in pairs and check your answers.

1 When did they leave their hotel?

2 Work in pairs.

Student A: Turn to Communication activity 6 on page 92.

Student B: Turn to Communication activity 39 on page 100.

3 Work in pairs. Ask and answer the questions you wrote in 1 and complete the passage.

4 Write about a special weekend.

Last month I went to Paris.

40 The end of the world?

Tense review: present simple, present continuous, past simple

GRAMMAR

Tense review
Present simple
They work very hard.
Present continuous
What's happening?
Past simple
I worked all my life on the railways.

1 Name the tense.

1 He speaks English.
2 We had dinner in a restaurant.
3 She's wearing a black dress.
4 They don't take credit cards.
5 He's writing a postcard.
6 I didn't hear you.

2 Choose the tense.

1 Ten years ago we (live) in a house in the country.
2 (Have) you dinner at the moment?
3 When (arrive) she arrive home last night?
4 What time (be) it now?
5 We usually (go) to the cinema at the weekend.
6 No, he's away at the moment. He (lie) on a beach in the South of France.

VOCABULARY

Listen and point.

waiting room ticket office platform passenger railway

READING AND LISTENING

1 Read and listen to part one of *The end of the world*. Answer the questions.

' My name is Joseph Finch. I live in a house in the country. My wife died a few years ago, and the children? Well, I don't see much of the children. They work very hard, they don't have much time for their father.

But, I've got a beautiful house. It 's an old railway station. It's got a ticket office, a waiting room and a platform. But there aren't any trains, oh no. There weren't many passengers around here so they closed the station when the last train left thirty years ago.

I worked all my life on the railways. When I was sixty-five, I stopped work, but I still liked trains so, when I saw the old station for sale,I bought it and made it my home.

I made a beautiful garden full of flowers where, in the past, the trains ran. My kitchen was the old ticket office, my living room was the waiting room, and the platform has got a table and chair where, on summer mornings, I have breakfast. In fact, I'm sitting in the garden now. It's quiet and peaceful.'

40

GENERAL COMMENTS

Revision and review

This is the last lesson in *Reward Starter* and the language focus is a review of the tenses taught in the book: present simple, present continuous and past simple. If you are going on to use *Reward Elementary*, you will find that the same tenses and other basic structures will be covered again within the first twenty or so lessons. As it should now be clear, the course design in the *Reward* series is based a careful cyclical organisation which revises and reviews all the structures it presents in a systematic way.

The end of the world?

The end of the world is a carefully graded story which makes allusions to the Cuba missile crisis in 1962. At this time, there was a very strong fear that another war would break out, in which the two superpowers would use nuclear weapons on each other and bring about the end of the world.

GRAMMAR

1 Aim: to review the tenses taught in *Reward* Starter.

- Ask the students to read the information in the grammar box and then to do the exercises.
- Ask the students to identify the tenses.

Answers
1 present simple 2 past simple
3 present continuous 4 present simple
5 present continuous 6 past simple

2 Aim: to review the tenses taught in *Reward* Starter.

- Ask the students to choose the best sense.

Answers
1 Ten years ago we lived in a house in the country.
2 Are you having dinner at the moment?
3 When did she arrive home last night?
4 What time is it now?
5 We usually go to the cinema at the weekend?
6 No, he's away at the moment. He's lying on a beach in the South of France.

VOCABULARY

1 Aim: to pre-teach some important vocabulary; to present the words in the vocabulary box.

- Ask the students to listen to the tape and point to the words in the illustration.

READING AND LISTENING

1 Aim: to practise reading and listening for main ideas.

● This activity is designed to extract the main story line in this part of the story. Ask the students to read and listen then answer the questions.

Answers
1 In a house in the country 2 No, he doesn't 3 No, he isn't. 4 Yes, he has. 5 an old railway station 6 thirty years ago. 7 railway worker 8 when he was sixty-five 9 the old ticket office 10 the old waiting room 11 Yes, he has.

2 Aim: to practise reading for text organisation.

● Ask the students to read the sentences and to put them in order.

Answers
d e c b a

3 Aim: to practise listening and checking.

● Play the tape and ask the students to listen and check their answers to activity 2.

4 Aim: to predict the next part of the story.

● Ask the students to think about the next part of the story by talking about their answers to the questions in pairs.

5 Aim: to practise reading and checking.

● Ask the students to read the rest of the story and check their predictions in activity 4.

6 Aim: to practise reading and enjoying the story.

● At this stage, the students should be reading with motivation and should not need any tasks to contribute towards their comprehension. Ask them to read the rest of the story in the Communication activity.

7 Aim: to practise speaking.

● Ask the students to talk about a possible explanation for the story. You may like to tell them about the Cuban missile crisis at this point. See the General comments at the start of this lesson.

1 Where does Joseph Finch live?
2 Does he live in a flat?
3 Is he married?
4 Has he got any children?
5 Describe his house.
6 When did they close the station?
7 What was Joseph's job?
8 When did he stop working?
9 In the past what was his kitchen?
10 What was the living room?
11 Has he got a garden?

2 Look at the next part of the story. Read the paragraphs and put them in order.

a 'The man stood by a poster. It said, "THE END OF THE WORLD?"'

b 'They all wore clothes from thirty years ago. "This is very strange," I thought. I saw an old taxi and two or three old cars, and a man selling newspapers outside the station.'

c 'Some people got out of the train and said hello to their friends, and others got in and said goodbye.'

d 'But one day, a strange thing happened. On the night of 28 October 1992 after a cold day in my garden, I had dinner, read my book and then I went to bed. I was asleep when suddenly I heard a noise like a train.'

e 'I got up and looked out of the window and saw a train in the garden. "What's happening? Am I dreaming?" I said. There were passengers on the platform.'

3 Listen and check your answer to 1.

4 Work in pairs and answer the questions. What do you think happened next?

1 Did Joseph Finch go back to sleep?
2 Did he get dressed?
3 Did he go downstairs?

5 Read and check.

'So I got dressed, ran downstairs and went outside. But when I got outside, no one was there. 'Hello!" I said. But no one replied. I walked up and down the platform. Then I went back inside. The ticket office was my kitchen again, and the waiting room was my dining room. The garden was full of flowers and everything was quiet and peaceful. "It was a dream," I thought.'

6 Turn to Communication activity 42 on page 101.

7 Work in pairs. Can you think of an explanation?

WAITING ROOM

Passenger

Platform

Railway

Progress check

1 Work in pairs. Look at all the vocabulary boxes in Reward Starter. Find:

– three words which you like

– three words which you don't like

– three words which you can use to talk about yourself

– three words which you often see in your country

– three words which sound nice

2 Tick (✔) the correct answers.

1 *September is*	
a a month	☐
b a day of the week	☐
c a job	☐
2 *A bank is*	
a a word to describe how you feel	☐
b a place where you put money	☐
c a drink	☐
3 *A car is*	
a a means of transport	☐
b an item of clothing	☐
c food	☐
4 *A detective is*	
a a job	☐
b a place	☐
c a member of the family	☐
5 *A dishwasher is*	
a a place of entertainment	☐
b an object you see at home	☐
c something you do on holiday	☐
6 *Mrs is*	
a a form of address for a married woman	☐
b a form of address for a single woman	☐
c a day of the week	☐

3 Look at the words in Lessons 31 – 40 again. Choose words which are useful to you and write them in your *Wordbank* in the Practice Book.

GRAMMAR

1 Write questions about what people are doing.

1 You/5th January?

2 Pete/5th November?

3 Jane/August?

4 Phil and Tim/this evening?

5 Ken/this weekend?

6 Julia and Philippa/this afternoon?

What are you doing on the fifth of January?

2 Answer the questions you wrote in 1.

1 fly to Thailand
2 have a party
3 stay with friends in Paris
4 go to the cinema
5 play football
6 go to an exhibition

1 We're flying to Thailand.

3 Write questions using the past simple.

1 you/thirsty?
2 he/dead?
3 you/hungry?
4 they/tired?
5 she/unhappy?
6 you/bored?

1 Were you thirsty?

4 Write answers to the questions in 3.

1 yes 2 no 3 yes 4 no 5 yes 6 no

1 Yes, I was.

5 Write sentences saying what people had or didn't have in the past.

1 televisions (✔)
2 videos (✗)
3 dishwashers (✗)
5 telephones (✔)
6 computers (✗)
7 cars (✔)

1 They had televisions. 2 They didn't have videos.

Progress check 31–40

GENERAL COMMENTS

You can work through this Progress check in the order shown, or concentrate on areas which may have caused difficulty in Lessons 31 to 40. You can also let the students choose the activities they would like or feel the need to do.

VOCABULARY

1 Aim: to revise the vocabulary presented in *Reward* Starter; to present some useful vocabulary categorisation techniques.

- These categories present a way of personalising the vocabulary acquisition process. Encourage the students to spend some time looking for words in the book.
- Ask the students to tell the rest of the class which words they have chosen.

2 Aim: to revise the vocabulary taught in *Reward* Starter.

Answers
1a 2b 3a 4a 5b 6a

3 Aim: to revise the vocabulary taught in Lessons 31 to 40.

- If the students have done this activity in every Progress check, they will now have a good collection of words in their *Wordbanks*. You may like to take this opportunity to ask them to show you the *Wordbanks* in their Practice Books.

GRAMMAR

1 Aim: to revise questions in the present continuous.

1 What are you doing on the fifth of January?
2 What's Pete doing on the fifth of November?
3 What's Jane doing in August?
4 What are Phil and Tim doing this evening?
5 What's Ken doing this weekend?
6 What are Julia and Philippa doing this afternoon?

2 Aim: to revise the present continuous.

Answers
1 I'm/We're flying to Thailand.
2 He's having a party.
3 She's staying with friends in Paris.
4 They're going to the cinema.
5 He's playing football.
6 They're going to an exhibition.

3 Aim: to revise past simple *yes/no* questions with *be.*

Answers
1 Were you thirsty?
2 Was he dead?
3 Were you hungry?
4 Were they tired?
5 Was she unhappy?
6 Were you bored?

4 Aim: to revise short answers with *be.*

Answers
1 Yes, I was. 2 No, he wasn't
3 Yes, I was./Yes, we were. 4 No, they weren't.
5 Yes, she was. 6 No, I wasn't./No, we weren't.

5 Aim: to revise affirmative and negative of past simple *have.*

Answers
1 They had televisions.
2 They didn't have videos.
3 They didn't have dishwashers.
4 The had telephones.
5 They didn't have computers.
6 They had cars.

6 Aim: to revise the past simple of regular and irregular verbs.

Answers
played worked painted was born
studied took went bought saw lived

7 Aim: to revise the past simple of regular and irregular verbs.

Answers
1 saw 2 lived 3 studied 4 painted 5 were born

8 Aim: to revise *yes/no* questions in the past simple.

Answers
1 Did you take a photo?
2 Did he go home?
3 Did she get lost?
4 Did you go out last night?
5 Did they see their friends at the weekend?
6 Did I answer your question?

9 Aim: to revise short answers in the past simple.

Answers
1 Yes, I did. 2 No, he didn't. 3 Yes, she did.
4 No, I didn't./No, we didn't. 5 Yes, they did.
6 No, you didn't.

10 Aim: to revise *wh*- questions in the past simple.

Answers
1 What did you do last weekend?
2 Where did you go on holiday last year?
3 Who did you see yesterday?
4 What did you have for breakfast today?
5 What did you buy at the weekend?
6 When did you get home last night?

11 Aim: to revise irregular form of the past simple.

● Ask the students to write true answers to the questions in activity 10.

SOUNDS

1 Aim: to focus on the difference between /ɪ/ and /iː/.

● Ask the students to listen and tick the words they hear.

● Ask the students to say all the words aloud.

2 Aim: to practise the pronunciation of /ɑ/, /əʊ/ and /ɔː/.

● Play the tape and ask the students to listen and repeat the words.

LISTENING

1 Aim: to listen and practise word boundaries.

● This activity focuses on the boundary where one word stops and another word starts. Ask the students to listen and mark / when they hear something extra. Play the tape.

Answers
Yesterday, all my troubles seemed / far away,
Now it looks as though they're here to stay,
/ I believe in yesterday.
Suddenly, I'm not / the man I used to be,
There's a shadow / over me,
Oh yesterday came suddenly
/ She had to go, I don't know
She wouldn't say
I said something /, now I long for yesterday.
Yesterday, love was / an easy game to play
Now I need a place to hide away
Oh, I believe in yesterday.
Why she had to go I don't know
She wouldn't say
I said something wrong, now I long for
Yesterday.
Yesterday, love was such an / game to play,
Now I need a / to hide away
Oh, I believe in yesterday.

2 Aim: to provide an opportunity for a second listening.

● Ask the students to try and remember what the missing words were.

● You may like to explain some new words, but don't try to explain them all as there will be too many.

● Play the song again.

6 Write the past simple of these verbs.

play work paint be born study take
go buy see live

7 Complete the sentences with the past simple form of the verbs in 6.

1 I _____ a good film at the cinema last night.
2 He ____ in London for a year.
3 She ____ English at school.
4 Picasso ____ Guernica.
5 They're French. They ____ in Paris.

8 Write questions.

1 you/take a photo?
2 he/go home?
3 she/get lost?
4 you/go out last night?
5 they/see their friends at the weekend?
6 I/answer your question?

1 Did you take a photo?

9 Write answers to the questions you wrote in 8.

1 yes 2 no 3 yes 4 no 5 yes 6 no

10 Write questions.

1 what/you do/last weekend?
2 where/you go/on holiday last year?
3 who/you see/yesterday?
4 what/you have for breakfast/today?
5 what/you buy/at the weekend?
6 when/you get home/last night?

1 What did you do last weekend?

11 Write answers to the questions in 10.

1 I went shopping on Saturday.

SOUNDS

1 Listen and tick (✔) the word you hear.

1 hit heat
2 sit seat
3 bit beat
4 sin seen
5 bin been
6 ill eel

2 Listen and repeat.

/ɑ/ dog orange shop stop
/əʊ/ poster boat hotel brochure go
/ɔː/ walk hall born

LISTENING

1 You're going to hear the song *Yesterday* by the Beatles. There are some words missing in the lines below. Listen and mark a line, like this /, when you hear an extra word.

Yesterday, all my troubles seemed far away,
Now it looks as though they're here to stay,
I believe in yesterday.
Suddenly, I'm not the man I used to be,
There's a shadow over me,
Oh yesterday came suddenly.
She had to go, I don't know
She wouldn't say.
I said something, now I long for yesterday.
Yesterday, love was an easy game to play,
Now I need a place to hide away,
Oh, I believe in yesterday.
Why she had to go I don't know
She wouldn't say
I said something wrong, now I long for
yesterday.
Yesterday, love was such an game to play,
Now I need a to hideaway
Oh, I believe in yesterday.

2 Work in pairs and check your answers. Can you remember what the extra words are?

Now listen again and check.

Communication activities

Lesson 4

Vocabulary and sounds, activity 5

Student A: Ask Student B to spell these words:

hello doctor student seven listen say

Now turn back to page 10.

Lesson 4

Listening and speaking, activity 3

Student A: You're Henry Schwarzkopf and you're a doctor. Here's some more information.

Ms Fiona Pink – teacher

Now turn back to page 11.

Lesson 5

Writing and speaking, activity 2

Student A: Read the information.

Terry Crystal is an actor.
The singer is from St Petersburg.
The secretary is Italian.

Now turn back to page 13.

Lesson 10

Functions, activity 1

Student A: Look at the words for these things.

sandwiches pizza telephone

Now turn back to page 23.

Lesson 11

Functions and grammar, activity 3

Student A: Ask Student B how much 1-3 are and write the price. Then answer Student B's questions about 4-6.

1 jeans	4 sweater	£25.99
2 jacket	5 shirt	£30.00
3 shoes	6 skirt	£45.99

Now turn back to page 27.

Lesson 39

Writing and speaking, activity 2

Student A: Read the passage and answer the questions you wrote in 1.

On Sunday morning, we left our hotel at (1) *eight o'clock* in the morning and took our (2) - to the airport. Then, we went to the (3) *Statue of Liberty* by boat. We spent (4) - there and then returned to Manhattan. We bought some (5) *sandwiches* for lunch and ate them in (6) - . We sat in the park for about (7) *two hours*. In the afternoon, we went to the (8) - and saw a (9) *film*. By now it was time to go to the airport for our flight home, so we took a (10) -. We got the plane at (11) *midnight* and flew home to (12) -. The end of a wonderful weekend!

Now turn to page 87.

Lesson 12

Speaking and writing, activity 1

Student A: Ask Student B where these objects are and put a cross (✗) on the picture on the right.

bag keys personal stereo wallet

Now answer Student B's questions.

Now turn back to page 29.

8 *Lesson 14*

Reading and speaking, activity 2

Student A: Match the questions with the missing information, then ask and answer to complete the E-mail. If you don't know how to spell the names, ask *How do you spell ...?*

What's her name? *What's her father's name?*

What's she like? *What's her sister's name?*

How old is her brother?

Dear Brad,

Thanks for your E-mail.

My name is (1)____. I'm an English teacher and I'm twenty-three years old. I've got (2)____ hair and (3)____ eyes. My family is from London.

My mother's name is Pippa and she's a teacher. My father's name is (4) ____. He's a doctor. He's got blue eyes, but he hasn't got any hair!

I've got a brother and a sister. My brother James is an engineer, too! He's (5)____ years old and he's got fair hair (he's very good-looking)! My sister's name is (6)____. She's eleven; she's also got (7)____ hair and (8)____ eyes.

Write soon,

Sue

Now turn back to page 33.

9 *Lesson 17*

Listening and reading, activity 3

Student A: Listen and find out what time they have breakfast in Russia, lunch in Hong Kong and dinner in Mexico.

Now turn back to page 39.

10 *Lesson 5*

Writing and speaking, activity 2

Student B: Read the information.

The actor is from Los Angeles.

Mischa Godonov is Russian.

The secretary is from Naples.

Now turn back to page 13.

11 *Lesson 19*

Vocabulary and sounds, activity 3

Student A: Look at the words for these sports.

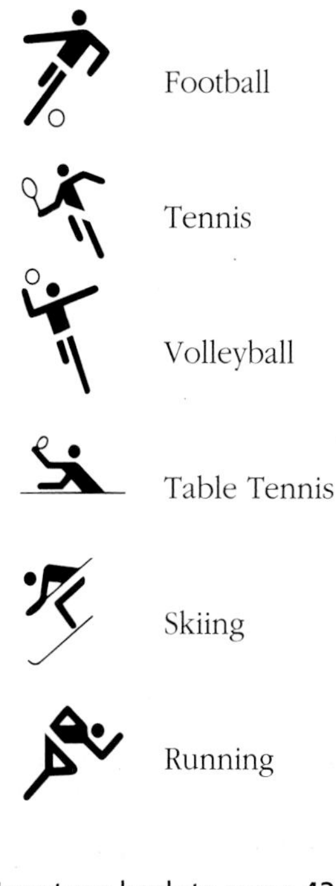

Now turn back to page 42.

12 *Lesson 21*

Vocabulary and sounds, activity 2

Look at the photos of different means of transport and check you know what the words mean.

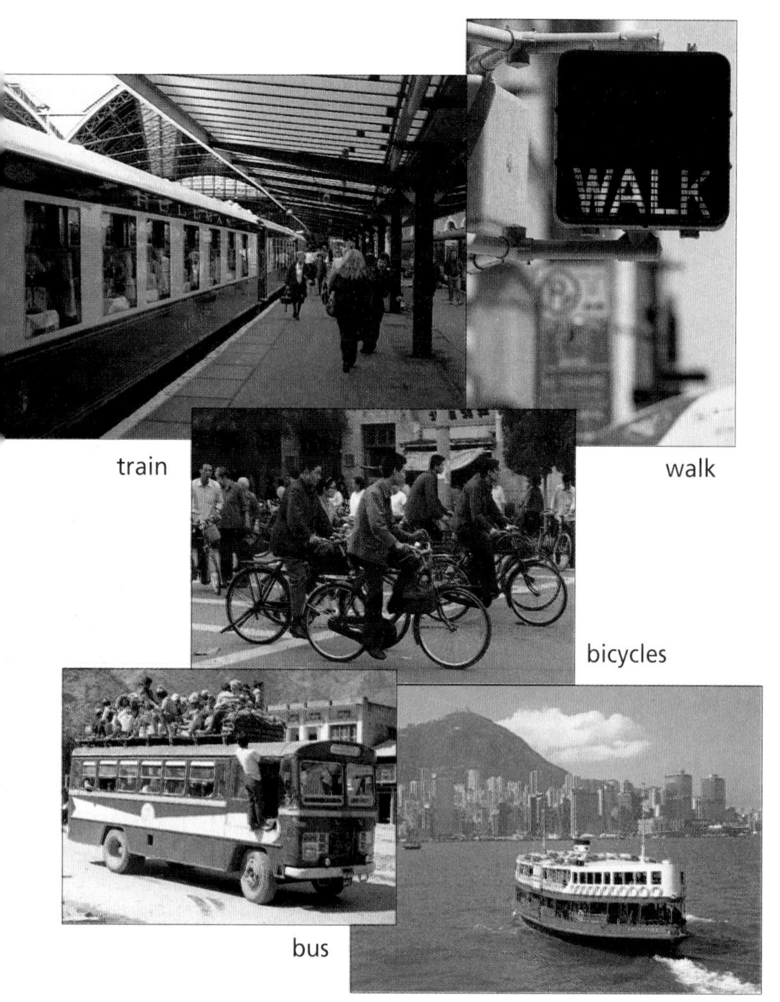

Now turn back to page 48.

13 *Lesson 22*

Vocabulary and sounds, activity 2

Student A: Look at the words for these things.

Now turn back to page 50.

14 *Lesson 22*

Grammar, activity 1

Student A: Listen and answer.

What food do they eat in Morocco?

What do they drink in India?

What do they have for breakfast in India?

Now turn back to page 51.

15 *Lesson 4*

Vocabulary and sounds, activity 5

Student B: Ask Student A to spell these words:

goodbye teacher singer eight repeat write

Now turn back to page 10.

16 *Lesson 4*

Listening and speaking, activity 3

Student B: You're Adam Hackett and you're a journalist. Here's some more information.

Mr Dave Dingle – student

Now turn back to page 11.

17 *Lesson 10*

Functions, activity 1

Student B: Look at the words for these things.

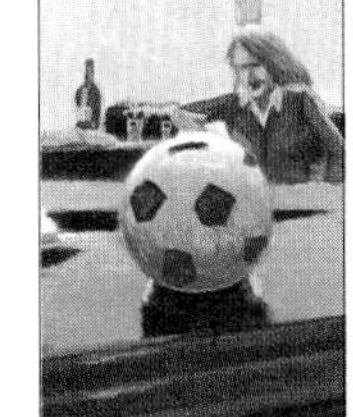

television taxis football

Now turn back to page 23.

18 *Lesson 11*

Functions and grammar, activity 3

Student B: Answer Student A's questions about 1-3. Then, ask Student A how much 4-6 are and write the price.

1 jeans £20.00	4 sweater
2 jacket £70.00	5 shirt
3 shoes £34.99	6 skirt

Now turn back to page 27.

19 *Lesson 12*

Speaking and writing, activity 1

Student B: Answer Student A's questions.

Ask Student A where these objects are and put a cross [✗] on the picture.

coat watch glasses book

Now turn back to page 29.

20 *Lesson 14*

Reading and speaking, activity 2

Student B: Match the questions with the missing information, then ask and answer to complete the E-mail. If you don't know how to spell the names, ask *How do you spell ...?*

How old is she?

What's he like?

What's her father's job?

What's her mother's name?

What's her brother's name?

(1) How old is she?

Dear Brad,

Thanks for your E-mail.

My name is Sue White. I'm an English teacher and I'm (1) ____ years old. I've got dark hair and brown eyes. My family is from London. My mother's name is (2)____ and she's a teacher. My father's name is Henry. He's a (3) _______. He's got
(4) ______ eyes, but he hasn't got any hair! I've got a brother and a sister. My brother (5)____ is an engineer, too! He's twenty-two years old and he's got (6)____ hair (he's very (7)____)! My sister's name is Sarah. She's eleven; she's also got fair hair and blue eyes.

Write soon,

Sue

Now turn back to page 33.

21 *Lesson 17*

Listening and reading, activity 3

Student B: Listen and find out what time they have breakfast in Mexico, lunch in Russia and dinner in Hong Kong.

Now turn back to page 39.

22 *Lesson 5*

Writing and speaking, activity 2

Student C: Read the information.

Terry Crystal is American.

Maria Agnelli is from Naples.

The singer is Russian.

Now turn back to page 13.

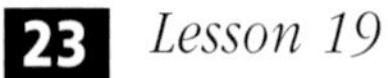

23 *Lesson 19*

Vocabulary and sounds, activity 3

Student B: Look at the words for these sports.

Basketball

Gymnastics

Swimming

Baseball

Sailing

Now turn back to page 42.

24 *Lesson 22*

Vocabulary and sounds, activity 2

Student B: Look at the words for these things.

Now turn back to page 50.

25 *Lesson 22*

Grammar, activity 1

Student B: Listen and answer.

What do they drink in Morocco?

When is the main meal in India?

What does he have for breakfast?

Now turn back to page 51.

26 *Lesson 4*

Listening and speaking, activity 3

Student C: You're Miss Fifi Lamour and you're an actress. Here's some more information.

Mr Frank Fearless – actor

Now turn back to page 11.

27 *Lesson 17*

Listening and reading, activity 3

Student C: Listen and find out what time they have breakfast in Hong Kong, lunch in Mexico and dinner in Russia.

Now turn back to page 39.

28 *Lesson 24*

Speaking and writing, activity 1

Student A: Ask about Student B's living room.Use the chart below. Add other items of your own.

Is there a television in your living room?

Living room	Yes/No
armchair	
window	
table	
telephone	
sofa	
television	

Now answer Student B's questions.

Now turn back to page 55.

29 *Lesson 22*

Grammar, activity 1

Student C: Listen and answer.

When is the main meal in Morocco?

What typical food do they eat in India?

What does she have for breakfast?

Now turn back to page 51.

30 *Lesson 26*

Vocabulary and sounds, activity 2

Match the words with the drawings.

dance swim draw cook sing drive type

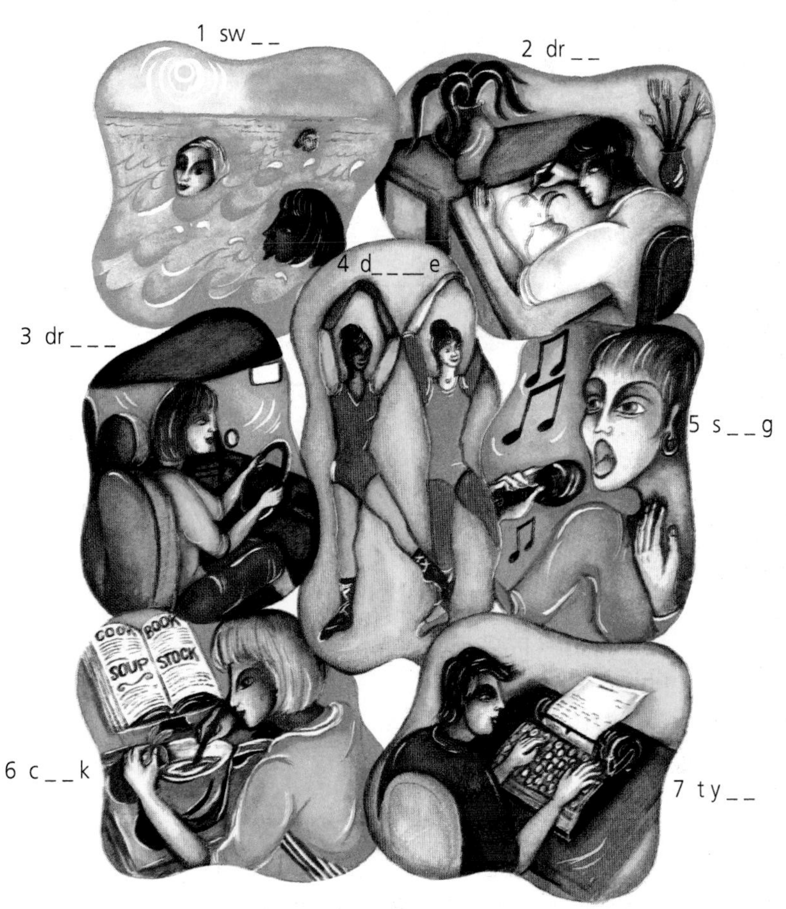

Now turn back to page 58.

31 *Lesson 28*

Vocabulary and sounds, activity 3

Student A: Look at the pictures.

Now complete the map on page 62

32 *Lesson 29*

Speaking, activity 1

Think of the photos in Unit 29 and describe them in detail.

Now turn back to page 65.

 *Lesson 30*

Speaking and writing, activity 1

Work together and say as many differences as you can between the pictures.

Now turn back to page 67.

34 *Lesson 33*

Speaking and writing, activity 1

Look at the photo for one minute only, then turn back to page 75.

35 *Lesson 24*

Speaking and writing, activity 1

Student B: Answer Student A's questions.

Now, ask about Student A's kitchen. Use the chart below. Add other items of your own.

Kitchen	Yes/No
cooker	
table	
chairs	
cupboards	
telephone	
television	

Is there a cooker in your kitchen?

Now turn back to page 55.

36 *Lesson 20*

Speaking, activity 1

Look at the card. Find out:

- who he/she is
- what his/her job is
- where he/she works
- where he/she lives

Merryfield School Library Card

Mary Ward
16 Green Street
Oxford

Now turn back to activity 2 on page 45.

37 *Lesson 38*

Reading and writing, activity 4

Dr Ueno was a teacher at a university in Tokyo. Every morning he walked with his dog, Hachiko, to the station to go to work. Hachiko walked home, but returned in the evening to meet Dr Ueno when he arrived at the station.

One day Hachiko arrived at the station and waited for Dr Ueno, but Dr Ueno didn't arrive that day. He died in the afternoon. Hachiko waited for six hours and then walked home.

The next day Hachiko returned to the station and waited for his friend Dr Ueno – and the next day and the next. He walked to the station every day at the same time – for nine years.

38 *Lesson 35*

Speaking and listening, activity 1

Look at the drawing from the nineteenth century.
What mistakes are there?

Now turn back to page 79.

39 *Lesson 39*

Writing and speaking, activity 2

Student B: Read the passage and answer the questions you wrote in 1.

On Sunday morning, we left our hotel at (1) - in the morning and took our (2) *cases* to the airport. Then we went to the (3) - by boat. We spent (4) *an hour* there, and then returned to Manhattan. We bought some (5) - for lunch and ate them in (6) *Central Park*. We sat in the park for about (7) -. In the afternoon, we went to the (8) *cinema* and saw a (9) -. By now, it was time to go to the airport for our flight home, so we took a (10) *taxi*. We got the plane at (11) - and flew home to (12) *London*. The end of a wonderful weekend!

Now turn back to page 87.

40 *Lesson 4*

Listening and speaking, activity 3

Student D: You're Tom James and you're a singer. Here's some more information.

Mike Handy – engineer

Now turn back to page 11.

41 *Lesson 28*

Vocabulary and sounds, activity 3

Student B: Look at the pictures.

Now complete the map on page 62.

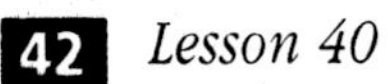
Lesson 40

Reading and listening, activity 6

Then I saw something on the ground. I picked it up and looked at it. It was a railway ticket. It had a date on it: 28 October 1962.

Now turn back to activity 7 on page 89.

Grammar review

CONTENTS

Present simple

Form

You use the contracted form in spoken and informal written English.

Be

Affirmative	**Negative**
I'm (I am)	I'm not (am not)
you we're (are) they	you we aren't (are not) they
he she's (is) it	he she isn't (is not) it

Questions	**Short answers**
Am I?	Yes, I am. No, I'm not.
Are you/we/they?	Yes, you/we/they are. No, you/we/they're not.
Is he/she/it?	Yes, he/she/it is. No, he/she/it isn't.

Have

Affirmative	**Negative**
I you've (have) we they	I you haven't (have not) we they
he she has it	he she hasn't (has not) it

Questions	**Short answers**
Have I/you/we/they?	Yes, I/you/we/they have. No, I/you/we/they haven't.
Has he/she/it?	Yes, he/she/it has.
Has he/she/it?	No, he/she/it hasn't.

Regular verbs

Affirmative	**Negative**
I you like we they	I you don't (do not) like we they
he she likes it	he she doesn't (does not) like it

Questions	**Short answers**
Do I/you/we/they like?	Yes, I/you/we/they do. No, I/you/we/they don't (do not).
Does he/she/it like?	Yes, he/she/it does. No, he/she/it doesn't (does not).

Question words with *is/are*
What's your name?
Who's your favourite singer?

Question words with *does/do*
What do they eat in Morocco?
Where does he live?

Present simple: third person singular

You add *-s* to most verbs
leaves, starts
You add *-es* to *do, go* and verbs which end in *-ch*, *-ss*, *-sh* and *-x*
goes, does, watches, finishes
You add *-ies* to verbs ending in *-y*
carries, tries

Use
You use the present simple:

- to talk about customs. (See Lesson 17)
  In Britain we have dinner at six o'clock in the evening.
  In Thailand we have breakfast at seven o'clock in the morning.
- to talk about habits. (See Lesson 25)
  I always get presents and birthday cards.
  I usually go out with friends.
- to talk about routines. (See Lesson 20)
  She leaves at 7.30 am and arrives at work at 8 am.
  On Saturday afternoon, he goes shopping with their sons.

Present continuous

Form

You form the present continuous with *be* + present participle (*-ing*). You use the contracted form in spoken and informal written English.

Affirmative	**Negative**
I'm (am) walking	I'm not (am not) walking
you we're (are) walking they	you we aren't (are not) walking they
he she's (is) walking it	he she isn't (is not) walking it

Questions	**Short answers**
Am I walking?	Yes, I am. No, I'm not.
Are you/we/they walking?	Yes, you/we/they are. No, you/we/they aren't.
Is he/she/it walking?	Yes, he/she/it is. No, he/she/it isn't.

Question words
Where are they staying? *Who is meeting them?*

Present participle (*-ing*) endings

You form the present participle of most verbs by adding *-ing*:
go – going, visit – visiting

You add *-ing* to verbs ending in *-e*:
make - making, have - having

You double the final consonant of verbs of one syllable ending in a vowel and a consonant, and add *-ing*:
get - getting, shop - shopping

You add *-ing* to verbs ending in a vowel and *-y* or *-w*:
draw - drawing, play - playing

You don't usually use these verbs in the continuous form.
believe feel hate hear know like love smell sound taste understand want

Use
You use the present continuous:

- to describe something that is happening at the moment. (see Lessons 29, 30)
  He's buying lunch.
  They're waiting for a bus.

- to talk about a definite arrangement in the future. (See Lesson 31)
  We're spending a week in a hotel.

Past simple

Form

You use the contracted form in spoken and informal written English.

Be

Affirmative		Negative	
I		I	
he	was	he	wasn't (was not)
she		she	
it		it	
you		you	
we	were	we	weren't (were not)
they		they	

Have

Affirmative		Negative	
I		I	
you		you	
we		we	
they	had	they	didn't (did not) have
he		he	
she		she	
it		it	

Regular verbs

Affirmative		Negative	
I		I	
you		you	
we		we	
they	listened	they	didn't (did not) listen
he		he	
she		she	
it		it	

Questions			Short answers			
	I			I		I
	you			you		you
	we			we		we
Did	they	listen?	Yes,	they did.	No,	they didn't.
	he			he		he
	she			she		she
	it			it		it

Question words

When did they arrive?
How much did Kate spend on her jacket?
How long did the journey take?
What did they buy?
How did they get to the hotel?

Past simple endings

You add *-ed* to most regular verbs:
walk - walked   watch - watched

You add *-d* to verbs ending in *-e*:
close - closed   continue - continued

You double the consonant and add *-ed* to verbs of one syllable ending in a vowel and a consonant:
stop - stopped   plan - planned

You drop the *-y* and and add *-ied* to verbs ending in *-y*:
study - studied   try - tried

You add *-ed* to verbs ending in a vowel and a *-y*
play - played

Irregular verbs

There are many verbs which have an irregular past simple. For a list of the irregular verbs which appear in **Reward Starter**, see page 108.

Pronunciation of past simple endings

/t/ *worked finished*
/d/ *played stayed*
/ɪd/ *wanted visited*

Use

You use the past simple:

- to talk about a past action or event that is finished. (See Lessons 33 - 39)
  Picasso was born in Malaga.
- to talk about a state, habit or routine in the past (See Lessons 33 - 39)
  They went to New York for the weekend.
  We took a taxi from the airport.

Questions

You can form questions in two ways:

- without a question word
  Are you James Bond? (See Lesson 4)
  Is she married? (See Lesson 6)
  Does he go to work by boat? (See Lesson 21)
  Did you take a photograph? (See Lesson 38)

- with a question word *who, what, how, when, where*
  Who's your favourite singer? (See Lesson 8)
  What's your name? (See Lesson 1)
  How did they get to the hotel? (See Lesson 39)
  When did they arrive? (See Lesson 39)
  Where did they go? (See Lesson 39)

You can put an adjective or an adverb after *how*.
How much are they? (See Lesson 11)
How old is she? (See Lesson 7)
How long did the journey take? (See Lesson 39)

You can also form questions about ability with *can*.
(See Lesson 26)
Can you swim?
Can you use a computer?

You can form more indirect, polite questions with *can*.
Can I have a sandwich, please? (See Lesson 27)

Imperatives

The imperative has exactly the same form as the infinitive (without *to*) and does not usually have a subject. You use the imperative:

- to give instructions (See Lesson 15)
  Stand up!
  Don't talk.
  Open your book.
- to give directions (See Lesson 28)
  Go along South Street.
  Turn left.
  Turn right.

You use *don't* + imperative to give a negative instruction.
Don't talk!
Don't look!

Verb patterns

like + *-ing* form verb

You can put an *-ing* form verb after *like*. (See Lesson 23)
I don't like swimming.
My girlfriend likes sightseeing, but she doesn't like walking.
We don't like staying in hotels.

When you *like doing something*, this is something you enjoy all the time.
I like travelling by train. I always go by train.

Have got

You use the contracted form in spoken and informal written English.

Affirmative	Negative
I	I
you 've (have) got	you haven't (have not) got
we	we
they	they
he	he
she's (has) got	she hasn't (has not) got
it	it

Questions	Short answers
Have I/you/we/they got?	Yes, I/you/we/they have. No, I/you/we/they haven't.
Has he/she/it got?	Yes, he/she/it has. No, he/she/it hasn't.

You use *have got*

- to talk about possession (See Lesson 13)
  We've got three children.
- to talk about appearance (See Lesson 14)
  She's got fair hair and blue eyes.
  He hasn't got any hair.

  Have got means the same as *have*. You use it in spoken and informal written English.
  She's got fair hair and blue eyes. (= She has fair hair and blue eyes)

Modal verbs

Can and *need* are modal verbs. Other modal verbs are *could must should will would.*

Form

Modal verbs:

- have the same form for all persons.
  I can swim.
  He can play the piano.
- don't take the auxiliary *do* in questions and negatives.
  Can you cook?
  I can't drive.
- take an infinitive without *to*.
  He can dance.
  She can cook.

Use

You use *can:*

- to talk about general ability, something you are able to do on most occasions. (See Lesson 26)
  I can swim. *I can play the piano.*
- to ask for something politely. (See Lesson 27)
  Can I have a sandwich, please?
  Can I have a cup of coffee?

Articles

There are many rules for the use of articles. Here are the rules presented in **Reward Starter.**

You use an indefinite article (*a/an*) with jobs. (See Lesson 2)
I'm a student.
I'm a doctor.
I'm an actor.
I'm an engineer.

You use *an* for nouns which begin with a vowel.
an actor *an engineer*

You use the definite article (*the*):

- when the listener or reader knows exactly which person or thing we mean (See Lesson 11)
  How much are the black shoes?
  How much is the green sweater?

You also use *the* when you talk in general about musical instruments.
He can play the piano.
She plays the guitar.
Before vowels you pronounce *the* /ə/.

Plurals

You form the plural of most nouns with *-s*. (See Lesson 9)
Singular: *friend* *neighbour* *boy* *girl* *brother* *sister* *twin*
Plural: *friends* *neighbours* *boys* *girls* *brothers* *sisters* *twins*

You add *-es* to nouns which end in *-o*, *-ch*, *-ss*, *-sh* and *-x*
glass - glasses *watch - watches* *sandwich - sandwiches*

There are some irregular plurals:
man - men *woman - women* *child - children*

Expressions of quantity

Any

You use *any* with *there aren't* and *are there?* (See Lesson 24)
There aren't any cupboards in the bathroom.
Are there any chairs in the kitchen?

Possessives

Possessive -*s*

You add *-s* to singular nouns to show possession. (See Lesson 12)
Jane's keys *Graham's wallet*
You add *-s'* to regular plural nouns.
My brothers' names are Pablo and Octavio.
You add *-'s* to irregular plural nouns.
The men's room.

Possessive adjectives

Pronoun	Possessive adjective	
I	my	(See Lesson 1)
you	your	(See Lesson 1)
he	his	(See Lesson 8)
she	her	(See Lesson 8)
it	its	
we	our	(See Lesson 13)
they	their	(See Lesson 13)

Adjectives

Position of adjectives

You can put adjectives in two positions.

- after the verb *to be* (See Lesson 5 and 33)
  He's British. She's Brazilian.
  It was warm. He was happy.
- before a noun (See Lesson 11)
  the black jacket *the blue jeans* *the green sweater*

Demonstrative adjectives

This, that, these and those (See Lesson 10)

You use *this* to point to singular nouns which are close.
What's this?
It's a watch.

You use *that* to point to singular nouns which are not close.
What's that?
It's an umbrella.

You use *these* to point to plural nouns which are close.
What are these?
They're glasses.

You use *those* to point to plural nouns which are not close.
What are those?
They're books.

Adverbs

Position of adverbs of frequency

You usually put adverbs of frequency before the verb. (See Lesson 25)

I always get presents and birthday cards.
I usually go out with friends.
I often go to a restaurant.

But you put them after the verb *to be.*

I never do anything special..
She was always cold in December.

Prepositions

from, in, to, at, on

You use *from:*

- with towns and countries to talk about people's homes. (See Lesson 5)
  He's from London.
  I'm from Bangkok.

You use *in:*

- to describe position. (See Lesson 12)
  Graham's wallet is in his coat pocket.
- with places (See Lesson 16)
  I live in a flat in Florence.
- with times of the day
  in the morning, in the afternoon, in the evening

You use *to:*

- with *go + school and work.* (See Lesson 16)
  I go to school in Fiesole.

You use *at*:

- with times of the day. (See Lesson 17)
  We have lunch at two o'clock.

You use *on*:

- to describe position. (See Lesson 12)
  Steve's wallet is on the table.
- with days of the week (See Lesson 18)
  on Monday on Tuesday on Monday morning on Tuesday afternoon

You use *under*:

- to describe position. (See Lesson 12)
  Joely's bag is under the table.

You use *by*:

- with means of transport (See Lesson 21)
  by car by train by bus by taxi

Pronunciation guide

/ɑː/	park
/æ/	hat
/aɪ/	my
/aʊ/	how
/e/	ten
/eɪ/	bay
/eə/	there
/ɪ/	sit
/iː/	me
/ɪə/	beer
/ɒ/	what
/əʊ/	no
/ɔː/	more
/ɔɪ/	toy
/ʊ/	took
/uː/	soon
/ʊə/	tour
/ɜː/	sir
/ʌ/	sun
/ə/	better

/b/	buy
/d/	day
/f/	free
/g/	give
/h/	house
/j/	you
/k/	cat
/l/	look
/m/	mean
/n/	nice
/p/	paper
/r/	rain
/s/	sad
/t/	time
/v/	verb
/w/	wine
/z/	zoo
/ʃ/	shirt
/ʒ/	leisure
/ŋ/	sing
/tʃ/	church
/θ/	thank
/ð/	then
/dʒ/	jacket

Irregular Verbs

Verbs with the same infinitive, past simple and past participle

cost	cost	cost
cut	cut	cut
hit	hit	hit
let	let	let
put	put	put
read /ri:d/	read /red/	read /red/
set	set	set
shut	shut	shut

Verbs with the same past simple and past participle but a different infinitive

bring	brought	brought
build	built	built
burn	burnt/burned	burnt/burned
buy	bought	bought
catch	caught	caught
feel	felt	felt
find	found	found
get	got	got
have	had	had
hear	heard	heard
hold	held	held
keep	kept	kept
learn	learnt/learned	learnt/learned
leave	left	left
lend	lent	lent
light	lit/lighted	lit/lighted
lose	lost	lost
make	made	made
mean	meant	meant
meet	met	met
pay	paid	paid
say	said	said
sell	sold	sold
send	sent	sent
sit	sat	sat
sleep	slept	slept
smell	smelt/smelled	smelt/smelled
spell	spelt/spelled	spelt/spelled
spend	spent	spent
stand	stood	stood
teach	taught	taught
understand	understood	understood
win	won	won

Verbs with same infinitive and past participle but a different past simple

become	became	become
come	came	come
run	ran	run

Verbs with a different infinitive, past simple and past participle

be	was/were	been
begin	began	begun
break	broke	broken
choose	chose	chosen
do	did	done
draw	drew	drawn
drink	drank	drunk
drive	drove	driven
eat	ate	eaten
fall	fell	fallen
fly	flew	flown
forget	forgot	forgotten
give	gave	given
go	went	gone
grow	grew	grown
know	knew	known
lie	lay	lain
ring	rang	rung
rise	rose	risen
see	saw	seen
show	showed	shown
sing	sang	sung
speak	spoke	spoken
swim	swam	swum
take	took	taken
throw	threw	thrown
wake	woke	woken
wear	wore	worn
write	wrote	written

Tapescripts

Lesson 1 **Listening and reading, activity 2**

ANNA Hello, I'm Anna. What's your name?
DAVID Hello, Anna. I'm David.
TONY Hello, I'm Tony. What's your name?
JANE Hello, Tony. I'm Jane.
JUDY Hello, I'm Judy. What's your name?
STEVE Hello, Judy. I'm Steve.

Lesson 2 **Vocabulary and sounds, activity 2**

JOSÉ What's your job, Pete?
PETE I'm a journalist. What's your job, José?
JOSÉ I'm a doctor.
MARIA What's your job, Hillary?
HILLARY I'm a secretary. What's your job, Maria?
MARIA I'm a teacher.
HASHIMI What's your job, Yıldız?
YILDIZ I'm a student. What's your job, Hashimi?
HASHIMI I'm an engineer.

Lesson 2 **Listening, activity 2**

MARIA What's your job, Hillary?
HILLARY I'm a secretary. What's your job, Maria?
MARIA I'm a teacher.

Lesson 3 **Listening and reading, activity 2**

Conversation A

MICHIKO Hello, Joan, how are you?
JOAN Hello, Michiko, I'm very well, thanks. How are you?
MICHIKO I'm fine, thanks.

Conversation B

PETE Kate, what's your telephone number, please?
KATE 0134 521 3987. What's your telephone number, Pete?
PETE 01967 328123.
KATE Thank you. Goodbye, Pete.
PETE Goodbye.

Lesson 4 **Listening and speaking, activity 1**

r-a-m-b-o
c-l-e-o-p-a-t-r-a
d-r-a-c-u-l-a
f-r-a-n-k-e-n-s-t-e-i-n
j-a-m-e-s- b-o-n-d

Lesson 5 **Vocabulary and sounds, activity 5**

American - The USA
Japanese - Japan
Italian - Italy
Brazilian - Brazil
Thai - Thailand
British - Britain
Turkish - Turkey
Russian - Russia.

Lesson 5 **Listening and reading, activity 3**

OLGA Hello, I'm Olga Maintz. I'm an engineer. I'm Russian and I'm from St Petersburg.
MUSTAFA Hi! I'm Mustafa Polat. I'm Turkish and I'm a teacher. I'm from Istanbul.
PATRIZIO Hello! I'm Patrizio Giuliani. I'm from Venice. I'm Italian and I'm an actor.

Lesson 6 **Vocabulary and sounds, activity 3**

One Two Thirteen Fourteen Five Six Seventeen Eighteen Nine Twenty

Lesson 6 **Listening and writing, activity 2**

Is Ken Stanwell from Kenton?
Yes, he is.
Is he married?
No, he isn't. He's seventeen.
Is he a student?
Yes, he is.
And is he British?
No, he isn't. He's American.

Lesson 6 **Grammar, activity 3**

Is Jane married?
Yes, she is.
Is Anna married?
No, she isn't.
Is Sema married?
No, she isn't.
Is Kazuo married?
Yes, he is.
Is Steve married?
Yes, he is.

Lesson 6 **Speaking and listening, activity 2**

Is Bill Clinton an engineer?
No, he isn't.
Is Tom Cruise an actor ?
Yes, he is.
Is pizza from Italy?
Yes, it is.
Is doctor a job?
Yes, it is.
Is San Francisco in the United States?
Yes, it is.
Are you from Japan?
No, I'm not./ Yes, I am.
Is Graham a French name?
No, it isn't.
Is Istanbul a country?
No, it isn't.
Is seventeen one-seven?
Yes, it is.
Is Whitney Houston American?
Yes, she is.
Are you President of the USA?
No, I'm not.
Is Argentinian a nationality?
Yes, it is.
Is Edinburgh in England?
No, it isn't.
Is Spain a country?
Yes, it is.
Is Roberto Baggio an actor?
No, he isn't.
Are you André Agassi?
No, I'm not.

Is Sony Korean?
No, it isn't.
Is champagne from France?
Yes, it is.
Is your name Queen Elizabeth?
No, it isn't.
Are you married.
Yes, I am. Are you married?
No, I'm not.

Lesson 7 Vocabulary and sounds, activity 3

Thirteen Forty Fifty Sixteen Seventeen Eighty Nineteen

Lesson 7 Listening, activity 1

How old is Tony?
He's twenty.
How old is Karen?
She's twenty-seven.
How old is Nick?
He's nineteen.
How old is Sarah?
She's twenty-three.
How old is Jill?
She's thirty-five.
How old is Alex?
He's seventeen.

Lesson 7 Listening and writing, activity 1

Ella isn't married. She's 42. She's an actress and she's American.
Miki's a student. She's 18. She isn't married and she's Japanese.
Maria's 24. She's Italian and she's a journalist. She isn't married.
Erol's Turkish. He's married and he's a waiter. He's 21.
Anant's married and he's a teacher. He's 30.
Carlos is 33. He's Brazilian and he's a doctor. He isn't married.

Lesson 8 Vocabulary and sounds, activity 2

One.	Car
Two.	Football team
Three.	TV programme
Four.	TV presenter
Five.	Group
Six.	Politician

Lesson 8 Writing and listening, activity 2

SALLY What's your favourite car, Max?
MAX My favourite car? A Porsche, I think. Yes, a Porsche.
SALLY And what's your favourite football team?
MAX Manchester .
SALLY Manchester United or Manchester City?
MAX Machester United, of course. What about you? Who's your favourite actor?
SALLY It's Arnold Schwarzenegger.
MAX Arnold Schwarzenegger, I see. And what's your favourite group?
SALLY Well, my favourite singer is Diana Ross. What's your favourite group?
MAX The Beatles.
SALLY The Beatles! Who are the Beatles?

Lesson 9 Reading and listening, activity 20

JANE Are you twins?
NICK Yes, we are. I'm Nick.
DAVE And I'm Dave.
JANE Are you from London?
NICK/DAVE No, we aren't. We're from Manchester.
JANE How old are you?
NICK/DAVE We're twenty-three.
JANE What are your jobs?
NICK/DAVE We're students.
JANE What's your favourite football team?
NICK/DAVE Manchester United!

Lesson 9 Reading and listening, activity 3

PAUL Who are they?
JANE They're ... er Nick and Dave.
PAUL Are they from London?
JANE No, they're from, er, ... Manchester.
PAUL And how old are they?
JANE They're twenty-three. They're students.

Lesson 10 Vocabulary and sounds, activities 2 and 3

One.	They're cassettes.
Two.	They're glasses.
Three.	It's a wallet.
Four.	It's a pen.
Five.	It's a clock.
Six.	It's an umbrella.
Seven.	They're keys.
Eight.	They're books.
Nine.	It's a watch.
Ten	It's a bag.

Progress check, lessons 1 to 10

Reading and listening, activity 2

One, two, three o'clock, four o'clock rock,
Five, six, seven o'clock, eight o'clock rock,
Nine, ten, eleven o'clock, twelve o'clock rock,
We're gonna rock around the clock tonight.
Put your glad rags on and join me, hon'
We'll have some fun when the clock strikes one,
Chorus
We're gonna rock around the clock tonight,
We're gonna rock, rock, rock til broad daylight
We're gonna rock, gonna rock around the clock tonight.
When the clock strikes two, three and four,
If the band slows down, we'll yell for more
Chorus
When the chimes ring five and six and seven
We'll be rockin' up in seventh heaven.
Chorus
When it's eight, nine, ten, eleven, too
I'll be going strong and so will you,
Chorus
When the clock strikes twelve, we'll cool off, then,
Start a rocking round the clock again.
Chorus

Lesson 11 Vocabulary, activity 4

MAN 1 How much is the jacket?
WOMAN 1 Fifty pounds.
MAN 2 How much are the jeans?
WOMAN 1 Twenty-seven, ninety-nine.
WOMAN 2 How much is the skirt?
WOMAN 1 Thirty-five, ninety-nine.
WOMAN 2 How much is the sweater?
WOMAN 1 Twenty one, fifty.
MAN 3 How much is the shirt?
WOMAN 1 Twelve, fifty.
WOMAN 2 How much are the shoes?
WOMAN 1 Forty, ninety-nine.

Lesson 11 Listening and sounds, activities 1 and 2

CUSTOMER How much are these black shoes?
ASSISTANT They're £29.50.
CUSTOMER And how much is that red sweater?
ASSISTANT It's £17.
CUSTOMER How much is this blue jacket?
ASSISTANT It's £40.
CUSTOMER How much are these black jeans?
ASSISTANT They're £35.99.

Lesson 11 Listening and speaking, activity 2

MAN How much is a big Mac in Britain?
WOMAN It's about two pounds.
MAN And how much are Levi jeans?
WOMAN They're thirty pounds.
MAN And Nike trainers? How much are they?
WOMAN They're forty pounds.
MAN And how much is a Cola?
WOMAN About thirty-five pence.

Lesson 12 Listening, activities 1 and 3

MAN Where're Jane's keys?
WOMAN They're on the chair.
MAN Where's Graham's wallet?
WOMAN It's in his coat pocket.
MAN And where's Frank's watch?
WOMAN It's on the chair.
MAN And where's Joely's bag?
WOMAN It's under the table.
MAN And where are Nicola's glasses?
WOMAN They're on the table.
MAN And where's Tom's personal stereo?
WOMAN It's on the table.

Lesson 12 Grammar, activity 3

TOM Where's my personal stereo?
JOELY It's on the table.
JOELY Where's my bag?
NICOLA It's under the table.
GRAHAM Where's my wallet?
JANE It's in your coat pocket.

Lesson 13 Listening and speaking, activity 2

INTERVIEWER Are you maried, Marco?
MARCO Yes, I am.
INTERVIEWER Have you got any children?
MARCO No, I haven't.
INTERVIEWER Have you got any brothers or sisters?
MARCO Yes, I have. I've got two brothers and one sister.
INTERVIEWER What are their names?
MARCO Paolo, Giovanni, and Patrizia.

Lesson 15 Vocabulary and listening, activity 6

Come in.
Take your coat off.
Sit down.
Open your book.
Pick your pen up.
Turn the cassette player on.

Lesson 15 Sounds and speaking, activity 3

Stand up.
Open your book.
Pick your pen up.
Sit down.
Close your book.
Put your pen down.
Pick your bag up.
Put your coat on.
Put your bag down.
Take your coat off.
Sit down.

Lesson 16 Reading and listening, activity 3. Photo 1

BOY Hello, I'm Erol. I'm from Turkey and I'm sixteen. I'm a student. My sister's name is Belma and we go to school in Istanbul. We live with our parents in a flat in Galata. My father is an engineer and my mother is a secretary. They work in an office in Beyoğlu.

Photo 2

MAN Hello, I'm Kazuo. I'm from Japan and I'm thirty-five. I'm a journalist and I work in an office in Tokyo. My wife's name is Michiko and we live in a flat in Ichikawa. We've got two children. Our son's name is Koji and our daughter's name is Miki. They go to school in Funabashi.

Lesson 17 Speaking and vocabulary, activity 4

MAN Hello, everybody and welcome to the Afternoon show. It's three o'clock. We've got some very interesting guests for you today ...
WOMAN This is the BBC World Service. It's eleven o'clock and here is the news.
MAN It's six o'clock and here is the news.
WOMAN And that was the end of the one clock news. Here's the weather forecast for all areas for the next twenty-four hours ...

Lesson 17 Listening and reading, activity 3

INTERVIEWER When do you have your meals in Russia?
MAN We have breakfast at seven o'clock, lunch at twelve o'clock and dinner at six o'clock.
INTERVIEWER And what about in Hong Kong? When do you have breakfast?
WOMAN 1 Oh, about seven o'clock in the morning. And we have lunch at about one o'clock.
INTERVIEWER And when do you have dinner?
WOMAN 1 About eight o'clock.
INTERVIEWER And when do you have breakfast in Mexico?
WOMAN 2 We have breakfast at about eight o'clock. Then we have lunch at two or three o'clock in the afternoon.
INTERVIEWER And dinner?
WOMAN 2 At about eight or nine o'clock in the evening.

Lesson 19 Listening and writing, activity 3

TIM Do you like gymnastics, Gwen?
GWEN Yes, I do. I like gymnastics very much.
TIM Do you like basketball?
GWEN No, I don't.

JAMES Do you like volleyball, Alison?
ALISON Yes, I do. I like volleyball very much.
JAMES Do you like skiing?
ALISON No, I don't.

Lesson 20 Vocabulary and speaking, activity 4

MAN It's half past five. Time to go home.
DJ Good morning! Good morning! It's a quarter to seven and this is the Pete Walker show...
TV PRESENTER It's a quarter past twelve. In fifteen minutes time we'll be talking to ...
MUM It's a quarter to six. Hurry up! We're leaving in five minutes.
DAD Get up, John! It's half past seven.
WOMAN Time for bed. It's a quarter past eleven. Goodnight!

Lesson 20 Listening and writing, activity 1

MAN1 Hello, and welcome to The British Abroad, the programme where we talk to British people living and working in other countries. Where do you live, Sarah?
WOMAN I live in Italy.
MAN 1 And where do you work?
WOMAN I work in an English school.
MAN 1 When do you have breakfast in Italy?
WOMAN At about half past seven.
MAN 1 When do you start work?
WOMAN I start work at three in the afternoon.
MAN 1 When do you finish work?
WOMAN At nine o'clock in the evening.
MAN 1 When do you go shopping in Italy?
WOMAN In the mornings and on Saturdays.
MAN 1 When do you visit friends in Italy?
WOMAN On Saturday evenings and on Sundays.
MAN 1 Where do you live, Mark?
MAN 2 I live in Acapulco.
MAN 1 And where do you work?
MAN 2 I work in a hospital. I'm a doctor.
MAN 1 When do you have breakfast?
MAN 2 At about half past six.
MAN 1 And when do you start work?
MAN 2 I start work at eight in the morning.
MAN 1 When do you finish work?
MAN 2 At seven o'clock in the evening.
MAN 1 When do you go shopping?
MAN 2 My wife goes shopping on Saturdays.
MAN 1 When do you visit your parents?
MAN 2 My parents live in Britain but my wife's parents live in Acapulco, too. We visit them on Sundays.

Progress check, lessons 11 to 20. Listening, activities 1 and 2

Don't worry about a thing
'Cause every little thing's gonna be all right
Singing 'Don't worry about a thing
'Cause every little thing's gonna be all right.'
Rise up this morning
Smiled with the rising sun
Three little birds beside my doorstep
Singing sweet songs of melodies pure and true
Singing 'This is my message to you.'

Lesson 21 Reading and listening, activity 2

SALLY Thank you Mehmet ... Excuse me!
LEYLA Yes.
SALLY Your name is...?
LEYLA My name is Leyla.
SALLY Do you walk to work, Leyla?
LEYLA Yes, I do.
SALLY And are you married?
LEYLA No, I'm not.
SALLY Have you got any brothers or sisters?
LEYLA Yes, I have a brother. His name's Mustafa.
SALLY And does he walk to work?
LEYLA No, he goes to work by boat.
SALLY Thank you very much. Excuse me, sir! What's your name?
JOHN My name's John.
SALLY Ah, you're American. Do you live here?
JOHN Yes, I do.
SALLY And do you work here?
JOHN No, I don't. I work in Asia.
SALLY And do you go to work by car?
JOHN No, I go by boat. My wife, Mary, goes to work by car.
SALLY Thank you, John. So, as you can see, people here are using many different ways of going to work...

Lesson 22 Listening, activity 1

RADIO PRESENTER Hello and welcome to food and drink around the world. Today we're looking at food in Argentina, Morocco, and India. Christina is from Argentina, what food do you eat in your country, Christina?
CRISTINA In Argentina, we eat meat, especially beef.
RADIO PRESENTER What do you drink?
CRISTINA We drink beer and wine with our meals, or water and juice.
RADIO PRESENTER When do you have the main meal of the day?
CRISTINA The main meal of the day is lunch. We have lunch at one o'clock in the afternoon. During the week, if you work, the main meal is dinner.
RADIO PRESENTER What do you have for breakfast?
CRISTINA We have coffee and bread.

Lesson 22 Grammar, activity 1

RADIO PRESENTER Nourredine, tell me what you eat in Morocco.
NOURREDINE Well, a typical dish is a dish with lamb and vegetables.
RADIO PRESENTER And what do you drink?
NOURREDINE Our national drink is tea and we drink a lot of juice as well.
RADIO PRESENTER And when do you have the main meal of the day?
NOURREDINE The main meal in Morocco is lunch. We have it at twelve o'clock.
RADIO PRESENTER And what do you have for breakfast?
NOURREDINE We have milk and yoghurt, and fruit: apples and oranges.
RADIO PRESENTER Ram, what do you eat in India?
RAM We eat alot of rice and vegetables.
RADIO PRESENTER And what do you drink?
RAM Tea or water.
RADIO PRESENTER And when do you have the main meal of the day?
RAM At 10 am in the morning or 7 pm in the evening.
RADIO PRESENTER And what do you have for breakfast?
RAM Tea.

Lesson 23 Reading and listening, activities 3 and 4

INTERVIEWER Gary, what do you like doing on holiday?
GARY Well, I like walking and sightseeing.
INTERVIEWER Anything else?
GARY Er, I like eating in restaurants and staying in hotels.
INTERVIEWER Is there anything you don't like doing?
GARY I don't like skiing. I don't like lying on the beach or swimming. Oh, and I don't like writing postcards.
INTERVIEWER Margaret, what do you like doing on holiday?
MARGARET I like lying on the beach and reading. I like swimming as well. And in the evening I like dancing.
INTERVIEWER And what don't you like doing?
MARGARET I don't like sightseeing.
INTERVIEWER Do you like writing postcards?
MARGARET No, I don't.

Lesson 24 Vocabulary and sounds, activity 6

Kitchen - cooker, table, cupboards, chair.
Dining room - table, chairs.
Living room - armchairs, sofa, television, table.
Bedroom 1 - armchair, bed.
Bedroom 2- bed, table, cupboard.
Bathroom - shower.
Hall - table, telephone.

Lesson 24 Reading and listening, activity 2

George Mandelson is a journalist. He isn't married. He lives in a small house. He doesn't have a garden. He likes watching football on TV, dancing and taking photos.
Angie Ashton is a singer. She's married with four children. She likes cooking, seeing her friends, playing tennis and reading newspapers. She

doesn't eat meat and she doesn't like watching television.
Frances Peters is an actress. She's married but she hasn't got any children. She lives in London. She likes seeing her friends, but she doesn't like cooking.

Lesson 25 Vocabulary and sounds, activity 2

January February March April May June July August September October November December.

Lesson 25 Vocabulary and sounds, activity 6

The seventh of July.
The eighth of August.
The ninth of September.
The tenth of October.
The eleventh of November.
The twelfth of December.

Lesson 25 Listening and speaking, activity 2

INTERVIEWER What do you for your birthday, Karen?
KAREN I usually have a party and I always get presents and birthday cards.
INTERVIEWER And Pete, what do you do?
PETE I usually go out with friends or I sometimes invite friends home.
INTERVIEWER Do you always get presents and birthday cards?
PETE Yes, I do.
INTERVIEWER What do you do for your birthday, Molly?
MOLLY I usually have a meal with my family. I often go to a restaurant and I always get presents and birthday cards.

Lesson 26 Reading and listening, activity 3

INTERVIEWER So, are you a student?
FRANK Yes, I am.
INTERVIEWER And you need a holiday job?
FRANK Yes, I do.
INTERVIEWER Can you swim?
FRANK Yes, I can.
INTERVIEWER And music? Can you play the piano?
FRANK No, I can't. But I can play the guitar.
INTERVIEWER OK, and can you speak any languages?
FRANK Yes, I can. I can speak French and German.
INTERVIEWER And what about sport. Can you play tennis and football?
FRANK Yes, I can.
INTERVIEWER Good.

Lesson 26 Listening and speaking, activity 1. Interview 1

INTERVIEWER Yes, come in.
JANIE Good morning.
INTERVIEWER Good morning. Come in and sit down. Take off your coat. What's your name?
JANIE Janie Ellis.
INTERVIEWER Are you a student?
JANIE Yes, I am. I need a holiday job at the moment.
INTERVIEWER Can you swim?
JANIE Yes, I can.
INTERVIEWER Can you play the piano?
JANIE Yes, I can.
INTERVIEWER Can you speak any languages?
JANIE I can speak a little Spanish.
INTERVIEWER And can you play tennis?
JANIE Yes, I can.
INTERVIEWER And what about football?
JANIE No, I can't.
INTERVIEWER All right. Where do you live, Janie? (FADE)

Interview two.

INTERVIEWER And your name is ...?
LOIS Lois Franks.
INTERVIEWER And you're a student?
LOIS Yes, I am. I'm a music student.
INTERVIEWER A music student! Excellent. So you can play the piano?
LOIS Yes, I can. I can play the piano, the guitar, the violin, the trumpet . . .
INTERVIEWER Excellent. And can you swim?
LOIS Yes, I can.
INTERVIEWER And can you speak any languages?
LOIS Yes, I can speak French, Italian, Russian and Spanish.
INTERVIEWER And do you like football and tennis?
LOIS Yes, they're my favourite sports.
INTERVIEWER Very good, Lois. Now, where are you from?

Lesson 27 Listening, activity 2

WAITER Can I help you?
JANE Yes, what's a Halley Court Special?
WAITER It's a sandwich with chicken, lettuce, tomato and mayonnaise.
JANE How much is it?
WAITER It's £2.50.
JANE OK, can I have a Halley Court Special, please?
WAITER Certainly. And anything to drink?
JANE A cup of coffee, please.
WAITER OK, a Halley Court Special and a cup of coffee. Anything else?
JANE A piece of chocolate cake, please.
WAITER Thank you . . . OK, a Halley Court Special, a cup of coffee and a piece of chocolate cake. Here you are.
JANE Thank you very much.
WAITER Enjoy your meal.

Lesson 27 Listening and speaking, activity 2

FINN What's your favourite food, Selina?
SELINA Well, I don't eat meat, so I like lots of salad things: lettuce and tomatoes etc, and vegetables. I like pizza and pasta very much,too, and I eat a lot of cheese. I like potatoes, but I don't eat them often.
FINN And what's your favourite drink?
SELINA I like mineral water and Cola. I don't like coffee, but I like tea. What about you? What's your favourite food?
FINN Well, I like chicken but I don't like beef. I like tomatoes and lettuce as well. I like potatoes, especially baked potatoes with tuna and mayonnaise.
SELINA What do you like to drink?
FINN Oh, I like tea. Do you know what my favourite food is, though?
SELINA No, what?
FINN Chocolate cake!
SELINA Oh yes! I like chocolate cake, too.

Lesson 27 Listening and speaking, activity 3

SELINA Can I have a cheese and tomato pizza and a mineral water, please?
WAITER Certainly. And for you, sir?
FINN Can I have a baked potato with tuna and mayonnaise?
WAITER Certainly. Anything to drink, sir?
FINN Oh, a cup of tea, please.
WAITER OK. That's a cheese and tomato pizza and a mineral water, one baked potato with tuna and mayonnaise, and a cup of tea. Anything else?
FINN Selina, look at that chocolate cake!
SELINA Wow! Great!
FINN And two pieces of chocolate cake, please.
WAITER Thank you.

Lesson 28 Listening, activity 1

MAN 1 Where's the station?
WOMAN 1 It's in East Street.
WOMAN 2 Where's the bookshop?
MAN 2 It's in West Street.
MAN 3 Where's the market?
WOMAN 3 It's in North Street.
WOMAN 4 Where's the chemist?
MAN 4 It's in South Street.

Lesson 28 Listening, activity 2

MAN 1 Where's North Street?
WOMAN 1 Go along West Street. Turn right into North Street.
WOMAN 2 Where's West Street?
MAN 2 Go straight ahead.
WOMAN 3 Where's South Street?
MAN 3 Turn right.
MAN 4 Where's East Street?
WOMAN 4 Turn right into South Street. Turn left into East Street.

Lesson 28 Listening, activity 3

MAN 1 Excuse me! Where's the post office?
WOMAN 1 It's in West Street.
MAN 1 Where's West Street?
WOMAN 1 Go straight ahead. It's on the left.
WOMAN 2 Where's the bank?
MAN 2 It's in East Street.
WOMAN 2 Where's East Street?
MAN 2 Turn right into South Street, and turn left into East Street. It's on the right.
MAN 3 Excuse me! Where's the cinema?
WOMAN 3 It's in South Street. Turn left and it's on the left.
MAN 3 Thank you.
WOMAN 4 Where's the car park?
MAN 4 It's in East Street. Go straight ahead, along West Street and turn right into North Street. Go along North Street and turn right into East Street. It's on the left.
WOMAN 4 Thank you.

Lesson 28 Listening and reading, activity 1

TOUR GUIDE Good morning, ladies and gentlemen, and welcome to Reward Walking Tours of London. I'm Jamie and I'm your guide this morning for our tour of Covent Garden and Trafalgar Square. Well, as you know, we're in Trafalgar Square, and the building over there is the National Gallery, and the building on my right is South Africa House. And the church between the National Gallery and South Africa House is St Martins-in-the Field. Now, the street on your right here is Whitehall, with Big Ben and the Houses of Parliament in the distance, and on your left is the Mall, with Buckingham Palace at the end.

Lesson 29 Sounds, activity 1

stand in, reading, shopping in, sit in, playing, running, lie in, writing

Lesson 30 Listening and vocabulary, activity 3

Picture 1	What's he doing? Is he listening to the radio?
Picture 2	What's she doing? Is she making tea?
Picture 3	What are they doing? Are they waiting for a bus?
Picture 4	What's he doing? Is he having a bath?
Picture 5	What's she doing? Is she talking to her daughter?
Picture 6	What are they doing? Are they having dinner?

Lesson 30 Listening and vocabulary, activity 6

one	He's listening to the cd.
two	She's making coffee.
three	They're waiting for a taxi.
four	He's having a shower.
five	She's talking to her son.
six	They're having lunch.

Progress check, lessons 21 to 30 Sounds, activity 2

bicycle vegetable telephone restaurant library
America December September computer

Progress check, lessons 21 to 30 Sounds, activity 3

Asia February November sightseeing eleventh

Progress check, lessons 21 to 30 Sounds, activity 5

MAN They aren't playing football. They're playing tennis.
WOMAN He isn't eating. He's drinking.
MAN She isn't washing. She's cooking.

Progress check, lessons 21 to 30

Listening, activities 1 and 2

Daniel is travelling tonight on a plane
I can see the red tail lights heading for Spain,
Oh, and I can see Daniel waving goodbye,
God, it looks like Daniel, must be the clouds in my eyes.
They say Spain's pretty, though I've never been,
Well, Daniel says it's the best place that he's ever seen,
Oh and he should know he's been there enough,
Lord, I miss Daniel, oh I miss him so much.
Oh, Daniel my brother,
You are older than me,
Do you still feel the pain
Of the scars that won't heal?
Your eyes have died, but you see more than I,
Daniel, you're a star in the face of the sky.

Lesson 31 Reading and listening, activity 2

TONY What are your plans for the holiday? Where are you going?
DON We're going to Australia.
TONY Australia!
SUE Yes, for three weeks. We're staying with Fran in Sydney. We're spending a week there.
DON And then we're driving to Port Stephens, about three hours away, and we're spending a week on the beach.
TONY Wonderful!
SUE Then we're going to a town called Cobar in the outback. We're camping there.
TONY Well, have a great time!
DON Thanks. What are you doing?
TONY Oh, I'm staying at home.

Lesson 31 Listening and speaking, activities 1 and 2

DON Hello, Don Fisher speaking.
FRAN Hello, Dad, it's Fran.
DON Fran, how are you?
FRAN I'm fine.
DON We're looking forward to seeing you.
FRAN So are we. But I'm ringing to tell you about a change of plan.
DON OK. Go ahead.
FRAN Well, Bruce's friend is staying with us at the moment, so Bruce isn't meeting you at the airport. I'm meeting you.
DON Great!
FRAN And, Dad, sorry about this, but there are only two bedrooms in our house, so you aren't staying with us. You're staying in a hotel near us. Is that ok?
DON Well, ok. But we're still spending a week with you in the city?
FRAN Yes, and then we're driving to Port Stephens, but we aren't spending a week there, we're spending longer- ten days, then we're camping for three days in the outback, not a week. We think a week camping in the outback is too long.
DON That's fine, Fran. Thanks for telling us.
FRAN OK, then, Dad. See you on the twenty-ninth! Love to Mum. Bye.
DON Bye Fran. See you soon.

Lesson 32 Listening, activity 2

JACK Let's go to the cinema.
ANNA I'm sorry but I don't like films.
JACK How about going to the theatre, then?
ANNA Yes, OK, What's on?
JACK An Agatha Christie play.
ANNA Where's it on?
JACK At the Theatre Royal.
ANNA Great!

Lesson 32 Sounds, activity 3

I'm sorry but I don't like music.
I'm sorry but I'm busy tomorrow evening.
I'm sorry but I don't like Spielberg.

Lesson 34 Reading and listening, activity 2

NARRATOR It was ten o'clock in the evening at Ripley Grange. It was quiet ... very quiet. Was there anyone in the dining room? No, there wasn't.
Then, there was a scream. It was Lady Scarlet. Was she in the kitchen? Yes, she was. Was she alone in the kitchen? No, she wasn't. Probe was also in the kitchen. He was dead.
Was there something on the table? Yes, there was – there was a knife on the table. It was red. Was it murder? Who was the murderer?

Lesson 34 Listening and speaking, activity 1

DETECTIVE PRUNE Please answer my questions very carefully. Colonel White, where were you at 8 pm last night?
COLONEL WHITE I was in the dining room. We were all in the dining room, Detective. It was dinner.
DETECTIVE PRUNE Where were you at ten o'clock, Colonel?
COLONEL WHITE I was in the living room. I was with Doctor Plum and Professor Peacock.
DETECTIVE PRUNE Thank you, Colonel. Please ask Miss Green to come in. Miss Green, where were you at ten o'clock last night?
MISS GREEN I was in the garden.
DETECTIVE PRUNE Were you alone?
MISS GREEN No, I was with Mrs Mustard. There was a scream! It was awful.
DETECTIVE PRUNE Thank you, Miss Green. Good morning, Professor Peacock. Where were you at ten o'clock last night?
PROFESSOR PEACOCK I was in the living room with Colonel White and Doctor Plum.
DETECTIVE PRUNE I see. Thank you. Mrs Mustard, where were you last night at ten o'clock?
MRS MUSTARD I was in the garden. It was a lovely evening. I was with Miss Green.
DETECTIVE PRUNE Thank you Mrs Mustard. Doctor Plum, where were you at ten o'clock last night?
DOCTOR PLUM I was in the kitchen.
DETECTIVE PRUNE In the kitchen?
DOCTOR PLUM Yes, Probe was dead. Lady Scarlet was there.
DETECTIVE PRUNE Where were you before you were in the kitchen?
DOCTOR PLUM I was in the living room with Professor Peacock and Colonel White.
DETECTIVE PRUNE Thank you, doctor. And Lady Scarlet, where were you at eight o'clock last night?
LADY SCARLET I was in the dining room with the other people. It was dinner time.
DETECTIVE PRUNE And where were you at ten o'clock?
LADY SCARLET I was in my bedroom. I was hungry and thirsty. There was some food and drink in the kitchen. Probe was there, but he was dead.
DETECTIVE PRUNE So there wasn't anyone in the bedroom with you?
LADY SCARLET Certainly not, constable. How dare you!
DETECTIVE PRUNE I'm a detective, Lady Scarlet. And I know who was Probe's murderer.

Lesson 34 Listening and speaking, activity 5

DETECTIVE PRUNE Thank you for coming to the living room. I now know who was Probe's murderer. You see, Doctor Plum, Colonel White and Professor Peacock were in the living room, and Mrs Mustard and Miss Green were in the garden. Only you, Lady Scarlet, were alone in your bedroom. You were Probe's murderer, weren't you, Lady Scarlet?
LADY SCARLET It's true. I was hungry! I was thirsty! I was bored with cold potatoes, cold meat and tired lettuce! I was tired of water to drink! I was unhappy with Probe.
DETECTIVE PRUNE Thank you, everyone. Lady Scarlet, please come with me.
COLONEL WHITE I say!
DOCTOR PLUM 'Pon my word!
PROFESSOR PEACOCK 'Straordinary.
MRS MUSTARD What's the time?
MISS GREEN One o'clock.
COLONEL WHITE Time for lunch!

Lesson 35 Vocabulary and sounds, activity 3

television video recorder telephone radio computer personal stereo
car bicycle fax machine dishwater vacuum cleaner

Lesson 35 Reading and listening, activities 3 and 4

MARY Well, when I was a child, we had a telephone in the hall, but we didn't have a television. No one had television when I was a child. And of course, we didn't have a video recorder.
INTERVIEWER What about a radio?
MARY Yes, we had a radio. The radio was in the living room. The radio programmes were very good.
INTERVIEWER And computers, did you have computers or personal stereos?
MARY Oh, no, we didn't have computers or personal stereos. And I was fifty before I had my own radio. It wasn't a personal stereo.
INTERVIEWER Did you have a car?
MARY Yes, some families had a car, but we didn't. We had bicycles, all six of us.
INTERVIEWER And no fax machine, of course. Or vacuum cleaner or dishwasher?
MARY No, we didn't have a fax machine. But we had a kind of vacuum cleaner, it was a Hoover. And we didn't have a dishwasher. The dishwasher was me!

Lesson 35 Speaking and listening, activity 6

WOMAN Right, let's see how much you know. Did they have aeroplanes in 1950?
MAN Yes, they did.
WOMAN And did they have them in 1850?
MAN No, they didn't.
WOMAN That's correct. How about trains? Did they have them in 1850?
MAN Yes, they did.
WOMAN And in 1750?
MAN No, they didn't.
WOMAN Correct. They had the first train in 1804. And did they have cameras in 1750?
MAN No, they didn't.
WOMAN And in 1850?
MAN Yes, they did.
WOMAN Just, yes. They had the first cameras in around 1830, 1840. Good and newspapers? Did they have newspapers in, let's say, 1550?
MAN Yes, they did.
WOMAN No, they didn't! Did they have newspapers in 1650?
MAN Yes, they did.
WOMAN That's correct. The world's first newspaper was in 1609.
MAN 1609! I didn't know that.
WOMAN Never mind. And the last one - steam engines. Did they have steam engines in, let me see now, in 1750?

MAN Yes, they did.
WOMAN And in 1650?
MAN No, they didn't.
WOMAN Correct. The world's first steam engine was in 1700. Good, well done. Only one wrong answer.

Lesson 36 Sounds, activity 2

lived arrived opened changed listened started hated
liked cooked stopped danced helped

Lesson 36 Listening and writing, activities 1 and 2

INTERVIEWER What did you do for entertainment when you were a child, Ben?
BEN We didn't have television, but we listened to the radio and we played cards a lot. It was fun!
INTERVIEWER And what about sport? Did you do any sport?
BEN I liked football. In fact, I still like football. I listened to the match on the radio. And I played football with friends in the park on Sunday mornings.
INTERVIEWER What else did you do on Sunday?
BEN We often had friends for lunch after I finished the football match. And then we played in the garden in the afternoon.
INTERVIEWER Where did you go on holiday?
BEN Most years we stayed in England. We stayed in a small hotel in Devon. The beach was very close.
INTERVIEWER And what about work. What did your parents do?
BEN My father was an engineer and he travelled a lot. My mother looked after the family. Sometimes I think it was quite hard for her.
INTERVIEWER Judy, tell me about your childhood. What did you do for entertainment at home?
JUDY We liked music very much. We're a very musical family. My brother played the violin and I played the piano. We had family concerts every evening.
INTERVIEWER And sport? Did you like sport?
JUDY Yes, I liked tennis very much. I played with my school friends. In fact I played tennis in my school team.
INTERVIEWER And how did you spend Sunday?
JUDY I stayed in bed until 9 o'clock. Then I did my homework for school. Then my mother cooked lunch for us all, there was always a traditional Sunday lunch at one o'clock. And in the afternoon, we had a walk in the country.
INTERVIEWER Where did you spend your holiday?
JUDY We were very lucky. My parents loved France, and we travelled around France several times, sometimes in the South, sometimes in the mountains, sometimes in Brittany. I still love France.
INTERVIEWER And what did your parents do? What was their job?
JUDY My parents worked in a hospital. My father and my mother were doctors.

Lesson 37 Sounds, activity 2

He <u>didn't</u> live in <u>Barcelona</u> in 1904. He <u>lived</u> in <u>Paris</u>.
He <u>didn't</u> return to <u>Spain</u> to live. He <u>lived</u> in <u>France.</u>
He <u>didn't</u> die in <u>1972</u>. He <u>died</u> in <u>1973</u>.

Lesson 38 Reading and listening, activity 1

STEVE When we started the weather was fine. We walked about fifteen kilometres. About four hours later, we started to come home. Suddenly the weather changed. It was very foggy. We were still in the mountains.
PHILIP Did you stay there?
STEVE No, we didn't. We walked for an hour but it was very cold and dark. We decided to stop walking and wait.
PHILIP Did you wait for a long time?
STEVE Well, no, we didn't. You see, after about two or three minutes, something happened. A dog, a big black dog suddenly appeared out of the fog. He had red eyes. Then he barked at us.
PHILIP Did he want to help you?
STEVE Yes, he did.
PHILIP So we walked for two hours behind the dog. Then we arrived back at the village.
STEVE Did the dog stay with you?
PHILIP No, he didn't. When we arrived at the village, he disappeared into the mountains .
STEVE Did you take a photograph?
PHILIP No, we didn't.

Lesson 39 Vocabulary and sounds, activity 5

drank-drink
spent-spend
got-get
left-leave
flew-fly
saw-see
took-take
ate-eat
sat-sit
went-go
bought-buy
thought-think

Lesson 40 Reading and listening, activity 3

MAN But one day, a strange thing happened. On the night of 28 October 1992 after a cold day in my garden, I had dinner, read my book and then I went to bed. I was asleep when suddenly I heard a noise like a train.
I got up and looked out of his window and saw a train in the garden.
"What's happening? Am I dreaming?" I said. There were passengers on the platform.
Some people got out of the train and said hello to their friends, and others got in and said goodbye.
They all wore clothes from thirty years ago. "This is very strange," I thought. I saw an old taxi and two or three old cars, and a man selling newspapers outside the station.
The man stood by a poster. It said, "THE END OF THE WORLD?"

Progress check, lessons 31 to 40 Listening, activity 1

Yesterday, all my troubles seemed so far away,
Now it looks as though they're here to stay,
Oh, I believe in yesterday.
Suddenly, I'm not half the man I used to be,
There's a shadow hanging over me,
Oh yesterday came suddenly.
Why she had to go I don't know
She wouldn't say.
I said something wrong, now I long for yesterday.
Yesterday, love was such an easy game to play,
Now I need a place to hide away
Oh, I believe in yesterday.
Why she had to go I don't know
She wouldn't say.
I said something wrong, now I long for yesterday.
Yesterday, love was such an easy game to play,
Now I need a place to hideaway
Oh, I believe in yesterday.

Wordlist

he first number after each word shows the lesson in which the word first appears in the vocabulary box. The numbers in *italics* show the later lessons in which the word appears again

a quarter past /ə kɔːtə pɑːst/20
a quarter to /ə kɔːtə tuː/ 20
actor /æktə/ 2
actress /æktrəs/ 2
address /ədres/ 6
afternoon /ɑːftənuːn/ 17
age /eɪdʒ/ 6
am /æm/ 17
America /əmerɪkə/ 21
American /əmerɪkən/ 5
apple /æpəl/ 22
apple pie / æpəl paɪ/ 27
April /eɪprəl/ 25
armchair /ɑːmtʃeə/ 24
arrive /əraɪv/ 20
Asia /eɪʃə/ 21
August /ɔːgəst/ 25
awful /ɔːfʊl/ 33

back /bæk/ 24
bag /bæg/ 10, 12, 15
baker /beɪkə/ 28
bank /bæŋk/ 28
bark /bɑːk/ 38
baseball /beɪsbɔːl/ 19
basket ball /bɑːskɪtbɔːl/ 19
bathroom /bɑːθruːm/ 24
be born /bɪ bɔːn/ 37
beach /biːtʃ/ 31
bed /bed/ 24
bedroom /bedruːm/ 24
beef /biːf/ 22
beer /bɪə/ 22
bicycle /baɪsɪkəl/ 21, 26, 35
bill /bɪl/ 39
bird /bɜːd/ 38
black /blæk/ 11, 14
blue /bluː/ 11, 14
boat /bəʊt/ 21
book /bʊk/ 15
books /bʊks/ 10
bookshop /bʊkʃɑp/ 28
bored /bɔːd/ 33
bottle /bɒtəl/ 27
boy /bɔɪ/ 9

Brazil /brəzɪl/ 5
Brazilian /brəzɪlɪən/ 5
bread /bred/ 22, 27
Britain /brɪtən/ 5
British /brɪtɪʃ/ 5
brochure /brəʊʃʊə/ 39
brother /brʌðə/ 9
brothers /brʌðəž/ 13
brown /braʊn/ 14
burger /bɜːgə/ 10
bus /bʌs/ 10, 21
buy /baɪ/ 29

cake /keɪk/ 27
camp /kæmp/ 31
car /kɑː/ 8, 21, 35
car park /kɑː pɑːk/ 28
cases /keɪsɪz/ 31
cassette player /kəset pleɪə/ 15
cassettes /kəsets/ 10
cat /kæt/ 38
chair /tʃeə/ 12
cheese /tʃiːz/ 27
chemist /kemɪst/ 28
chicken /tʃɪkɪn/ 22
children /tʃɪldrən/ 13
cinema /sɪnəmə/ 10, 28, 32
city /sɪtiː/ 31
climb /klaɪm/ 38
clock /klɒk/ 10
club /klʌb/ 32
coat /kəʊt/ 15
coat pocket /kəʊt pɒkɪt /12
coffee /kɒfiː/ 10, 22, 27
cold /kəʊld/ 33
computer /kəmpjuːtə/ 26, 35
concert /kɒnsət/ 32
concert hall /kɒnsət hɔːl /32
cook /kʊk/ 26
cooker /kʊkə/ 24
country /kʌntriː/ 5
cup /kʌp/ 27
cupboard /kʌbəd/ 24

dance /dɑːns/ 26, 29
dancing /dɑːnsɪŋ/ 23
dark /dɑːk/ 14, 38
daughters /dɔːtəz/ 13
December /dɪsembə/ 25
die /daɪ/ 37
dining room / daɪnɪŋ ruːm/ 24

disappear /dɪsəpɪə/ 38
dishwasher /dɪʃwɒʃə/ 35
doctor /dɒktə/ 2
dog /dɒg/ 38
door /dɔː/ 15
downstairs /daʊnsteəz/ 24
draw /drɔː/ 26
drink /drɪŋk/ 22, 29
drive /draɪv/ 26, 29, 29

eating in restaurants /iːtɪŋ ɪn restrɒnts/ 23
eight /eɪt/ 3
eighteen /eɪtiːn/ 6
eighth /eɪθ/ 25
eighty /eɪtiː/ 7
eleven /ɪlevən/ 6
eleventh /ɪlevənθ/ 25
engineer /endʒɪnɪə/ 2
English /ɪŋglɪʃ/ 26
Europe /jʊərəp/ 21
evening /iːvnɪŋ/ 17
exhibition /eksɪbɪʃən/ 32
eyes /aɪs/ 14

fair /feə/ 14
father /fɑːðə/ 13
favourite /feɪvrət/ 8
fax machine /fæks məʃiːn/ 35
February /febjʊəriː/ 25
fifteen /fɪftiːn/ 6
fifth /fɪθ/ 25
fifty /fɪftiː/ 7
film /fɪlm/ 32
fine /faɪn/ 33
finish /fɪnɪʃ/ 20, 37
first /fɜːst/ 25
five /faɪv/ 3
flat /flæt/ 16
foggy /fɒgiː/ 38
food /fuːd/ 22
football /fʊtbɔːl/ 10, 19, 26
football team /fʊtbɔːl tiːm/ 8
forty /fɔːtiː/ 7
four /fɔː/ 3
fourteen /fɔːtiːn/ 6
fourth /fɔːθ/ 25
French /frentʃ/ 26
Friday /fraɪdeɪ/ 18
friend /frend/ 9
friendly /frendliː/ 14

front /frʌnt/ 24
fruit /fru:t/ 22

gallery /gæləri:/ 32
garden /gɑ:dən/ 24
get /get/ 31
get dressed /get drest/ 29
get up /get ʌp/ 29
girl /gɜ:l/ 9
glass /glɑ:s/ 27
glasses /glɑ:sɪz/ 10, 12
go /gəʊ/ 16
go for a walk /gəʊ fɔ: a wɔ:k/ 18
go home /gəʊ həʊm/ 20
go shopping /gəʊ ʃɒpɪŋ/ 18
go straight ahead /gəʊ streɪt əhed/ 28
go to the cinema /gəʊ tu: ðə sɪnəmə/ 18
good-looking /gʊdlʊkɪŋ/ 14
goodbye /gʊdbaɪ/ 2
green /gri:n/ 11, 14
group /gru:p/ 8
guitar /gɪtɑ:/ 26
gymnastics /dʒɪmnæstɪks/ 19
hair /heə/ 14
half past /hɑ:f pɑ:st/ 20
hall /hɔ:l/ 24
happy /hæpi:/ 33
hat /hæt/ 31
have /hæv/ 29, 30
have breakfast /hæv brekfəst/ 17
have dinner /hæv dɪnə/ 17
have lunch /hæv lʌntʃ/ 17
hello /heləʊ/ 1
hot /hɒt/ 33
house /haʊs/ 16
hungry /hʌngri:/ 34
husband /hʌzbənd/ 13

individual sport /ɪndɪvɪdjʊəl spɔ:t/ 19
Italian /ɪtælɪən/ 5, 26
Italy /ɪtəli:/ 5

jacket /dʒækɪt/ 11
January /dʒænjʊəri:/ 25
Japan /dʒəpæn/ 5
Japanese /dʒæpəni:z/ 5
jeans /dʒi:nz/ 11
job /dʒɒb/ 2, 6
journalist /dʒɜ:nəlɪst/ 2
juice /dʒu:s/ 22
July /dʒu:laɪ/ 25
June /dʒu:n/ 25

keys /ki:z/ 10, 12
kitchen /kɪtʃɪn/ 24

lamb /læm/ 22
large /lɑ:dʒ/ 24
last month /lɑ:st mʌnθ/ 36
last week /lɑ:st wi:k/ 36
last year /lɑ:st jɪə/ 36
leave /li:v/ 20
lemon /lemən/ 22
lettuce /letɪs/ 27
library /laɪbri:/ 28
lie /laɪ/ 29
light /laɪt/ 15
like /laɪk/ 19
listen /lɪsən/ 30
live /lɪv/ 16, 37
living room /lɪvɪŋ ru:m/ 24
lying on the beach /laɪɪŋ ɒn ðə bi:tʃ/ 23

make /meɪk/ 30
man /mæn/ 9
March /mɑ:tʃ/ 25
market /mɑ:kɪt/ 28
married /mærɪd/ 6
May /meɪ/ 25
meat /mi:t/ 22
meet /mi:t/ 31
milk /mɪlk/ 22, 27
Monday /mʌndeɪ/ 18
morning /mɔ:nɪŋ/ 17
mother /mʌðə/ 13
mountains /maʊntɪns/ 31
music /mju:sɪk/ 32

name /neɪm/ 6
nationality /næʃənælɪtɪ:/ 5, 6
neighbour /neɪbə/ 9
nice /naɪs/ 14
nine /naɪn/ 3
nineteen /naɪnti:n/ 6
ninety /naɪnti:/ 7
ninth /naɪnθ/ 25
November /nəʊvembə/ 25

o'clock /əklɒk/ 17
October /ɒktəʊbə/ 25
office /ɒfɪs/ 16
one /wʌn/ 3
one hundred /wʌn hʌndrəd/ 7
orange /ɒrɪndʒ/ 22, 27
outback /aʊtbæk/ 31

pack /pæk/ 31
paint /peɪnt/ 37
painting /peɪntɪŋ/ 37
passenger /pæsɪndʒə/ 40
pen /pen/ 10, 15

pence /pens/ 11
personal stereo /pɜ:sənəl sterɪəʊ/ 12, 35
piano /pjænəʊ/ 26
piece /pi:s/ 27
pizza /pi:tzə/ 10
plane /pleɪn/ 31
platform /plætfɔ:m/ 40
play /pleɪ/ 26, 29, 32
pm /pi: em/ 17
politician /pɒlɪtɪʃən/ 8
post office /pəʊst ɒfɪs/ 28
potato /pəteɪtəʊ/ 22
pound /paʊnd/ 11
pretty /prɪti:/ 14
pub /pʌb/ 28

quiet /kwaɪət/ 14
quite /kwaɪt/ 14

radio /reɪdi:əʊ/ 35
railway /reɪlweɪ/ 40
read /ri:d/ 29
reading /ri:dɪŋ/ 23
receipts /rɪsi:ts/ 39
red /red/ 11, 14
restaurant /restrɒnt/ 28
rice /raɪs/ 22
ride /raɪd/ 26
run /rʌn/ 29
running /rʌnɪŋ/ 19
Russia /rʌʃə/ 5
Russian /rʌʃən/ 5

sailing /seɪlɪŋ/ 19
sandwich /sænwɪdʒ/ 10
Saturday /sætədeɪ/ 18
school /sku:l/ 16
sculpture /skʌlptʃə/ 37
sea /si:/ 31
second /sekənd/ 25
secretary /sekrəteri:/ 2
see /si:/ 29
see friends /si: frends/ 18
September /septembə/ 25
seven /sevən/ 3
seventeen /sevənti:n/ 6
seventh /sevənθ/ 25
seventy /sevənti:/ 7
shirt /ʃɜ:t/ 11
shoes /ʃu:s/ 11
shop /ʃɒp/ 16, 29
short /ʃɔ:t/ 14
shower /ʃaʊwə/ 24
sightseeing /saɪtsi:ɪŋ/ 23
sing /sɪŋ/ 26

singer /sɪŋə/ 2
sister /sɪstə/ 9
sisters /sɪstəz/ 13
sit /sɪt/ 29
sitting in the sun /sɪtɪŋ ɪn ðə sʌn/ 23
six /sɪks/ 3
sixteen /sɪksti:n/ 6
sixth /sɪkθ/ 25
sixty /sɪksti:/ 7
skiing /ski:ɪŋ/ 19, 23
skirt /skɜ:t/ 11
small /smɔ:l/ 24
sofa /səʊfə/ 24
sons /sʌnz/ 13
speak /spi:k/ 26
spend /spend/ 31
stand /stænd/ 29
start /stɑ:t/ 20, 37
station /steɪʃən/ 28
staying in hotels /steɪjɪŋ ɪn həʊtels/ 23
stop /stɒp/ 29
student /stu:dənt/ 2
study /stʌdi:/ 37
Sunday /sʌndeɪ/ 18
sweater /swetə/ 11
swim /swɪm/ 26
swimming /swɪmɪŋ/ 19, 23

table /teɪbəl/ 12
table tennis /teɪbəl tenɪs/ 19
talk /tɔ:k/ 30
tall /tɔ:l/ 14
taxi /tæksi:/ 10, 21
tea /ti:/ 22
teacher /ti:tʃə/ 2
team sport / ti:m spɔ:t/ 19
telephone /teləfəʊn/ 10, 35
telephone number /teləfəʊn nʌmbə/ 3
television /teləvɪʒən/ 10, 35
ten /ten/ 3
tennis /tenɪs/ 10, 19, 26
tenth /tenθ/ 25
Thai /taɪ/ 5
Thailand /taɪlənd/ 5
the United States of America /ðə ju:naɪtɪd steɪts ɒv əmerɪkə/ 5
theatre /θɪətə/ 10, 32
third /θɜ:d/ 25
thirsty /θɜ:sti:/ 34
thirteen /θɜ:ti:n/ 6
thirty /θɜ:ti:/ 7
thirty-one /θɜ:ti: wʌn/ 7
this month /ðɪs mʌnθ/ 36
this week /ðɪs wi:k/ 36
this year /ðɪs jɪə/ 36
three /θri:/ 3
Thursday /θɜ:zdeɪ/ 18
ticket office /tɪkɪt ɒfɪs/ 40
tickets /tɪkɪts/ 31, 39
tired /taɪəd/ 33
today /tədeɪ/ 36
tomato /təma:təʊ/ 22, 27
train /treɪn/ 21
Tuesday /tju:zdeɪ/ 18
Turkey /tɜ:ki:/ 5
Turkish /tɜ:kɪʃ/ 5
turn left /tɜ:n left/ 28
turn right /tɜ:n raɪt/ 28
TV presenter /ti: vi: prɪzentə/ 8
TV programme /ti: vi: prəʊgræm/ 8
twelfth /twelθ/ 25
twelve /twelv/ 6
twenty /twenti:/ 6
twenty- eight /twenti: eɪt/ 7
twenty-five /twenti: faɪv/ 7
twenty-four /twenti: fɔ:/ 7
twenty-nine /twenti: naɪn/ 7
twenty-one /twenti: wʌn/ 7
twenty-seven /twenti: sevən/ 7
twenty-six /twenti: sɪks/ 7
twenty-three /twenti: θri:/ 7
twenty-two /twenti: tu:/ 7
twin /twɪn/ 9
two /tu:/ 3
type /taɪp/ 26

umbrella /ʌmbrelə/ 10
understand /ʌndəstænd/ 26
unhappy /ʌnhæpi:/ 33
upstairs /ʌpsteəz/ 24
use /ju:z/ 26

vacuum cleaner /vækju:m kli:nə/ 35
vegetable /vedʒtəbəl/ 22
very /veri:/ 14
video /vɪdɪəʊ/ 10
video recorder /vɪdɪəʊ rekɔ:də/ 35
village /vɪlɪdʒ/ 38
visit /vɪzɪt/ 20
volleyball /vɒlɪbɔ:l/ 19

wait /weɪt/ 30
waiter /weɪtə/ 2
waiting room /weɪtɪŋ ru:m/ 40
walk /wɔ:k/ 21, 29
walking /wɔ:kɪŋ/ 23
wallet /wɒlɪt/ 10, 12
warm /wɔ:m/ 33
wash /wɒʃ/ 29
watch /wɒtʃ/ 10, 12, 29
watch television /wɒtʃ teləvɪʒən/ 18
water /wɔ:tə/ 22, 27
wear /weə/ 31
weather /weðə/ 38
Wednesday /wenzdeɪ/ 18
white /waɪt/ 11
wife /waɪf/ 13
window /wɪndəʊ/ 15
wine /waɪn/ 22
woman /wʊmən/ 9
work /wɜ:k/ 16, 37
write letters /raɪt letəz/ 18
writing postcards /raɪtɪŋ pəʊstkɑ:dz/ 23

yesterday /jestədeɪ/ 36
yoghurt /jɒgət/ 22

zero /zɪərəʊ/ 3

Progress Test 1 Lessons 1 – 10

SECTION 1: VOCABULARY (15 marks)

1 Write the numbers in words. (5 marks)

Example: 25 *twenty-five*

1 18 ________
2 97 ________
3 45 Smith St ________
4 0171 281002 ________
5 100 metres ________

2 Complete the chart. (5 marks)

country	**nationality**
Example: *Brazil*	Brazilian
1 Britain	________
2 ________	Japanese
3 Russia	________
4 ________	Thai
5 Turkey	________

3 Put a word from the box under the correct heading below. (5 marks)

American doctor read mother forty-six

1 **numbers** ________
2 **nationalities** ________
3 **jobs** ________
4 **classroom language** ________
5 **family** ________

PHOTOCOPIABLE

 © Macmillan Publishers Limited 1997.

Progress Test 1 Lessons 1 – 10

SECTION 2: GRAMMAR (15 marks)

4a Choose five of these words to complete the first five spaces in the conversation. (5 marks)

Example: a) How b) What c) Who

1 a) thank b) thanks c) thanks you
2 a) that b) these c) those
3 a) Listen b) Look c) Read
4 a) his b) our c) their
5 a) Their b) They c) They're

b Complete the last five spaces with five of your own words. (5 marks)

JANE Hello, Mark. How are you?
MARK Hello, Jane. I'm very well, (1) ________.
JANE What's (2) ________?
MARK It's a photo. (3) ________! These are my neighbours.
JANE What are (4) ________ names?
MARK Paul and Katya. (5) ________ from Los Angeles.
JANE Are they married?
MARK No, they (6) ________.
JANE How old (7) ________ Paul?
MARK He's 25. He's a student. Katya's 23.
JANE How (8) ________ you spell Katya?
MARK K-A-T-Y-A.
JANE And what's (9) ________ job?
MARK She's (10) ________ actress.

5 Tick (✓) the correct sentence. (5 marks)

Example: a He's American. ☑
b His American. ☐

1 a We're student. ☐
b We're students. ☐
2 a What are these? ☐
b What are this? ☐
3 Is she married?
a Yes, she's. ☐
b Yes, she is. ☐
4 a They're woman. ☐
b They're women. ☐
5 a Is he your brother? ☐
b Is he your sister? ☐

© Macmillan Publishers Limited 1997.

PHOTOCOPIABLE

Progress Test 1 Lessons 1 – 10

SECTION 3: READING AND WRITING (20 marks)

6 Complete the conversation. Write questions and your own answers. (20 marks)

CHRIS Hello, I'm Chris. What's your name?

1 YOU ______________________________

CHRIS Are you from England?

2 YOU ______________________________

CHRIS Where are you from?

3 YOU ______________________________

CHRIS Are you a student?

4 YOU ______________________________

CHRIS How old are you?

5 YOU ______________________________

CHRIS You aren't very old!

6 YOU ______________________________

CHRIS Married? No, I'm not.

7 YOU ______________________________

CHRIS I'm a teacher. A music teacher.

8 YOU ______________________________

CHRIS My favourite group? Oasis, I think.

9 YOU ______________________________

CHRIS Bjork's my favourite singer. She's from Iceland.

10 YOU ______________________________

CHRIS At home it's 655804.

YOU Thank you, Chris.

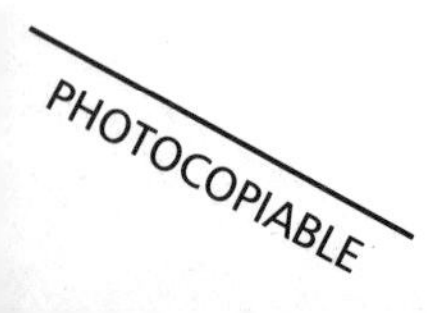

 © Macmillan Publishers Limited 1997.

Progress Test 2 Lessons 11 – 20

SECTION 1: VOCABULARY (15 marks)

1 Write the prices and times in words. (5 marks)

Example: £20 *twenty pounds*

1 3.15 ________
2 £9.99 ________
3 11.00 ________
4 50 p ________
5 12.40 ________

2 Underline the odd-one-out. (5 marks)

Example: jeans keys shoes sweater

1 black green tall white
2 children daughter mother wife
3 friendly nice quiet very
4 light listen read talk
5 basketball sailing shopping tennis

3 Match the five verbs below with words from the box. (5 marks)

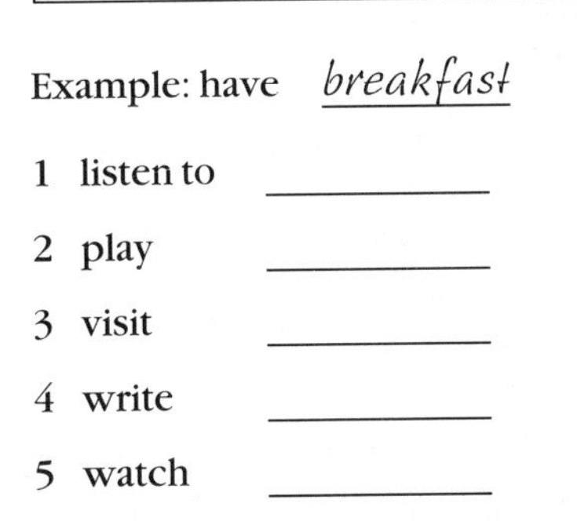

breakfast cassettes chairs cinema
football friends homework letters
school television work

Example: have *breakfast*

1 listen to ________
2 play ________
3 visit ________
4 write ________
5 watch ________

© Macmillan Publishers Limited 1997.

PHOTOCOPIABLE

Progress Test 2 Lessons 11 – 20

SECTION 2: GRAMMAR (15 marks)

4a Choose five of these words to complete the first five spaces in the passage. (5 marks)

Example: a) are b) has c) <u>is</u>

1	a) at	b) in	c) on
2	a) has	b) have	c) got
3	a) at	b) in	c) on
4	a) flat	b) job	c) son
5	a) arrives	b) goes	c) leaves

b Complete the last five spaces with five of your own words. (5 marks)

Julia Brown ___*is*___ twenty-eight years old. She lives (1) __________ London with her husband and their son. They (2) __________ a flat in north London. She works (3) __________ an office from Monday to Friday. She likes her (4) __________!

Julia (5) __________ home at quarter past eight and goes (6) __________ work. She starts work at nine o'clock and finishes at one o'clock (7) __________ the afternoon. After work she goes shopping and (8) __________ lunch. Then she goes home. (9) __________ Wednesday afternoon Julia goes swimming. She goes swimming with (10) __________ sister.

5 Tick (✓) the correct sentence. (5 marks)

Example: a What's the time? ☑

b What the time? ☐

1 a How much is the shirt white? ☐

b How much is the white shirt? ☐

2 a John's keys are in his pocket. ☐

b John's key's are in his pocket. ☐

3 a Take your coat off. ☐

b Take your coat on. ☐

4 Do you like skiing?

a Yes, I do. ☐

b Yes, I like. ☐

5 a I don't like football. ☐

b I no like football. ☐

PHOTOCOPIABLE

 © Macmillan Publishers Limited 1997.

Progress Test 2 Lessons 11 – 20

SECTION 3: READING AND WRITING (20 marks)

6 Complete the conversation. Write questions. (10 marks)

Example: YOU Hello, Bob. How are you?

BOB I'm fine, thanks.

1 YOU ______________________________?

BOB Yes, I am. My wife's name is Joanne.

2 YOU ______________________________?

BOB Joanne? She's got dark hair and she's quite pretty.

3 YOU ______________________________

BOB Yes, we have. We've got a son and a daughter.

4 YOU ______________________________

BOB Robert and Elizabeth.

5 YOU ______________________________

BOB Robert's two and Elizabeth's a baby.

7 Write 5–10 sentences about yourself, your work/school, your family and your home. (10 marks)

Hello, I'm __________ . I'm from ______________

© Macmillan Publishers Limited 1997.

PHOTOCOPIABLE

Progress Test 3 Lessons 21 – 30

SECTION 1: VOCABULARY (15 marks)

1 Complete the chart with five words from the box. (5 marks)

apple cupboard eat juice lamb milk pasta piece pub shower water

food	**drink**
apple	________
________	________
________	________

2 Underline the odd one out. (5 marks)

Example: bottle cup glass <u>sandwich</u>

1 America Asia English Europe
2 baker bookshop chemist party
3 eighth first number third
4 France May June November
5 bus taxi train walk

3 Complete the phrases with verbs. (5 marks)

Example: You *use* a computer.

1 You ________ the guitar.
2 You ________ a hat.
3 You ________ something to eat.
4 You ________ a bicycle.
5 You ________ the shopping.

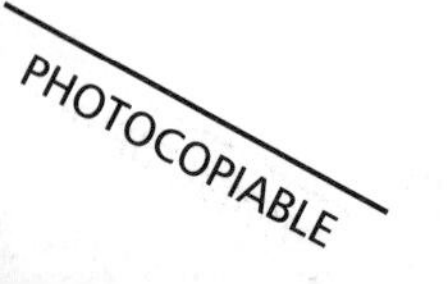

 © Macmillan Publishers Limited 1997.

Progress Test 3 Lessons 21 – 30

SECTION 2: GRAMMAR (15 marks)

4a Choose five of these words to complete the first five spaces in the passage. (5 marks)

Example: a) for b) in c) on

	a)	b)	c)
1	a) at	b) in	c) on
2	a) He	b) She	c) They
3	a) at	b) in	c) to
4	a) ski	b) skiing	c) skis
5	a) go	b) goes	c) going

b Complete the last five spaces with five of your own words. (5 marks)

Susan likes going ___on___ holiday. She goes skiing (1) __________ February or March with her sister. (2) __________ usually go to Italy or France for a week. Sometimes their mother goes (3) __________ Italy with them. Susan's mother can't (4) __________ but she likes sitting in the sun.

Susan's favourite city is Paris. She (5) __________ there every year with her husband, David. They go there for her birthday and (6) __________ in the same hotel near the centre.

It's the sixteenth (7) __________ April today. It's Susan's birthday. Susan and David are (8) __________ Paris. They (9) __________ standing in a queue outside an art gallery. Susan is (10) __________ a newspaper.

5 Tick (✓) the correct sentence. (5 marks)

Example: a When's she eat? ☑
b When does she eat? ☐

1 a Where does the station? ☐
b Where is the station? ☐

2 Is there a table?
a Yes, there is. ☐
b Yes, there's. ☐

3 a How much does it? ☐
b How much is it? ☐

4 a Turn on the right. ☐
b Turn right. ☐

5 a Is he listening the radio? ☐
b Is he listening to the radio? ☐

© Macmillan Publishers Limited 1997.

PHOTOCOPIABLE

Progress Test 3 Lessons 21 – 30

SECTION 3: READING AND WRITING (20 marks)

6 Match the questions with five of the answers. (10 marks)

Example: Do you go to work by car? [d]

1 What do you have for breakfast? [ ]
2 What do you do on your birthday? [ ]
3 Can you speak any languages? [ ]
4 Anything to drink? [ ]
5 What are you doing? [ ]

a I'm reading the newspaper.
b Yes, I do. It's my favourite drink.
c I have a cup of coffee. I don't eat anything in the morning.
d No, I don't. I walk there. It's not far.
e Yes, I do. I usually drink tea.
f No, I can't. I can't drive.
g A cup of coffee, please.
h We stay at home. My wife cooks a nice meal. We sometimes invite friends to eat with us.
i French and English. My wife's French.
j Yes, we are. We're having breakfast.

7 Write 5–10 sentences about your home. Write about the rooms. Say what's in one or two rooms. (10 marks)

PHOTOCOPIABLE

 © Macmillan Publishers Limited 1997.

Progress Test 4 Lessons 31 – 40

SECTION 1: VOCABULARY (15 marks)

1 Match five words from the box with the words in the list and make phrases. (5 marks)

case cleaner exhibition game knife machine music office room station team

Example: dining *room*

1 fax ___________
2 vacuum ___________
3 computer ___________
4 football ___________
5 railway ___________

2 Underline the odd one out. (5 marks)

Example: city club gallery theatre

1 awful bored office unhappy
2 cook detective engineer murder
3 computer dishwasher hall television
4 month today week year
5 American French Spanish Turkey

3 Complete the phrases with verbs. (5 marks)

Example: You *take* photographs.

1 You ___________ the piano.
2 You ___________ a shirt.
3 You ___________ in a hotel.
4 You ___________ in a village.
5 You ___________ a great time.

© Macmillan Publishers Limited 1997.

PHOTOCOPIABLE

Progress Test 4 Lessons 31 – 40

SECTION 2: GRAMMAR (15 marks)

4a Choose five of these words to complete the first five spaces in the passage. (5 marks)

Example: a) in b) the c) this

1 a) I go b) I'm go c) I'm going

2 a) doing b) eating c) having

3 a) then b) tomorrow c) yesterday

4 a) film b) films c) the films

5 a) go b) goes c) going

b Complete the last five spaces with five of your own words. (5 marks)

STEVE Let's do something _this_ evening.

ANNA I'm sorry but I'm busy. (1) __________ out with my sister. We're (2) __________ a meal at the new French restaurant.

STEVE Well, let's go to the cinema (3) __________ .

ANNA I'm sorry but I don't like (4) __________ .

STEVE OK. How about (5) __________ to the theatre, then?

ANNA Yes! I like (6) __________ to the theatre. What's (7) __________ ?

STEVE Romeo and Juliet's (8) __________ the Theatre Royal.

ANNA Oh no! I (9) __________ it last week! It was great!

STEVE Who (10) __________ you go with?

ANNA My sister. We go out every week.

5 Complete the short answers for these questions. (5 marks)

Example: Are you well? Yes, _we are_.

1 Does he like music? No, __________

2 Have they got the tickets? Yes, __________

3 Did she like the play? No, __________

4 Am I going home? Yes, __________

5 Were you happy? No, __________

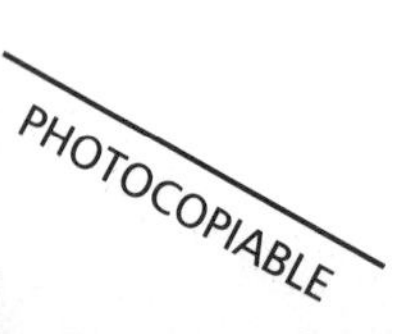

 © Macmillan Publishers Limited 1997.

Progress Test 4 Lessons 31 – 40

SECTION 3: READING AND WRITING (20 marks)

6 Match the questions with five of the answers. (10 marks)

Example: Did you sleep well? [c]

1 What are your plans for the holiday? [ ]

2 Where were you yesterday? [ ]

3 Where was Agatha Christie born? [ ]

4 Where did you go on holiday? [ ]

5 What are you doing at the weekend? [ ]

a We were at home. Why?

b I was born in 1964.

c Yes, I did.

d Robert's going walking in Italy and I'm staying at home.

e To Italy. We went walking for three weeks in the north-east.

f No, thank you.

g Yes, we were.

h In south-west England. She was born in 1890.

i Yes, I am.

j We're tired. We're staying at home.

7 What did you do at the weekend? Write 5 – 10 sentences about your weekend. (10 marks)

© Macmillan Publishers Limited 1997.

PHOTOCOPIABLE

Answers Progress Test 1 Lessons 1 – 10

SECTION 1: VOCABULARY [15 marks]

1 (5 marks: 1 mark for each correct answer.)
1 eighteen
2 ninety-seven
3 forty-five
4 oh one seven one two eight one oh oh two
5 a/one hundred

2 (5 marks: 1 mark for each correct answer.)
1 British
2 Japan
3 Russian
4 Thailand
5 Turkish

3 (5 marks: 1 mark for each correct answer.)
1 forty-six
2 American
3 doctor
4 read
5 mother

SECTION 2: GRAMMAR [15 marks]

4a (5 marks: 1 mark for each correct answer.)
1 b)
2 a)
3 b)
4 c)
5 c)

b (5 marks: 1 mark for each appropriate answer.)
6 aren't
7 is
8 do
9 her
10 an

5 (5 marks: 1 mark for each correct answer.)
1 b
2 a
3 b
4 b
5 a

SECTION 3: READING AND WRITING [20 marks]

6 (20 marks: 2 marks for each correct question or answer.)
1 I'm (+ name).
2 No, I'm not.
3 I'm from (+ country).
4 Yes, I am. OR No, I'm not.
5 I'm (+ age).
6 Are you married?
7 What's your job?
8 What's your favourite group?
9 Who's your favourite singer?
10 What's your (tele)phone number?

PHOTOCOPIABLE

 © Macmillan Publishers Limited 1997.

Answers Progress Test 2 Lessons 11 – 20

SECTION 1: VOCABULARY [15 marks]

1 (5 marks: 1 mark for each correct answer.)

1 (a) quarter past three
2 nine pounds ninety-nine (pence)
3 eleven o'clock
4 fifty pence
5 twenty to one/twelve forty

2 (5 marks: 1 mark for each correct answer.)

1 tall
2 children
3 very
4 light
5 shopping

3 (5 marks: 1 mark for each correct answer.)

1 cassettes
2 football
3 friends
4 letters
5 television

SECTION 2: GRAMMAR [15 marks]

4a (5 marks: 1 mark for each correct answer.)

1 b)
2 b)
3 b)
4 b)
5 c)

b (5 marks: 1 mark for each appropriate answer.)

6 to
7 in
8 has
9 On
10 her

5 (5 marks: 1 mark for each correct answer.)

1 b
2 b
3 a
4 a
5 a

SECTION 3: READING AND WRITING [20 marks]

6 (10 marks: 2 marks for each correct question.)

1 Are you married?
2 What's she/your wife like?
3 Have you got any children?
4 What are their names?
5 How old are they?

7 (10 marks)

Tell students what you will take into consideration when marking their written work. Criteria should include:

* efficient communication of meaning (4 marks)
* grammatical accuracy (4 marks)
* coherence in the ordering or the information or ideas (1 mark)
* layout, capitalisation and punctuation (1 mark)

It is probably better not to use a rigid marking system with the written part of the test. If, for example, you always deduct a mark for a grammatical mistake, you may find that you are over-penalising students who write a lot or who take risks. Deduct marks if students haven't written the minimum number of sentences stated in the test.

© Macmillan Publishers Limited 1997.

PHOTOCOPIABLE

Answers Progress Test 3 Lessons 21 – 30

SECTION 1: VOCABULARY [15 marks]

1 (5 marks: 1 mark for each correct answer.)

food	drink
apple	juice
lamb	milk
pasta	water

2 (5 marks: 1 mark for each correct answer.)

1 English
2 party
3 number
4 France
5 walk

3 (5 marks: 1 mark for each correct answer.)

1 play
2 wear
3 have
4 ride
5 do

SECTION 2: GRAMMAR [15 marks]

4a (5 marks: 1 mark for each correct answer.)

1 b)
2 c)
3 c)
4 a)
5 b)

b (5 marks: 1 mark for each appropriate answer.)

6 stay
7 of
8 in
9 are
10 reading

5 (5 marks: 1 mark for each correct answer.)

1 b
2 a
3 b
4 b
5 b

SECTION 3: READING AND WRITING [20 marks]

6 (10 marks: 2 marks for each correct answer.)

1 c
2 h
3 i
4 g
5 a

7 (10 marks)

Tell students what you will take into consideration when marking their written work. Criteria should include:

* efficient communication of meaning (4 marks)
* grammatical accuracy (4 marks)
* coherence in the ordering or the information or ideas (1 mark)
* layout, capitalisation and punctuation (1 mark)

It is probably better not to use a rigid marking system with the written part of the test. If, for example, you always deduct a mark for a grammatical mistake, you may find that you are over-penalising students who write a lot or who take risks. Deduct marks if students haven't written the minimum number of sentences stated in the test.

PHOTOCOPIABLE

 © Macmillan Publishers Limited 1997.